T0287829

Mirrors to One Another

New Directions in Aesthetics

Series editors: Dominic McIver Lopes, University of British Columbia, and Berys Gaut, University of St Andrews.

Blackwell's New Directions in Aesthetics series highlights ambitious single- and multiple-author books that confront the most intriguing and pressing problems in aesthetics and the philosophy of art today. Each book is written in a way that advances understanding of the subject at hand and is accessible to upper-undergraduate and graduate students.

1. **Robert Stecker** *Interpretation and Construction: Art, Speech, and the Law*
2. **David Davies** *Art as Performance*
3. **Peter Kivy** *The Performance of Reading: An Essay in the Philosophy of Literature*
4. **James R. Hamilton** *The Art of Theater*
5. **James O. Young** *Cultural Appropriation and the Arts*
6. **Scott Walden, ed.** *Photography and Philosophy: Essays on the Pencil of Nature*
7. **Garry Hagberg, ed.** *Art and Ethical Criticism*
8. **Eva M. Dadlez** *Mirrors to One Another: Emotion and Value in Jane Austen and David Hume*

Mirrors to One Another

Emotion and Value in Jane Austen and David Hume

E.M. Dadlez

A John Wiley & Sons, Ltd., Publication

This edition first published 2009
© 2009 E.M. Dadlez
Blackwell Publishing was acquired by John Wiley & Sons in February 2007.
Blackwell's publishing program has been merged with Wiley's global Scientific,
Technical, and Medical business to form Wiley-Blackwell.

Registered Office
John Wiley & Sons Ltd, The Atrium, Southern Gate, Chichester, West Sussex,
PO19 8SQ, United Kingdom

Editorial Offices
350 Main Street, Malden, MA 02148-5020, USA
9600 Garsington Road, Oxford, OX4 2DQ, UK
The Atrium, Southern Gate, Chichester, West Sussex, PO19 8SQ, UK

For details of our global editorial offices, for customer services, and for information
about how to apply for permission to reuse the copyright material in this book please
see our website at www.wiley.com/wiley-blackwell.

The right of E.M. Dadlez to be identified as the author of this work has been asserted
in accordance with the Copyright, Designs and Patents Act 1988.

Library of Congress Cataloging-in-Publication Data

Dadlez, E.M. (Eva M.), 1956–
   Mirrors to one another : emotion and value in Jane Austen and David Hume /
E.M. Dadlez.
       p. cm. — (New directions in aesthetics)
   Includes bibliographical references and index.
   ISBN 978-1-4051-9348-1 (hardcover : alk. paper)   1. Austen, Jane, 1775–1817
—Philosophy.   2. Austen, Jane, 1775–1817—Knowledge—Ethics.   3. Hume,
David, 1711–1776—Ethics.   4. Literature and morals.   5. Ethics in literature.
6. Literature—Philosophy.   I. Title.
   PR4038.P5D33 2009
   823'.7—dc22
                                                                2008052918

A catalogue record for this book is available from the British Library.

Set in 10/12.5pt Galliard by Graphicraft Limited, Hong Kong
Printed and bound in Singapore by Fabulous Printers Pte Ltd

01   2009

CONTENTS

Preface		vii
Acknowledgments		xiv
Abbreviations		xvi

1 How Literature Can Be a Thought Experiment:
   Alternatives to and Elaborations of Original Accounts   1
2 Literary Form and Philosophical Content   20
3 Kantian and Aristotelian Accounts of Austen   37
4 Hume and Austen on Pleasure, Sentiment, and Virtue   58
5 Hume and Austen on Sympathy   76
6 Hume's General Point of View and the Novels of
   Jane Austen   88
7 The Useful and the Good in Hume and Austen   100
8 Aesthetics and Humean Aesthetic Norms in the Novels
   of Jane Austen   114
9 Hume and Austen on Good People and Good Reasoning   135
10 "Lovers," "Friends," and other Endearing Appellations:
    Marriage in Hume and Austen   157
11 Hume and Austen on Pride   168
12 Hume and Austen on Jealousy, Envy, Malice, and the
    Principle of Comparison   181
13 Indolence and Industry in Hume and Austen   195
14 What Hume's Philosophy Contributes to Our
    Understanding of Austen's Fiction; what Austen's Fiction
    Contributes to Our Understanding of Hume's Philosophy   206

Bibliography   223
Index   229

PREFACE

It is a truth universally acknowledged that any philosopher with an appreciation of moral perspicacity must harbor some weakness for the works of Jane Austen.[1] Gilbert Ryle, when asked if he still read novels, promptly responded: "Yes, all six every year," referring to those very works.[2] Many academics, although most of them are not philosophers, have commented at length on the normative content of Austen's novels. Normative analyses of works like Austen's are to be expected. Austen is one of the exemplars of what Robert Alter refers to as the "worldly literature of the quotidian," the kind of writing that addresses questions about character and human interaction, inviting readers to discriminate among character types and reflect on moral dilemmas and predicaments set in a variety of naturalistic contexts.[3] The central questions for those attempting an analysis of this aspect of Austen's writing are not about her familiarity with the work of some particular philosopher, because there is insufficient evidence of such familiarity. Austen herself denied any knowledge of philosophy, though the circumstances under which she did so (declining to base one of her characters on an importunate correspondent) may incline

---

[1] All examples of Austen's work will be derived from the following editions of her novels: *The Novels of Jane Austen*, 5 volumes, ed. R.W. Chapman, 3rd edition (Oxford: Oxford University Press, 1988) and to *The Works of Jane Austen*, ed. R.W. Chapman, volume 6, *Minor Works* (Oxford: Oxford University Press, 1988). Titles will be abbreviated as is standard: SS, *Sense and Sensibility* (v. 1); PP, *Pride and Prejudice* (v. 2); MP, *Mansfield Park* (v. 3); E, *Emma* (v. 4); NA, *Northanger Abbey* (v. 5); P, *Persuasion* (v. 5); MW, *Minor Works* (including *Lady Susan*, *The Watsons*, *Sanditon* (v. 6).
[2] Natalie Tyler, *The Friendly Jane Austen: A Well-Mannered Introduction to a Lady of Sense and Sensibility* (New York: Viking, 1999), p. 205.
[3] Robert Alter, Introduction, in Frank Kermode, *Pleasure and Change: The Aesthetics of Canon* (Oxford: Oxford University Press, 2004), p. 9.

us to regard the claim as disingenuous.[4] In any case, we cannot assume that Austen read or reflected on philosophy without indulging in speculation. Of course, Peter Knox-Shaw does speculate to some purpose in the *Times Literary Supplement*,[5] when he agrees with his reviewer Michael Caines that Austen may well have been exposed to Adam Smith's *Theory of Moral Sentiments*. Gilbert Ryle[6] and Alisdair MacIntyre[7] both propose an Aristotelian influence, one which Ryle believes may derive from exposure to Shaftesbury. Less plausible candidates such as Kant and Hobbes have also been brought forward. But whether or not such speculation is permissible is beside the point of the present enterprise. Asking what philosophy Jane Austen read involves us in a question independent of inquiries about the philosophical position to which her writing commits her. We can still make perfectly reasonable assumptions about the theories and systems into which the normative (and sometimes meta-ethical) points of view taken up in Austen's works best fit. It will be argued here that the best "fit" is with the approach to ethics and value taken by David Hume.

I should stress at the outset that no single correspondence between Hume and Austen to which I will draw attention is absolutely unique. The importance of sympathy in moral contexts is something which both Hume and Austen emphasize, but we may see the same emphasis in Adam Smith and Francis Hutcheson. Austen and Hume both see connections between morality and sentiment, but so do Aristotle, Smith, and Shaftesbury. The normative ethical stance most often endorsed in Austen's novels is much like the utility-based virtue ethics which can most plausibly be ascribed to Hume, but the parallel to Aristotle is equally obvious. Writing this book has not lent itself to the happy practice of submitting individual chapters to journals, since most such submissions incur requests for comparative analysis that would inflate any individual offering beyond an acceptable length. In a book, at least, one may explore such questions more at one's leisure. My point about Hume really is intended to be a point about degree of fit, and my demonstration of

---

[4] We are told that Jane Austen "disclaimed any knowledge of science and philosophy." Letter 132 (D) December 11, 1815, in *Jane Austen's Letters*, 3rd ed., ed. D. Le Faye (Oxford: Oxford University Press, 1995). Cited in David Gallop, "Jane Austen and the Aristotelian Ethic," *Philosophy and Literature* 23.1 (1999): 96–109, at 106.
[5] Peter Knox-Shaw, "Austen's Reading," in Letters to the Editor, *Times Literary Supplement* March 18, 2005, p. 15.
[6] Gilbert Ryle, "Jane Austen and the Moralists," in *Critical Essays on Jane Austen*, ed. B.C. Southam (London: Routledge & Kegan Paul, 1968).
[7] Alisdair MacIntyre, *After Virtue: A Study in Moral Theory* (Indiana: University of Notre Dame, 1981).

this is intended to be cumulative. It is not that Austen is *more* like Hume than Smith on the subject of sympathy, it is that her general normative stance, all told, is a great deal more like that which we can find in or infer from Hume's *Treatise* than that which we can locate in the corpus of any other philosopher. The third chapter will address, albeit briefly, proposed alliances between Austen and Kant, Austen and Shaftesbury, and, most famously, Austen and Aristotle (discussions of Adam Smith are reserved for the chapter on sympathy). I will then begin to explore correspondences between Hume and Austen, no one of which is unique but all of which, taken together, appear to demonstrate a closer correspondence than may be found by drawing comparisons between Austen and some other philosopher. This is my first thesis.

Establishing the preceding would enable us to characterize Austen's work as deriving in most respects from the traditions of the Enlightenment rather than those of the Victorian era, something that I very much wish to do. In fact, Peter Knox-Shaw accomplishes this in his *Jane Austen and the Enlightenment*, allying Austen with the skeptical tradition of the empiricists.[8] I hope only to add to the evidence for that contention. Although Austen's novels were published early in the nineteenth century, three were begun before the end of the eighteenth. And although Hume left this world a scant eight months after Austen had entered it, his way of thinking about the world and the people in it did not depart with him. I aim to show, at least, that many of Hume's insights about human nature survive more or less intact in Austen's work, and thereby hope to augment the grounds for maintaining Austen's affinity for Enlightenment thought. I regard this as a kind of secondary thesis, if a derivative one.

Austen herself believed fictions could prove a source of insights about human nature, calling a novel a "work in which . . . the most thorough knowledge of human nature, the happiest delineation of its varieties," is to be observed (NA 38). It is assumed here that novels can and do make ethical, meta-ethical, aesthetic, and even epistemic endorsements, many of them centered on human character and the manner in which it may be assessed. These assumptions are compatible with Hume's own contentions about fiction in the essay "Of the Standard of Taste."[9] Hume criticizes works in which "vicious manners are described, without being marked with the proper characters of . . . disapprobation," maintaining that

---

[8]   Peter Knox-Shaw, *Jane Austen and the Enlightenment* (Cambridge: Cambridge University Press, 2004).

[9]   David Hume, "Of the Standard of Taste," in Eugene F. Miller, ed., *Essays: Moral, Political, and Literary* (Indianapolis: Liberty Classics, 1987), pp. 226–49. Henceforth designated ST.

one cannot enter into such a writer's sentiments or "bear an affection to characters which we plainly discover to be blameable" (ST 246). People ought not to "pervert the sentiments of" their own hearts "in complaisance to any writer whatsoever" (ST 247). In the *Treatise*, Hume tells us that "A generous and noble character affords a satisfaction even in the survey; and when presented to us, tho' only in a poem or fable, never fails to charm and delight us."[10] So fictions engage their audience on a moral level. They have moral content and present moral perspectives which can be entered into or resisted. Most heavy-handedly, fictions present endorsements by means of the pronouncements of an omniscient narrator, but this is a literary crudity in which Austen herself seldom indulged. Works may be taken to endorse a course of action or a way of thinking or a mode of evaluation when they make it clear that – in the world of the work – this course or method is right (or correct or appropriate or preferable to the alternatives). As we know, this can be made entirely apparent even in the course of a novel when nothing of the sort is explicitly mentioned. Likewise, no reader must be directly informed that Fanny Dashwood of *Sense and Sensibility* is contemptible. One has but to read one of Austen's more ruthless passages about Fanny's rationalizations to understand that this is the case and, more to the point, to feel the contempt.

Austen's works taken as a whole, as do most works of fiction, endorse particular perspectives on the rightness and wrongness of various courses of action in various contexts. They sometimes endorse modes of reasoning and methods for the evaluation of character. They put forward a distinctive view of human nature, and particularly of human foibles. These perspectives may be thought to converge more closely with one philosopher's normative and meta-ethical stance than they do with another's. As I have indicated, I hope to establish that they converge with views concerning human nature and morality put forward by David Hume in Books II and III of his *Treatise of Human Nature*.

Why should such a convergence be philosophically interesting? There is, after all, an enormous difference between novels and philosophical treatises. Treatises may enlighten the reader about the rationale which underlies a policy or course of action. Novels, on the other hand, can lead that reader to imagine a situation in which she would adopt such a stance or course herself. Fiction can supply a moral point of vantage, not by telling people what it is, but by showing them how to have it. Austen's

---

[10] David Hume, *Treatise of Human Nature*, ed. L.A. Selby-Bigge (Oxford: Clarendon Press, 1978), p. 296. Henceforth designated T.

novels don't just provide examples that illustrate Hume's points. They can sometimes function as thought experiments which offer a demonstration of Hume's normative assumptions in regard to ethics (and sometimes epistemology or aesthetics), as well as the ways in which he encouraged us to think about such things. To investigate the aforementioned convergence may be to explore the way in which Austen's works enable readers to see the world through the lens of a Humean perspective. This is my third thesis.

I believe that Austen's novels encourage us to respond in a distinctively Humean way to hypothetical situations by rehearsing our responsive dispositions. All novels, of course, enable us to adopt an attitude reminiscent of what Hume calls a general point of view (free of personal bias and prejudice based on degree of proximity), and all encourage us to consider the effects of character traits on the narrow circle of their possessor. That is, literature in general is suited to the exercise of moral as well as emotional responsiveness, as Hume describes such responsiveness. My claim is that Austen's literature is better suited to the enterprise than most, because of its intimate focus on character traits and their hypothetical and actual effects and because of the significance of utility in the assessment of those traits. More importantly, there are passages in Austen that read very much like thought experiments which establish some of Hume's assumptions and hypotheses, experiments that sometimes go even further by expanding the arena of these assumptions' application or following out their implications. That is, Austen and Hume can serve as complements to one another. So Austen can help us to understand and to expand upon Hume. That represents a part of my third thesis, already discussed above. Next, Hume, by making salient for us insights in Austen which are often given short shrift, can help us to understand and to expand upon Austen. That represents a fourth thesis, emphasizing the advantages of adopting a Humean perspective in reading Austen. The question of how literature in general, and Austen's literature in particular, can act as a thought experiment will be addressed in the first chapter, with an eye to establishing the groundwork for specific examples and analyses that appear in each succeeding chapter. The second chapter will pick up a thread of this discussion and pursue some questions about the effects of literary form on such an enterprise.

It is important to note that Austen's works are among those that have, as Hume puts it, "survived all the caprices of mode and fashion" (ST 233). Indeed the spate of film adaptations of Austen's novels (although I will have some harsh things to say about a few of them) has continued in a way that has exceeded the critics' expectations, and is considered to be a consequence rather than the cause of Austen's popularity.[11] Austen's reputation among highbrows and common readers alike is described as undiminished.[12] With assessments such as these in the contemporary critical literature, it seems fair to maintain that Austen's novels have stood the test of time, and have stood it rather better than a lot of other works.

Works of art often have, in respect to tests of time, a longer shelf life than other products of human intellectual endeavor. No alteration in government, religion, or language can obscure the glory of a Homer, says Hume. On the other hand, theologies, philosophical theories, and the hypotheses of science are often overturned or superseded. Indeed, "nothing has been experienced more liable to the revolutions of chance and fashion than . . . decisions of science" (ST 242) while "Terence and Virgil maintain an universal, undisputed empire over the minds of men" (ST 243). Hume makes these points in order to show that finding a criterion or standard of taste is not as difficult as it might seem at first glance – or even as difficult as it might be to find a standard for evaluation in other apparently more objective contexts. I make them again in order to stress that Hume himself saw a kind of resistance to inessentials, a kind of universal accessibility in art, and especially in literature, that could be counted on to engage the faculties, including the rational faculties, irrespective of cultural context. This is reminiscent of the Aristotelian claim that poetry deals with the universal while history deals with the particular. And this in turn is relevant to the present project because it provides us with an independent Humean argument for the continuing relevance of many of Hume's insights.

I remember a Hume conference during the course of which a young epistemologist was holding forth on Hume's account of knowledge, working well within the conceptual schemes employed by Alston and Goldman and Lehrer and other contemporary epistemologists. A Hume scholar of my acquaintance rose up like an avenging angel during the question-and-answer period and pointed out that those concepts would not even have been recognized by Hume, that Hume's use of "idea" does not correspond to our contemporary understanding of "belief," that Hume's epistemology cannot – at least not without dozens of caveats and amendments – fit into the relevant conceptual schemes. I have elsewhere heard not dissimilar things said of Hume's philosophy of mind – that it fails, or proves inapplicable within a more advanced philosophical framework,

---

[11] See, for instance, Richard Jenkyns, *A Fine Brush on Ivory: An Appreciation of Jane Austen* (Oxford: Oxford University Press, 2004), p. vii.

[12] Jenkyns, *A Fine Brush on Ivory*, p. vii.

or is no longer relevant to our inquiries and interests. Some of Hume's philosophy, then, is thought by at least some philosophers to have met the very fate of speculative opinion that Hume outlines: "other theories and systems have supplied . . . [its] place, which again gave place to their successors" (ST 242).

My point, of course, is that if a novelist's work has proved more or less impervious to changes and innovations of various kinds and speaks almost as readily to a contemporary audience as it does to people of the late eighteenth and early nineteenth centuries, then a few circumspect claims of universality do not seem out of place. Consider that the focal interest of the works in question involves their ethical perspicacity and that those very insights and modes of ethical reasoning are closely aligned, if I can make my case, with those of David Hume. It may be held, given the preceding, that Austen's novels can provide us both with thought experiments and with outright illustrations that support or demonstrate particular points which Hume himself made about morality or moral reasoning, about aesthetic or epistemic norms. If so, and this would be my fifth and final thesis, then we can claim for Hume's ethics, and for some of his philosophy of mind and epistemology and aesthetics as well, a similar universality and breadth of accessibility. That is, much of Hume's philosophy (in particular the part that he believed was most important) retains both immediacy and relevance.

As is evident from the preceding, establishing the second and fifth theses depends on my ability to establish the other three. That is, if it can be established that there is a close correspondence between the various norms endorsed by Hume and Austen, that Austen's novels can elicit from us distinctively Humean responses, insights and methods of evaluation, and that Hume can help us better to take advantage of what is there in Austen, then I will have shown something both about the contemporary relevance of those insights and about Austen's affinity for the worldview of the Enlightenment.

ACKNOWLEDGMENTS

Parts of the Preface first appeared in: "Dense Insensibility: Hume's Vices and Virtues in the Work of Jane Austen," *1650–1850*, 12 (2006): 147–74, © 2006 AMS Press, Inc.; "David Hume and Jane Austen on Pride: Ethics in the Enlightenment."

Part of Chapter 1 ("How Literature Can Be a Thought Experiment") first appeared in *Theory and Practice in Eighteenth Century Britain: Writing Between Philosophy and Literature*, ed. Christina Lupton and Alex J. Dick (London: Pickering & Chatto Publishers, 2008). Reproduced by permission of Pickering & Chatto Publishers.

Chapter 2 ("Literary Form and Philosophical Content") first appeared as: "How Literary Form Affects Content: Reading Jane Austen," *Philosophy and Literature*. Reprinted with permission from Johns Hopkins University Press.

Parts of Chapter 4 ("Hume and Austen on Pleasure, Sentiment, and Virtue") first appeared in: "Dense Insensibility: Hume's Vices and Virtues in the Work of Jane Austen," *1650–1850* 12 (2006): 147–74. © 2006 AMS Press, Inc. All rights reserved.

An earlier version of Chapter 8 ("Aesthetics and Humean Aesthetic Norms in the Novels of Jane Austen") first appeared in: *Journal of Aesthetic Education* 42.1 (Spring 2008), published by University of Illinois Press. © Board of Trustees of the University of Illinois. Used with permission of the University of Illinois Press.

Chapter 11 ("Hume and Austen on Pride") first appeared in from "David Hume and Jane Austen on Pride: Ethics in the Enlightenment," in *Theory and Practice in Eighteenth Century Britain: Writing Between Philosophy and Literature*, ed. Christina Lupton and Alex J. Dick (London: Pickering & Chatto Publishers Ltd., 2008). Reproduced by permission of Pickering & Chatto Publishers.

ABBREVIATIONS

Austen

All examples of Austen's work will be derived from the following editions of her novels: *The Novels of Jane Austen*, 5 vols, ed. R.W. Chapman, 3rd edition (Oxford: Oxford University Press, 1988) and to *The Works of Jane Austen*, ed. R.W. Chapman, vol. 6, *Minor Works* (Oxford: Oxford University Press, 1988).

Titles will be abbreviated as is standard:

E   *Emma* (vol. 4)
MP   *Mansfield Park* (vol. 3)
MW   *Minor Works* (including *Lady Susan*, *The Watsons*, *Sanditon*; vol. 6)
NA   *Northanger Abbey* (vol. 5)
P   *Persuasion* (vol. 5)
PP   *Pride and Prejudice* (vol. 2)
SS   *Sense and Sensibility* (vol. 1)

Hume

The following abbreviations are used:

EPM *An Enquiry Concerning the Principle of Morals* in *Enquiries Concerning Human Understanding and Concerning the Principles of Morals*, ed. L.A. Selby-Bigge and P.H. Nidditch (Oxford: Clarendon, 1995)
T   *Treatise of Human Nature*, ed. L.A. Selby-Bigge (Oxford: Clarendon Press, 1978)

1
How Literature Can Be a Thought Experiment: Alternatives to and Elaborations of Original Accounts

Much has been written about the relationship between literature and moral philosophy and about how literature contributes to our moral education. I have claimed at the outset of this book that literature can make such contributions not just by providing striking illustrations of particular moral insights (although it certainly does that) but sometimes by leading us to have such insights, insights that reflective thinking alone is unlikely to produce. This is not the first occasion on which I have made such claims in print. More importantly, I am by no means the first philosopher to do so, which makes me beholden to those whose endeavors and observations precede my own, or whose work has paralleled my personal efforts. I will begin by addressing the work of the most prominent of these investigators, and eventually branch out to discuss the observations of others who are, I am afraid, too numerous to be done justice to in a single chapter. Divergences between the former and my own project will be employed as a template to guide the direction of the discussion.

Martha Nussbaum claims that literature, or at least the best literature, can evoke from us the fineness of perception requisite for moral judgment. She maintains that literature contributes to moral knowledge in two ways. First, it offers paradigms of conduct. Next, and perhaps more important, it draws us into a form of imaginative engagement and awareness that is vital for the deployment of what Nussbaum regards as a characteristically Aristotelian ethical perspective in all its complexity and responsiveness to human experience, a kind of awareness that is less accessible from the standpoint of "excessively simplistic and reductive approaches to human experience . . . that can be found in some parts of philosophy."[1] Nussbaum

[1] Martha C. Nussbaum, "Exactly and Responsibly: A Defense of Ethical Criticism," *Philosophy and Literature* 22.2 (1998): 343–65, 347–8.

emphasizes that "it is seeing a complex concrete reality in a highly lucid and richly responsive way; it is taking in what is there, with imagination and feeling"[2] that makes some kinds of fiction an adjunct to ethical judgment. Vital to the exploration of such a moral stance are "(1) an insistence on the plurality and non-commensurability of a well lived life; (2) an insistence on the importance of contextual complexity and particularized judgment in good deliberation; (3) an insistence on the cognitive role of the emotions; (4) an insistence on human vulnerability and the vulnerability of the good."[3] In the preceding claims and explorations Nussbaum has come much closer than most philosophers to the provision of a satisfying and convincing account of what can happen at the intersection of ethics and aesthetics and of how it is that one can *do* ethics by perusing or creating literature. The claims which I will make throughout this book owe a great deal to some of the ground that Nussbaum has already broken, but depart from her assumptions in three ways.

First, while I absolutely agree that the ethical significance of literature crucially involves its eliciting of emotion, I do not believe that emotions are value judgments, as Nussbaum has maintained,[4] nor am I convinced that such an account of emotion is compatible with an emphasis on the role of emotion in our moral engagement with fiction. Second, I am more inclined to regard literature as a thought experiment which articulates hypothetical cases, elicits moral responses, and allows readers to test moral intuitions, to see whether different circumstances do or would make a fundamental difference in moral judgments or outcomes. This is not something that I see as being fundamentally at odds with Nussbaum's project, but it does involve a considerable difference in focus: on clarity rather than the kind of complexity and obscurity that make Nussbaum "see literary works as guides to what is mysterious and messy and dark in our experience."[5] I am inclined to see the tack I am taking, though perhaps Nussbaum would think it a mistake to do so, as another chapter of the *same* project she pursues, whose different concerns stem at least in part from the fairly radical difference we see in the style, tone, and axiological

---

[2]   Nussbaum, "Finely Aware and Richly Responsible: Moral Attention and the Moral Task of Literature," *The Journal of Philosophy* 82.10 (1985): 516–29, 521.

[3]   Nussbaum, "Exactly and Responsibly," 348.

[4]   Nussbaum, "Emotions as Judgments of Value and Importance," in *What Is an Emotion? Classic and Contemporary Readings*, 2nd edn, ed. Robert C. Solomon (New York: Oxford University Press, 2003), pp. 271–83. Originally published in *Relativism, Suffering, and Beyond: Essays in Memory of Bimal K. Matilal*, ed. P. Bilimoria and J.N. Mohanty (New Delhi: Oxford University Press, 1997).

[5]   Nussbaum, "Exactly and Responsibly," 348.

predilections of Jane Austen and Henry James. And my third departure emerges from this, for I want to claim that the kind of Jamesian role that Nussbaum finds for fiction in moral discourse does not exhaust or, indeed, begin to exhaust the potentialities of fiction as an adjunct to practical reason. As is evident, the latter two departures are in the nature of friendly amendments rather than disagreements, and the first need not constitute an objection to Nussbaum's more general position on emotion and cognition, since she has been known to stress what she refers to as "the cognitive role of the imagination" in the context of her observations about literature and ethics.[6] It is to a discussion of that issue that I will first turn.

In "Emotions as Judgments of Value and Importance" Nussbaum contends that emotions are forms of judgment, explicitly arguing against accounts that would make relevant beliefs and perceptions mere constituents of the emotion (among other constituents which were not beliefs), or necessary or sufficient conditions for the emotion.[7] Thus, as seems clear from the preceding restrictions, judgments, as Nussbaum uses the term, are beliefs, or at least embody beliefs. Emotions "embody not simply ways of seeing an object, but beliefs – often very complex – about the object."[8] It is this outright identification of emotion with belief, however complex and incisive that belief happens to be, that is at the root of my difficulty. For it is not clear that such an account of emotion sits at all comfortably with intentional objects that are not believed to exist but are merely imagined. Nussbaum repeatedly emphasizes the particularity, the fine-tunedness, of the reader's attention. The proposition entertained by the reader in the course of an emotional response to a fiction could not, given this emphasis, involve some universal of which the fictional event represented a particular instance. Rather, the thought of the reader would have to be about a *particular* fictional event or entity. This means that, as Noel Carroll would put it, the relevant proposition would be entertained unasserted[9] – entertained in imagination *rather* than believed.

There are ways, of course, to make a belief-based account of emotion compatible with a story about an emotional response to fiction: by

[6] Nussbaum, "Exactly and Responsibly," 348.
[7] Nussbaum, "Emotions as Judgments of Value and Importance," 278.
[8] Nussbaum, "Emotions as Judgments of Value and Importance," 276 – this, despite a footnoted caveat to the effect that in some human and all animal emotions "the presence of a certain kind of *seeing as* ... is sufficient for emotion" (fn. 5, p. 276).
[9] Noel Carroll, "Critical Study: *Mimesis as Make-Believe*," *Philosophical Quarterly* 45 (1995): 93.

resorting to the aforementioned universals. Such an approach would be quite at odds with Nussbaum's insistence on particularity of focus, though it would provide us, as philosophers like Bijoy Boruah have pointed out, with a candidate belief that is not at odds with one's belief that one is dealing with a fiction.[10] Consider someone's emotional response of disapprobation upon contemplating some fictional depiction of injustice – Sir Thomas Bertram's attempt to bully Fanny Price into accepting Henry Crawford's proposal, say. This need not be tied to some specific thought about the very particular injustice which is done to Fanny: the purposeful aim that is taken at her vulnerabilities, the false charges of ingratitude, the sincere horror that is expressed at the idea of female autonomy. These things are, after all, merely entertained in imagination and are not believed real. Instead, the belief in question could be the belief that to be treated as the character is treated constitutes an injustice, that to induce unjustified guilt and self-loathing in others in order to get them to do something which they do not want to do can be a serious moral wrong. This would be a belief about a type or kind of action rather than about particular people and their treatment of one another, for the latter are things that one is well aware are fictional. However, this solution to the problem is unavailable to Nussbaum, for it does not accord with the kind of focused specificity of response that she believes the right kind of reading can involve, a reading in the course of which no paraphrase or summary can hope to capture what is morally valuable about a given literary passage.[11]

As will become evident, I am quite convinced that fictions very often give rise to just such universal beliefs as I have described and that these are extremely important in any assessment of the impact of literature on our moral lives, for beliefs about situation types or about kinds of people apply equally well to the fiction and to the world, a topic to which I return later. It is worth noting at this juncture, however, that such beliefs really cannot explain all of our emotional reactions to literature, some of which are clearly directed toward quite specific individuals and events, just as Nussbaum's stress on particularity leads us to believe they are. The latter must be addressed in any account that hopes to explain moral and emotional reactions to the fictional. Luckily, nothing suggests that we have to choose between the two approaches, for they are not mutually exclusive. My position is that literature elicits *both* kinds of responses and that no account of the moral impact of fiction can be complete without

[10]   Bijoy H. Boruah, *Fiction and Emotion: A Study in Aesthetics and Philosophy of Mind* (Oxford: Clarendon Press, 1988), pp. 108–17.
[11]   Nussbaum, "Finely Aware," 522.

addressing each. But that does little to solve the problem which presently confronts us.

Neither beliefs about situation types nor far more specific beliefs about what is fictionally the case will have the right kinds of intentional objects, if what we are searching for is a cognition that corresponds to an emotional response to fiction as Nussbaum has described it. If we delight in Elizabeth Bennett's defiance of Lady Catherine or empathetically share her regret over having made critically over-hasty judgments, then our delight and regret are about something we have imagined, not something that we believe has occurred. Setting aside the important question of the way in which what we imagine is guided by how it is that an author has put things, something that I believe Nussbaum is perfectly right about, but which will overcomplicate the present discussion, we need to consider the intentional object of a belief about what is fictionally the case. We do believe, after all, that Elizabeth Bennett is a fictional character, and that her courage and her feelings are likewise the products of an author's pen. We believe that it is fictional that Elizabeth Bennett has a witty and acerbic father, that she is brave, that she regrets having made certain judgments about Darcy and his motives. That is, we may believe any number of things about what is fictionally the case, but a fictional character remains a theoretical entity of literary criticism,[12] and as such it can have neither virtues nor sensitivities nor, indeed, non-metaphorical parents. And the belief that it is fictional that Elizabeth Bennett is brave is rather about the fictionality of a state of affairs than about something that would elicit our admiration. I suppose that a belief about the fictionality of something *could* elicit our admiration in circumstances where the fictionality itself is admirable: "You made that *up*? What an imagination you have!" But this is certainly not the kind of case under consideration. If admiration of Elizabeth Bennett on account of her courage, or disapproval of Sir Thomas Bertram on account of his maddening and narrow-minded certainty that he has a right to make everyone's decisions for them, involve cognitions (thinking that is liable to rational assessment), as I agree with Nussbaum that they do, then these are thoughts entertained in imagination rather than beliefs. I am therefore happy to concede that there is a cognitive aspect of emotional reactions to fictional entities and events, but must insist that the candidate cognition is a thought entertained in imagination. This does not rule out the possibility that emotions with

---

[12] Peter Van Inwagen, "Creatures of Fiction," *American Philosophical Quarterly* 14 (1977): 299–308. See also, Nicholas Wolterstorff on characters as person-kinds in *Works and Worlds of Art* (Oxford: Clarendon Press, 1980), pp. 144–9.

connections to beliefs can be aroused by literature, as has been indicated above. However, the latter have broader intentional objects – they would not be responses to specific fictional characters and incidents.

My second departure from Nussbaum's approach, though I hope to have shown that the initial difference is not a vast one, is in regard to my contention that literature serves some of the same functions that thought experiments do in ethics, though often with considerably more effectiveness. I describe this as a departure not because I think Nussbaum's account is in some way incompatible with it, but because the Jamesian concern with subtleties and mysterious or obscure distinctions seems rather different from the stark simplicity of the (often maligned) intuition pump, the kind of thought experiment with which fiction is most frequently associated. The term, I am told, originates with Daniel Dennett, in whose capable hands I leave the explanation:

> If you look at the history of philosophy, you see that all the great and influential stuff has been technically full of holes but utterly memorable and vivid. They are what I call "intuition pumps" – lovely thought experiments. Like Plato's cave, and Descartes's evil demon, and Hobbes' vision of the state of nature and the social contract, and even Kant's idea of the categorical imperative. I don't know of any philosopher who thinks any one of those is a logically sound argument for anything. But they're wonderful imagination grabbers, jungle gyms for the imagination. They structure the way you think about a problem. These are the real legacy of the history of philosophy. A lot of philosophers have forgotten that, but I like to make intuition pumps.
>
> I like to think I'm drifting back to what philosophy used to be, which has been forgotten in many quarters in philosophy during the last thirty or forty years, when philosophy has become a sometimes ridiculously technical and dry, logic-chopping subject for a lot of people – applied logic, applied mathematics. There's always a place for that, but it's nowhere near as big a place as a lot of people think.
>
> I coined the term "intuition pump," and its first use was derogatory. I applied it to John Searle's "Chinese room," which I said was not a proper argument but just an intuition pump. I went on to say that intuition pumps are fine if they're used correctly, but they can also be misused. They're not arguments, they're stories. Instead of having a conclusion, they pump an intuition. They get you to say "Aha! Oh, I get it!"[13]

If fiction is to be regarded as a thought experiment, then it will most often be so regarded with Dennett's intuition pump firmly in mind.

---

[13]   http://www.edge.org/documents/ThirdCulture/r-Ch.10.html

I will try to show that Nussbaum's Jamesian approach, however subtle and amenable to our apprehension of the obscure and the ambiguous, nonetheless encourages a clear and disambiguating alliance between literary works and certain kinds of ethical arguments. I will also attempt to establish that considering literary works outright as thought experiments requires one to take into account various kinds of subtleties and ambiguities in content and to consider as well the impact of literary form on how it is one takes that content. That is, I believe that Nussbaum's approach, in some respects at least, *does* treat literature as a thought experiment, and that different literary styles and concerns give rise to quite distinct forms of thought experiment. But, as some readers will doubtless note, I use the term "thought experiment" rather broadly.

First, in arguing against Posner's criticism of her work, Nussbaum makes it clear that the moral import of many works hinges on neither complexity nor obscurity. Dickens' novels, for instance, are said to "take us into the lives of those who are different in circumstance from ourselves and enable us to understand how similar hopes and fears are differently realized in different social circumstances."[14] This is clearly much the same process that we employ when we empathize with actual people. We form beliefs about their distinct situations and then proceed to imagine what it would be like to experience them. Although Nussbaum maintains that empathy in itself isn't always sufficient for compassion, it seems clear that both fiction and empathy lead us to inhabit the worlds of others in imagination, just as they both encourage the adoption of alien perspectives. This is surely not insignificant when we choose to regard literature with an eye to its impact on our ethical lives. Neither need this aspect of our encounters with fiction be hindered by complexities and obscurity. In the case of the Dickens example, at least, much of the ethical impact of the work centers on dispelling illusions and clarifying facts.

My own contention about Hume and Austen isn't simply that Austen provides us with illustrations of Hume's ethical stance, though it will be necessary to establish a range of such similarities at the outset. I would like to establish further, beyond these initial parallels, that Austen's novels may be regarded as thought experiments that *demonstrate* (at least in the loose sense employed by devotees of the intuition pump) something about the kind of moral reasoning that Hume advocates, that engage us in that rational/emotional process as part and parcel of our imaginative participation in the work.

---

[14] Nussbaum, "Exactly and Responsibly," 350.

Consider the simplest kinds of thought experiments, especially thought experiments in ethics, and how they work. Many of these are intended to test the effectiveness or applicability of moral principles (often by providing counterexamples) in a way that depends almost entirely on our immediate reactions to particular cases. Utilitarians present us with examples in which a rigid adherence to moral rules – the rule of promise-keeping, say – prevents an agent from saving a life. Deontologists, on the other hand, muster an arsenal of cases in which insignificant increases in utility are obtainable only at the expense of someone's life or someone's rights, attempting to show that utilitarians would be required by their ethical system to take lives and trample rights without compunction. Such examples cannot assume the truth of the presenter's ethical stance without begging the question. They clearly do not assume the truth of the principle they are intended to criticize. The point of such thought experiments *must* be to confront the audience with a case to which they *react* as wrong, in order to demonstrate the inadequacy of the principle under consideration. Since this reaction should properly depend neither on the principle under review nor on that preferred by the presenter of the example, it seems clear that what is essential to the entire process is the emotional reaction of the auditor. That is, thought experiments, and the manner in which ethicists deploy them, suggest in themselves that emotion can play a serious role in ethics, something that Hume maintains from the outset when he claims that the source of morality is to be found in sentiment, and that our emotional reactions of approbation and disapprobation provide the key to identifying virtue and vice.

Some may maintain that if Austen were conducting thought experiments, she would have joined Hume as a *teller* of moral principles, assuming with Roy Sorensen that literary works cannot be regarded as thought experiments because their authors didn't create them with this purpose in mind.[15] But philosophers like Noel Carroll, Eileen John, Martha Nussbaum, and others suggest, as we have seen, that fiction can cause us to examine what concepts mean and can lead readers to apply them to characters and events on the basis of their actual conceptual commitments, ascribing to fiction the kind of clarificatory function typically associated with thought experiments. The same mechanism is thought to govern our reactions to fiction and to the world, leading these philosophers, just as Hume has done, to stress the connection between ethical salience and emotional response.

---

[15]   See Simon Blackburn, "Thought Experiment," in *The Oxford Dictionary of Philosophy* (Oxford: Oxford University Press, 1994), p. 377; Roy A. Sorensen, *Thought Experiments* (New York: Oxford University Press, 1992), p. 289.

Fiction is not a work of philosophy, but it can have philosophical value nonetheless. In this sense, then, it can be held by even the most conservative to do some of the work of a thought experiment.

Of course, Martha Nussbaum is not the only philosopher who has proposed treating fiction as the kind of thought experiment whose nature has just been sketched here, though she and Eileen John[16] are among the few to focus in considerable detail on literature itself – and on *the manner in which* literature may fulfill such a function. They are also among the few who do so with reference to the effects of literary form on this function. But there are other philosophers with a good deal to say about the matter. Noel Carroll, Berys Gaut, Matthew Kieran, Bashshar Haydar, James Harold, Amy Mullin, Mary Devereaux, and a score of others have all written, many at length, on the moral evaluation of art.[17] I cannot hope to do justice to the impressive body of philosophy that is represented by these names, but I can attempt to offer a general account of my own of the relationship between fiction and moral knowledge, an account that

[16]   Eileen John, "Art and Knowledge," in *The Routledge Companion to Aesthetics*, ed. Robert C. Solomon (New York: Routledge, 2001), pp. 329–40. See also: "Reading Fiction and Conceptual Knowledge: Philosophical Thought in Literary Context," *Journal of Aesthetics and Art Criticism* 56 (1998): 331–48; "Subtlety and Moral Vision in Fiction," *Philosophy and Literature* 19 (1995): 308–19.

[17]   Noel Carroll, "Moderate Moralism," *British Journal of Aesthetics* 36 (1996): 223–38. Carroll goes on in several articles to argue that literature can be a source of moral knowledge and education. See, e.g., "The Wheel of Virtue: Art, Literature, and Moral Knowledge," *Journal of Aesthetics and Art Criticism* 60.1 (2002): 3–26. See also "Art, Narrative, and Moral Understanding," in *Aesthetics and Ethics: Essays at the Intersection*, ed. Jerrold Levinson (Cambridge: Cambridge University Press, 1998), pp. 126–60. Roughly similar approaches have been taken by: Berys Gaut, "The Ethical Criticism of Art," in *Aesthetics and Ethics: Essays at the Intersection*, ed. Jerrold Levinson (Cambridge: Cambridge University Press, 1998), pp. 182–205; Oliver Conolly and Bashshar Haydar, "Narrative Art and Moral Knowledge," *British Journal of Aesthetics* 41 (April 2001): 109–24; Matthew Kieran, "In Defence of the Ethical Evaluation of Narrative Art," *British Journal of Aesthetics* 41 (January 2001): 26–38; Amy Mullin, "Evaluating Art: Significant Imagining v. Moral Soundness," *Journal of Aesthetics and Art Criticism* 60.2 (2002): 137–49. Contributions have been made by Mary Devereaux in "Beauty and Evil: The Case of Leni Riefenstahl's *Triumph of the Will*," in *Aesthetics and Ethics*, ed. Levinson, pp. 227–56 and "Moral Judgments and Works of Art: The Case of Narrative Literature," *Journal of Aesthetics and Art Criticism* 62 (2004): 3–11. There are also significant contributions from James Harold in "On Judging the Moral Value of Narrative Artworks," *Journal of Aesthetics and Art Criticism* 64 (2006): 259–70; "Infected by Evil," *Philosophical Explorations* 8 (2005): 173–87; "Narrative Engagement with *Atonement* and *The Blind Assassin*," *Philosophy and Literature* 29 (2005): 130–45; and "Flexing the Imagination," *Journal of Aesthetics and Art Criticism* 61 (2003): 247–57.

arises out of the discussion in which I and the aforementioned philosophers have for some time been engaged.[18]

Any investigation of fiction as a contributor to moral knowledge, whether or not one regards that knowledge as relevant to the aesthetic value of a work, brings with it as a corollary the assumption that fiction may be implicated in negative moral effects. My own entry into the discussion came as the result of my interest in David Hume's contentions about our disinclination to enter into moral perspectives that are alien to us. In "Of the Standard of Taste" Hume speaks of works in which "vicious manners are described, without being marked with . . . disapprobation" (ST 246).[19] We cannot "enter into such sentiments; and however [we] . . . may excuse the poet, on account of the manners of his age, [we] . . . never can relish the composition" (ST 246). There is a wide literature on imaginative resistance, spearheaded by some fascinating work by Tamar Szabo Gendler, who takes the preceding to identify "the puzzle of imaginative resistance: the puzzle of explaining our comparative difficulty in imagining morally deviant worlds," a conundrum especially in view of the fact that we experience no difficulty whatsoever in imagining empirically deviant ones.[20] Although she considers and rejects Kendall Walton's claim that we're unable to engage imaginatively with a work which requires us to imagine conceptual impossibilities,[21] she concedes in the end (at least in the last conference paper I heard) that there may be a few cases of this kind. I want to say that they are more frequent than Gendler and other philosophers are willing to allow, and that a stance which focuses our attention on conceptual impossibilities has a direct bearing on the question of moral knowledge. Consider the following as a rough approximation of the central point. We cannot imagine what we cannot conceive. If we are asked to imagine the acceptability of conduct of a kind we believe is never

---

[18]   I have published on related topics in the fourth chapter of my book *What's Hecuba to Him? Fictional Events and Actual Emotions* (University Park, PA: Penn State Press, 1997) and in "Only Kidding: the Connection between Amusement and Our Attitudes," *Southwest Philosophy Review* 22.2 (2006): 1–16; "Knowing Better: The Epistemic Underpinnings of Moral Criticism of Fiction," *Southwest Philosophy Review* 21.1 (2005): 35–44; "Pleased and Afflicted: Hume on the Paradox of Tragic Pleasure," *Hume Studies* 30.2 (November 2004): 213–36; and "The Vicious Habits of Entirely Fictive People: Hume on the Moral Evaluation of Art," *Philosophy and Literature* 26 (2002): 38–51.

[19]   Thanks to Susan Feagin and Aaron Meskin, who argued with me about issues related to this claim, thereby forcing me into a position of greater consistency.

[20]   Tamar Szabo Gendler, "The Puzzle of Imaginative Resistance," *Journal of Philosophy* 47 (February 2000): 55–81.

[21]   Kendall Walton, "Morals in Fiction and Fictional Morality (I)," *Proceedings of the Aristotelian Society*, suppl. 68 (1994): 27–50.

permissible (via the endorsement of an omniscient narrator say), if we are asked to imagine it approvingly, we may well encounter imaginative resistance unless, of course, the fiction leads us to change our minds and come to consider that it is possible, at least on occasion, for such conduct to be acceptable. I concede that the moral cases of imaginative resistance that are most plausible tend to be extreme ones: white supremacist literature is a case in point. It is most obvious in such cases that our concept of what is morally permissible undermines our ability to adopt attitudes of approval toward what we imagine, and that is just because we cannot imagine what we cannot conceive (and we cannot conceive that genocide, say, is an admirable course of action). Naturally, it is a simple matter to imagine that some character or other believes that the conduct in question is permissible even if we do not. But we ourselves cannot imagine that conduct is permissible unless we believe it is *possible* for actions of that kind to be right.

Of course, the kinds of endorsements made in fictions do not typically challenge our moral concepts in such blatant ways. We will usually imagine that it is possible that the kind of behavior endorsed in a fiction is permissible in one circumstance or another. As regards endorsement, while some works are ambiguous on this score, there exist a considerable number in which endorsements are indisputable, in which it is true in the world of the work that certain conduct is correct or laudable – perhaps only in the special circumstances with which the fiction presents us. In such cases, our entering into the work's endorsement may merely amount to our believing that conduct of this kind is permissible in some carefully delimited range of cases. We will often enter into such endorsements. But the fact that we cannot *always* do so is something which strongly suggests that moral (and probably other) attitudes transcend fictional contexts. It is the negative case, more than the positive one, that clarifies the connection between moral concepts and the imagination.

The central matter of interest here is not about how often it turns out that we are afflicted by imaginative resistance, but about the epistemic underpinnings of the imagination. The resistance phenomenon suggests that imaginatively entering into a fiction's endorsements makes us complicit in its perspective on the world. I have described fictions as thought experiments because fictions engage us at the level of our epistemic and conceptual commitments, and a thought experiment is a device which enables us to discern possibilities and to clarify concepts. Thought experiments in ethics can reinforce or refine or even revise our conceptions of what is right or virtuous or just. And fictions can do the same. To imaginatively engage with a fiction and imaginatively enter into its endorsements can be to accede to certain judgments – that some behaviors are permissible given a particular set of alternatives, that some forms of decision-making morally mandate an initial attempt to acquire information, that one thing can count as evidence for another. We don't believe in the existence of fictional characters or states of affairs, but we have plenty of beliefs about what can count as evidence, about what is permissible in different ranges of situations, about what kind of information is necessary if one is to make a competent decision. Those beliefs may be reinforced by our perusal of a literary work. They may be undermined when a work invites us to imagine exceptions or presents us with counterexamples. A belief may even be refined, as a fiction leads us to imagine a new way of considering evidence or justifying a decision. Imagination and hypothetical thinking in general cannot be severed from their conceptual underpinnings. If we cannot imagine what we cannot conceive, then what we can imagine is something to the possibility of which we have acceded.

I hope that the preceding has established at least a few grounds for regarding fiction as a particular kind of thought experiment. I will next try to show that differences in the style and content of literary works will yield very different kinds of contributions to moral knowledge and to moral reasoning. As Nussbaum says, "not all readers will have the same ethical view or project; thus a work that bores or offends one reader ethically may be exactly what the other is looking for."[22] So, for those of us who find Henry James perhaps a little impenetrable, a little muffled in ambiguities, for those who are sometimes a little dizzied by the unremitting insistence on fineness of perception, there is still hope. There is more than one kind of ethical project. More to the point, as philosophers like Adam Morton have suggested, the deployment of reliable moral principles is only one part of an exponentially larger ethical story about how it is one ought to live one's life. Much human misery occurs, not because of sadism and cruelty and other commonplace vices and transgressions, "but because a large number of people act with limited care and imagination."[23] It is safe to assume that most literature will have what moral impact it does, not on account of the mere depiction of the applicability of various principles to different situations, but on account of an exploration of a multitude of other possible phenomena that can affect our moral lives. I will claim that both the phenomena so explored and the mode of exploration will differ with the pen.

---

[22] Nussbaum, "Exactly and Responsibly," 356.
[23] Adam Morton, *On Evil* (New York: Routledge, 2004), p. 5.

One of the things that a Jamesian literary approach will incline us toward, according to Nussbaum, will be the adoption of an Aristotelian ethical perspective. That is, "to respond 'at the right times, with reference to the right objects, towards the right people, with the right aim, and in the right way, is what is appropriate and best,'" a clear characteristic of the virtuous life.[24] This is a kind of responsiveness that Jamesian characters are said to demonstrate (although I am inclined to argue that their way is not the only way to demonstrate it) and that is elicited from readers of James by both the content and form of his prose (although, again, other types of form and content may do so as well). Just as Jamesian character may show "a respect for the irreducibly concrete moral context . . . [and] a determination to scrutinize all aspects of this particular with intensely focused perception,"[25] so the reader is invited to pay the very kind of moral attention that the novel demonstrates, to share the character's scrutiny of appearances and deploy a sensitivity to nuance that, in the end, can cultivate such habits for exercise in life.

And just as a reader of James may, in the end, pay the kind of moral attention to events in her own life that James' characters do to events in their lives and that James does to what he writes about, so an inveterate reader of Austen may, in the course of reading her work, begin to exhibit a pattern of moral attention that is cultivated by this practice. But here the differences begin, and they are enormous. Where James is complex and obscure and subtle, and prone to delve into a kind of moral microscopy of observation, Austen is direct, naturalistic, acerbic, and more than a little cold. There are no sensitive, metaphorical images or delvings into the minutiae of a given motivation. Rather, Austen mocks, strips away rationalizations, and reveals what is contemptible quite ruthlessly.

I will indulge myself here in a restrained and abbreviated diatribe simply to forestall confusion on the part of those readers who are more familiar with film versions of Austen's work and to whom the above description will probably seem utterly alien. A few recent screen offerings, *Pride and Prejudice* (written by Deborah Moggach and directed by Joe Wright)[26] and *Mansfield Park* (the 1999 Miramax iteration) for example, seem almost exclusively to be populated by Brontë people, swooning and sighing,

---

[24]   Nussbaum, "Finely Aware," 525.
[25]   Nussbaum, "Finely Aware," 526.
[26]   For a splendidly enraged review of this film, which happily led me to the first of the Virginia Woolf quotations below, see Gina Fattore, "Pride and Pathetic," on Salon.com, December 21, 2005. http://dir.salon.com/story/ent/movies/feature/2005/12/21/pride/index.html

rather than any such persons as Austen may have had in mind (with the possible exception of Marianne Dashwood in any version of *Sense and Sensibility*). Here is my heretical thought on the matter, or at least heretical by Hollywood standards. Austen is not a romantic novelist. She writes novels about romantic entanglements, but she in not often inclined to be sentimental in the pejorative sense. I defer to Virginia Woolf's description of Austen's writing: "Never, even at the emotional age of fifteen, did she . . . obliterate a sarcasm in a spasm of compassion, or blur an out line in a mist of rhapsody. Spasms and rhapsodies, she seems to have said, pointing with her stick, end THERE; and the boundary line is perfectly distinct."[27] Austen's novels raise questions about character and human nature, present moral dilemmas, and address concerns about human interaction in a naturalistic setting, as do James' novels. But Austen addresses such questions in a way that shows just how infernally proximity can chafe, how ludicrous pretensions and overgenerous self-assessments really are, how narrow is the point of vantage from which it is possible for most people to see the world. Austen holds the world up for ridicule by pinpointing its idiocies. She doesn't inevitably make us aware of the myriad subtleties in human interaction and decision. What is inevitable is her drawing our attention to what is salient in those interactions and those choices. She is not, as it were, a focuser in, but a refiner. Delusions and self-deceptions are burned away with the kind of unscrupulous clarity that makes her very much a child of the Enlightenment. Austen's writing is spare – it is both less beautiful and less poetic than that of James. Austen writes about ordinary things in a direct way, with no heroics in her prose or her subject matter. Virginia Woolf compares certain aspects of Austen's writing to Greek drama:

> It is thus, with a thousand differences of degree, that in English literature Jane Austen shapes a novel. There comes a moment – "I will dance with you," says Emma [Watson] – which rises higher than the rest, which, though not eloquent in itself, or violent, or made striking by beauty of language, has the whole weight of the book behind it. In Jane Austen, too, we have the same sense, though the ligatures are much less tight, that her figures are bound, and restricted to a few definite movements. She, too, in her modest, everyday prose, chose the dangerous art where one slip means death.[28]

[27]   Virginia Woolf, *The Common Reader*, First Series (1925). Project Gutenberg of Australia ebook. http://gutenberg.net.au/ebooks03/0300031.txt
[28]   Ibid.

But this does not, I think, make her work any less likely to engage us morally than that of James. The nature of that engagement will simply be different – more amenable to the tastes and predispositions and ethical projects of some readers than others, as Nussbaum has pointed out. It is possible, of course, to profit from both.

Yet it is easy to see how a James person, an inveterate reader of James, would find Austen too ordinary, too narrow, too unreflecting and unlyrical. And one can see how an Austen person might look at the passage from *The Golden Bowl* as Nussbaum has explicated it for us, the passage in which Maggie realizes that "she cannot love her husband except by banishing her father. But if she banishes her father, he will live unhappy and die alone."[29] It is not that the passage would not be moving for an Austen person. The fantastic and lyrical sea metaphor, the father's recognition of and wish for his daughter's freedom, his sacrifice and renunciation, could not fail to move most readers. But an Austen person would wipe his eyes and proceed to irritate a devotee of James to distraction by wondering, after due consideration, why it had to happen just that way, why such a sacrifice was necessary, why no compromise was possible. Since when are loves mutually exclusive? Why could not the relationship with the father grow and evolve to make room for the relationship with the husband? Would everyday people with an understandable distaste for supererogation not, in everyday parlance, try to have their cake and eat it too? Or at least give it a try before deciding it had to be one or the other? This is not, I absolutely concede, the right way to read that passage in James. At least it is not the way to read it if one hopes to learn the things that Henry James has to teach us. But it illustrates just the kind of thing that can happen when someone with a different ethical attunement, an ear to different kinds of ethical concerns, gets ahold of James. It sometimes isn't pretty. If the experience of reading James does involve us in a thought experiment of sorts, it is of a different species from the kind in which reading Austen involves us.

For purposes of comparison, let me finish this chapter with an illustration of the kind of ethical and even aesthetic attunement that I believe is fostered by reading Jane Austen without, at this stage, resorting to Hume. Most of the rest of this book is replete with comparisons between David Hume and Jane Austen. At the present juncture, however, let us allow Austen to stand on her own, if only as a promissory note that suggests how it is that Austen may help us understand some things that philosophical writing alone may not. I have purposely chosen an example in

---

[29]   Nussbaum, "Finely Aware," 518.

which no argument or counterexample is embedded (many examples of the latter type will be offered later) in an effort to simplify the process. The following is a single, albeit capacious, sentence from *Persuasion*. Captain Benwick has not yet recovered from the loss of his fiancée a year past. Anne Elliot is sympathetic, and engages him in conversation about things literary:

> Though shy, he did not seem reserved; it had rather the appearance of feelings glad to burst their usual restraints; and having talked of poetry, the richness of the present age, and gone through a brief comparison of opinion as to the first-rate poets, trying to ascertain whether *Marmion* or *The Lady of the Lake* were to be preferred, and how ranked the *Giaour* and *The Bride of Abydos*; and moreover, how the *Giaour* was to be pronounced, he showed himself so intimately acquainted with all the tenderest songs of the one poet, and all the impassioned descriptions of hopeless agony of the other; he repeated, with such tremulous feeling, the various lines which imaged a broken heart, or a mind destroyed by wretchedness, and looked so entirely as if he meant to be understood, that she ventured to hope he did not always read only poetry, and to say, that she thought it was the misfortune of poetry to be seldom safely enjoyed by those who enjoyed it completely; and that the strong feelings which alone could estimate it truly were the very feelings which ought to taste it but sparingly. (P 100–1)

Here we have a young man who has lost someone he loves, and whose loss is blunted just enough by time to enable him to indulge in a little literary wallowing. He sees himself, a little absurdly, in the suffering heroes of Scott and Byron. He wants others to identify him as just such a sufferer: destroyed, wretched, deprived of love forever by a cruel fate – a tragic hero. Yet, just as is true in the case of the paradox of tragedy, it is clear that this identification and the requisite self-image are not devoid of enjoyment, that there is some compensation in casting oneself in a role typically taken on by poetic principals. Benwick has, clearly, become a little too fond of exercising his distress and sorrow, awakening and reawakening them in a passionate identification with characters too romantic for real life. Indeed, Austen conveys with greater subtlety here something that she is more direct about in *Northanger Abbey*: a critical attitude toward melodrama and high romanticism. Yet doubt is never cast on Benwick's distress. It is simply made clear that this distress can coexist with pleasanter experiences. And Anne's genuine kindness, her wish to help Benwick and, without injuring his pride, to detach him from his habits of identification are also made clear. The depiction of Benwick here is absolutely characteristic of Austen. We are led to see through the Byronic pretensions with amusement and contempt. But the contempt is not unkind and our amusement so benign that we cannot help but like him. Austen is less kind to other characters: no villain escapes being laughed at. It is a signal virtue of her prose to uncover the ridiculous in the least expected places. It is another virtue of her stories that she offers us blended people, always composites: never entirely bad, though sometimes entirely irritating, never entirely good, though sometimes frustrated by aspiring to such impossibilities, usually a combination of the admirable and the less so. That is, Jane Austen does not present us with ideals to live up to but with versions of ourselves, or our annoying college roommates, or our husband's mother, or the Vice President of Academic Affairs: always vivid, always believable, often as irritating as their real-life counterparts. And she teaches us how not to take them (or our expectations of them) too seriously. This is a moral lesson of a usefulness that cannot be underestimated.

Most remarkable, perhaps, is how Austen illustrates in one sentence the development of a friendship. The very rhythms of the prose that delimit the progress of the conversation mimic the emotional progress of that friendship. We begin with delight in discovery of a common interest and even greater delight in the identification of favorite authors, exhibited in a flurry of swift interchanges and excited questions. There is the happy discovery of a willing ear, open to confidences and questions, the sheer satisfaction of commonality. Then, on the basis of the mutuality which has been established, a different tone is adopted. Something personal, flimsily disguised in poetic allusion, is tentatively exposed. This is the beginning of vulnerability. A segue from the literary to the almost intimate. Will the other person be put off? Will she pretend not to understand? Is it permissible? Yes. The intimacy is not only acknowledged, but accepted. Only friends can give advice with concern and affection. The relationship, which began with books, is cemented into friendship by advice about books. More prose, says Anne, to leaven the poetry, more work by the moralists of the day. She recommends memoirs of real-life non-Byronic sorts who have had a hard time of it but refrain from wailing. The pattern here, both vivid and convincing, is of a swiftly evolving friendship, created through and by conversation, and through and by literature as well, beginning with commonalities and likemindedness, turning to timid but hopeful self-exposure, moving through acceptance and a kind of joining of interests. Benwick's imperfections are no bar to friendship. Indeed, later in the same book, we learn that the best company is "is the company of clever, well-informed people, who have a great deal of conversation" (P 150). Stupidity and ignorance and uncommunicativeness form more of a bar to companionship than a few personal foibles.

Without belaboring the point, it is worth noting that a few other interesting things are suggested by the passage. We learn that sentiment is a necessary adjunct to the understanding of art, but that such sentiments must be regulated. We also learn that misery may sometimes be ameliorated not by changing one's circumstances, but by changing the objects of one's attention. Finally, we learn that literature, and reading in general, has the power to change the emotional tenor of one's life, that it resonates with and can reflect that life. Benwick uses literature as a kind of model in accordance with which to reinvest himself in his personal tragedy. Anne, seeing this, suggests a shift in literary subject from abject despair to fortitude, counting on a resonance of emotion between literary or biographical subject and reader. We, seeing Anne's sympathy for Benwick and (possibly also understanding exactly how it is that one can make friends over books), share it, and feel with her both the mild amusement and the affectionate concern. Benwick appeals to us because he appeals to Anne. He literally appeals to her for understanding, and figuratively appeals to her as a slightly absurd but endearing companion.

It would be difficult to regard a single sentence, however commodious, as a thought experiment. But there is something to be said here for the possibility that our conception of what constitutes an acceptable companion, or our conception of the role of vulnerability in the forming of a friendship, or our conception of the effects of literature on the emotional tone and attunement of our lives, may expand to accommodate some of the ideas conveyed by means of that sentence. In James, what is characteristic of a reading that holds ethical significance is the concentration, the ever finer focus, the transition to a sudden poetic metaphor or symbol that leaves us grasping for associations, sometimes bewildered by the loveliness of the images, often following out an unexpected analogy it presents. In Austen, such a reading is entirely different, for it counts on our *recognition* of the kinds of character traits and situations and interactions it presents. It takes our familiarity and then reconfigures it, shows us incongruities that hitherto escaped us, always noticing the absurdity of people and their desirable and undesirable connectedness to one another. If there is a laughing gaze that can be cast upon the world then Austen has it. It is a gaze that is at best sporadically kind. It is more often sympathetic in the sense Hume used that word, for we can enter into a given character's perspective without a touch of pity. It reveals the ordinary for what it is – an arena for the exhibition of human character.

With that in mind, we will soon proceed to consider correspondences between Hume and Austen. I have stated at the outset that Austen's works enable readers to see the world through the lens of a Humean perspective. But I will want to make a few further claims, which will also have to rest on the investigation of the aforementioned correspondences. I believe that a Humean reading or interpretation of Austen can provide the most satisfying and complete picture of the insights her works convey, more so than would a Shaftesburian or Kantian or Aristotelian reading. That is, I believe that a Humean perspective can help us see things in Austen we haven't seen before. And conversely, I believe that Austen's prose can help to elaborate productively, and sometimes surprisingly, on elements of Hume's philosophy. These two claims will be reserved for the final chapter. But before we begin delving into the correspondences whose investigation must precede it, a final foray must be made into the question of literary form, the impact it has on content, and the role it might play in literature when it is conceived of as a thought experiment. What are the crucial differences between literary prose and philosophical exposition? It should not come as a shock that someone who takes a consuming interest in producing a naturalistic depiction of human virtues and foibles, who likes to trace out with her characters how life could be and could have gone and the impact we can have on it, is going to have a radically different agenda from a philosopher. And it should also not surprise us that some of those depictions can venture into arenas less accessible or not accessible at all to typical philosophical prose, or even the far less typical prose of David Hume.

2

Literary Form and Philosophical Content

In "Of Tragedy,"[1] David Hume reflects, to some purpose if not at length, on the role form may play in explaining the paradox of tragedy. How is it that we can derive pleasure from the tragic? Hume indicates that: "This extraordinary effect proceeds from that very eloquence, with which the melancholy scene is represented. The genius required to paint objects in a lively manner, the art employed in collecting all the pathetic circumstances, the judgment displayed in disposing them: the exercise . . . of these noble talents, together with the force of expression, and the beauty of oratorial numbers, diffuse the highest satisfaction on the audience" (OT 219–20). For our purposes, which involve the investigation of the role of literary form in literature's functioning as a thought experiment, we can derive the following insights from Hume's reflections. Like a conductor, the author orchestrates our attention. In literature, unlike life, inessentials are eliminated and relevant considerations are cast into sharp relief. The author decides which facets of an experience to bring within our purview, which aspects of a character's thinking will be foregrounded, which circumstances are crucial or significant. It is the author who governs and directs our attention and who, in so doing, determines at once the perspective we inhabit and the emotional attitude which it inclines us to adopt, because the *manner* in which we attend to something is as much within his or her power to dictate as is the subject to which we attend, the two proving to be interconnected.

So far, that is just "the art employed in collecting all the pathetic circumstances" and "the judgment displayed in disposing them." Yet to be considered are the impact of metaphor and symbol and irony, even the

---

[1] David Hume, "Of Tragedy," in *Essays: Moral, Political and Literary*, ed. Eugene F. Miller (Indianapolis: Liberty Classics, 1987), pp. 216–25. Henceforth abbreviated OT.

effects of the rhythm and cadence of the prose. I will not pretend to give anything like a complete account of the effects of these on the reader, but it seems possible at least to offer an adequate explanation of what Martha Nussbaum may have meant when she indicated that the morally valuable aspects of a literary passage "could not be captured in a summary or paraphrase," that any alteration in the description of an act "seems to risk producing a different act" from the one described.[2] With literature, it is not just content that can lend genuine insights, that can lead us to rehearse or alter our moral judgments, that can enhance our moral understanding. It is also the way that content is presented to us. In investigating the impact of form on readers, an attempt will be made not just to contrast literature with exposition, but to investigate unique aspects of *Austen's* literary style.

The most obvious point to be made here in relation to the effect of literature on our moral lives is about its particularity. Literature presents us with specific cases: not roughly sketched out in the way an example is when it is used in a philosophical argument, but fully fleshed. Indeed, we can know more about the plights of fictional characters than we do about those of actual people, since an author can make us privy to a character's thoughts and feelings and experiences, whereas we are forced to make (sometimes inadequate) inferences to determine the mental states of other people. Now, so far, this is just a matter of a sufficiency of information. But, of course, real literature goes far beyond the mere detailed presentation of events, for it will make salient for us the aspects of those events that are critical to moral judgment. It will show them to us in an order, with a subtext and associations, and in a way that elicits (or at least is intended to elicit) attitudes and emotions of a particular kind. That some of those emotions are feelings of approbation and disapprobation certainly buttresses the contention that our reactions to fictions can be moral ones.

Part of what complicates any discussion of such matters is the interdependence of what are typically referred to as form and content. Eloquent or poetic writing on behalf of the characters one has created makes it fictional that the characters themselves are eloquent. Offering a version of *Othello* in contemporary English, something Andrew Davies tried recently to surprisingly good effect, presents us with an entirely new fictional world. In that world, the characters say different things (eschewing iambic pentameter) and occupy a different place than do the denizens of the original

---

[2] Martha Nussbaum, "Finely Aware and Richly Responsible: Moral Attention and the Moral Task of Literature," *The Journal of Philosophy* 82.10 (1985): 516–29, at 522–3.

play, despite the fact that they all experience the same tragic sequence of personal disasters outlined in the original script. Indeed, it seems evident that all performance worlds of the same work must differ substantially, in that they will have to differ in fictional facts concerning character appearance, delivery, and so on. In all such cases it seems clear that the mode of presentation to some extent determines what we can take it has been presented. That is, if what we want to call content is, as I assume, what is true in the world of the work, then the manner in which that content is presented to a reader or to an audience will in part determine what the content turns out to be.

As has been indicated, Martha Nussbaum contends that conception and form are intimately interrelated: were we to attempt a paraphrase of a work "in a very different form and style [it would] . . . not, in general, express the same conception."[3] It is tempting in this context to compare the two endings of *Persuasion* which Jane Austen wrote and which bring about the same denouement, for chapters 10 and 11 of the second volume were entirely revised before she completed the book. Engaging in a full-blown comparison at the present juncture is impossible, though an attempt will be made to contrast film adaptations, one of which takes an episode in Austen's earlier draft of chapter 10 as its point of departure (the Simon Burke iteration of *Persuasion* discussed below). We will begin by embarking on a more straightforward comparison, however: one involving the mere *placement among events* of a particular passage. I think here of a comparison between the novel and a recent television adaptation of *Persuasion* scripted by Simon Burke, or a comparison between the Burke adaptation and the much more faithful 1995 adaptation by Nick Dear, which for the most part retained the novel's sequence of events. The Burke adaptation differs from both the Dear adaptation and the novel (among many differences) in the placement of a particular conversation: Anne Elliot's argument with another character (Captain Harville in the novel and the Dear adaptation, Captain Benwick in the Burke). The argument centers on whether women or men are more devoted, on which is likely to love longest.

In Austen's novel and in Nick Dear, this speech is the crucial event upon which Captain Wentworth's decision to declare his feelings turns. The overcoming of Wentworth's pride and resentment, which have prevented him from giving voice to his affection, hinge on his having heard Anne's words. She says to Harville,

[3]   Martha Nussbaum, *Love's Knowledge: Essays on Philosophy and Literature* (New York: Oxford University Press, 1990), p. 5.

"we certainly do not forget you, so soon as you forget us. It is, perhaps, our fate rather than our merit. We cannot help ourselves. We live at home, quiet, confined, and our feelings prey upon us. You are forced on exertion. You have always a profession, pursuits, business of some sort or other, to take you back into the world immediately, and continual occupation and change soon weaken impressions." (P 232)

The conversation is remarkable to me, personally, for Austen's keen appreciation, evidenced in Anne's keen appreciation, of the psychological effects of living a circumscribed, restricted life with no formal occupation, of her complete awareness that most women knew no other kind of life, and of her suggestion that they were on that account more liable to be obsessive in their devotion than men, having literally nothing better to think about. This is my language and understanding rather than Anne Elliot's or Jane Austen's, yet these ideas are so prominent in the passage that it seems impossible to reinterpret them into some less incisive and more sentimental panegyric concerning women's proper lot. Austen doesn't recommend changes, of course. As usual, she merely observes. But Anne Elliot's observations have effects, for it is also clear that Wentworth's offer is an offer of an alternative to just such a lot as Anne describes. The ideal marriage, as it is indisputably presented in *Persuasion*, is between Admiral Croft and Wentworth's sister, and this is just the kind of relationship the Wentworth and Anne seem most likely to emulate, if only on account of their admiration of the Crofts. It shows us the diametrical opposite of confinement and limitation for women, since it is a marriage of equals. Mrs. Croft does not stay at home and brood while the Admiral sails. Instead, she sails everywhere with him – she is not left behind to pine in the approved manner, with nothing to dwell on but absent people. So Wentworth's immediate declaration, upon hearing Anne's description of women's lot, offers her an alternative in offering her a life less restricted and confined than the one she has described.

The conversation culminates in Anne's making the following statement to Harville:

"No, I believe you [i.e., men] capable of everything great and good in your married lives. I believe you equal to every important exertion, and to every domestic forbearance, so long as – if I may be allowed the expression – so long as you have an object. I mean while the woman you love lives, and lives for you. All the privilege I claim for my own sex (it is not a very enviable one; you need not covet it), is that of loving longest, when existence or when hope is gone." She could not immediately have uttered another sentence; her heart was too full, her breath too much oppressed. (P 235)

In the novel and the Nick Dear adaptation, Wentworth overhears Anne's conversation with Harville, and his overhearing it changes everything. The pivotal moment in the book rests on misdirection: Anne speaks to Harville but addresses Wentworth, Wentworth pretends to be writing a letter to a third party while eavesdropping, he then pretends to have forgotten his gloves in order to deliver a different letter written hastily in response to what Anne has said, Anne feigns indisposition to hide her agitation and provide an excuse for leaving and perhaps catching up with Wentworth to assure him that his affections are returned. One piece of misdirection falls out of the other, but Anne's disquisition on men and women is what begins the increasingly inevitable cascade of events, each following from the other in true Aristotelian fashion, and following a pattern of reversals and misdirection that seem Aristotelian as well. Nick Dear adds, not inappropriately, a closing scene in which we see Anne aboard Wentworth's ship, circumscribed no more, embarking on a life of at least modest adventure and about to see the world. She is not at home, not quiet, not confined.

In the adaptation by Burke, the argument is situated much earlier in the story. Only a few remnants of the original argument are retained, and these are inserted into dinner table chatter between Anne and Captain Benwick in a scene set at the Harvilles' during the ill-fated visit to Lyme. Anne's reflections about the confining nature of women's lives and the effects of such confinement are entirely eliminated. Wentworth is engaged in a noisy, laughing conversation at the other end of the dinner table, and does not overhear the argument. In fact, the argument has no causal impact on the plot. It now squats ineffectually in the middle of the story, whittled down almost to nothing, a mere reflection of Anne's hopeless feeling that she will love Wentworth forever despite the fact that she believes all hope is gone. It is a sentiment more worthy of the melodramatic Benwick than Austen's Anne who, in the novel at least, has considerable reason to believe her affections are returned and that Wentworth is eavesdropping on her conversation when she makes the statement about women loving longest when all hope is gone. *Everything* seems to be changed by this change in sequence: in my opinion, not for the better. The entire course of events that is precipitated by Anne's argument must now be managed in another way. In Burke, the *denoument* is set in motion when Wentworth pays Anne a visit in order to discover (allegedly on the Admiral's behalf) whether she will be marrying Elliot, a contrivance in part lifted, with many amendments, from the earlier version of chapter 10 which Austen had the good sense to replace. Anne tells him that she has no intention of marrying Elliot. They are then interrupted and

Wentworth (rather inexplicably) leaves. Anne soon follows in pursuit, meeting several people in the streets of Bath along the way to tie up loose plot elements, including Harville, who hands her the proposal letter Wentworth apparently nipped home to write before dashing out again. We see her racing for some considerable time through the streets of Bath, huffing and puffing, for all the world (as one mean-spirited blogger put it) as if she were in an episode of *The Amazing Race: Regency Edition*. What we have here is not the happy confluence of events that Austen describes, but a footrace, with Anne determined to chase Wentworth down before he changes his mind. The closing scene, in complete contrast to the Dear adaptation, presents an initially blindfolded Anne being surprised by the sight of Kellynch Hall, which Wentworth has just purchased for her. She has come full circle. She will be staying in just the place where she initially felt confined.

It is unfair, I suppose, to compare films and novels, which is part of my motivation for including the Nick Dear adaptation in the discussion. However, the primary purpose of the comparison was to allow us to examine two plotlines which differ slightly in respect of their sequencing of events. And here it really does seem that the two cannot express the same conception. Anne's argument with Harville is the stimulus for succeeding events in both the novel and the Dear adaptation. In being their causal antecedent, it makes these events different from those in the Burke adaptation, and it gives Wentworth a different motive for deciding to write the letter and thereby deciding to make himself vulnerable. There is kind of reciprocity at work in Wentworth's letter to Anne, as it is described in the novel and the more faithful adaptation. All in the room know Anne speaks, but none know her words are for (and about) Wentworth, to whom she has made herself vulnerable by speaking them. All know Wentworth writes, but none know he writes to Anne, to whom he makes himself vulnerable by admitting his feelings. When Wentworth writes "you pierce my soul" and "I am every instant hearing something which overpowers me" (P 237) he is speaking of Anne's *words*, of her veiled communication to him, and his communication to her is also veiled. Anne and Wentworth affect one another subtly, almost delicately, and very privately – just beneath the surfaces of things. Nothing of the sort is the case in the Burke adaptation. Wentworth is not overpowered. His letter is simply the result of Anne's announcement that she is available. Anne pierces his soul (we hear it in a voiceover) as a tidy romantic convention of proposal letters, not on account of what she has said about men and women and love. The relationship between this Anne and this Wentworth is not subtle or private or delicate. And I would argue that it is none of these things just because a crucial causal antecedent has been summarily relocated. That is, I believe that a shift in the sequence of events, coupled with excisions and amendments that may seem minor on the surface, can actually result in an entirely different story populated by entirely different people.

Even seemingly incidental features of a text may have crucial or symbolic roles to play, such that their elimination may entirely alter meaning. Consider the following scene from *Sense and Sensibility*, in which Robert Ferrars is caught in the act of ordering a toothpick-case at the jeweler's. His fussiness inconveniences the Miss Dashwoods, and keeps them waiting an unconscionable time at the counter:

> On ascending the stairs, the Misses Dashwood found so many people before them in the room, that there was not a person at liberty to tend to their orders; and they were obliged to wait. All that could be done, was, to sit down at that end of the counter which seemed to promise the quickest succession; one gentleman only was standing there, and it is probable that Elinor was not without hope of exciting his politeness to a quicker despatch. But the correctness of his eye, and the delicacy of his taste, proved to be beyond his politeness. He was giving orders for a toothpick-case for himself; and till its size, shape, and ornaments were determined, all of which, after examining and debating for a quarter of an hour over every toothpick-case in the shop, were finally arranged by his own inventive fancy, he had no leisure to bestow any other attention on the two ladies than what was comprised in three or four very broad stares; a kind of notice which served to imprint on Elinor the remembrance of a person and face of strong, natural, sterling insignificance, though adorned in the first style of fashion. Marianne was spared from the troublesome feelings of contempt and resentment, on this impertinent examination of their features, and on the puppyism of his manner in deciding on all the different horrors of the different toothpick-cases presented to his inspection, by remaining unconscious of it all. . . . At last the affair was decided. The ivory, the gold, and the pearls, all received their appointment; and the gentleman having named the last day on which his existence could be continued without the possession of the toothpick-case, drew on his gloves with leisurely care, and bestowing another glance on the Misses Dashwood, but such a one as seemed rather to demand than express admiration, walked off with a happy air of real conceit and affected indifference. (SS 220–1)

Austen is masterly in her derision in this passage. She is so effective that D.A. Miller, in his *Jane Austen, or the Secret of Style*[4] not only showcases the

---

[4]   D.A. Miller, *Jane Austen, or the Secret of Style* (Princeton: Princeton University Press, 2003).

example, but also adorns the cover of his book with the very toothpick-case in question.

The toothpick-case is clearly not an object that is at all replaceable by a snuffbox, say, or any number of fobs and seals. Manifestly, Robert in all his sartorial resplendence is just like the toothpicks in his case-to-be: an insignificant little prick, all dressed up. So far, Miller and I are in complete agreement. But I am not in accord with Miller[5] when he contends that

> style here is not merely another general name . . . for the particular insuffi-
> ciencies of substance . . . that we have seen characterize the toothpick case
> and its personification in Robert. Unlike insignificance, which denotes a con-
> dition, style presupposes a deliberately embraced project. . . . "All style and
> no substance": the formula helps us recognize not that style is different,
> or even opposite, to substance . . . but that one is incompatible with, and even
> corrosive of the other. Style can only emerge at the expense of substance.[6]

Yet surely a deliberately embraced project – like writing, say – need not exhibit a style only at the expense of substance. Much writing, I concede, is like Robert Ferrars in concealing its sterling insignificance beneath rhetorical adornments. Such embellishments are often intended to present an appearance of profundity and substance without putting the author to the trouble of having to achieve them, though of course no such thing is true of Austen's writing. I am being unfair, however, in failing to note that Miller's deployment of the style/substance dichotomy is intended to focus our attention on cases in which style is assumed to eat away at individual identity, as the disjunction in the title of his book broadly hints. (Austen is taken by Miller to have effaced herself from the pages of her work in adopting, among other things, the third person omniscient, but I believe this isn't relevant to a discussion of the aforementioned episode, *contra* Miller.) To return to the passage under consideration, a corrosion of identity really does not seem to be a key factor. Robert lacks substance, of course, but that is just to say that he lacks character and intelligence, not that personal identity is at issue. His 'style' does not erode or eat away at some individual essence. Rather, Robert Ferrars mistakes wealth and ostentation for genuinely laudable traits on account of which a man can and should be admired. That is, he confuses being a man of substance

---

[5] Here, and in an earlier review of his book. E.M. Dadlez, Review of D.A. Miller, *Jane Austen, or the Secret of Style* (Princeton University Press), *Journal of Aesthetics and Art Criticism* 64:3 (2006): 397–9.
[6] Miller, *Jane Austen*, p. 17.

in one sense with being a man of substance in quite another. And noth-ing shows this better than the ornate, overdecorated shell which contains nothing whatsoever of significance.

What are toothpicks good for, exactly? Dislodging food from between the teeth. What is Robert Ferrars good for? In *Sense and Sensibility*, he dislodges his older brother from the clutches of Lucy Steele and inserts himself in Edward's place in her affections. It is the only useful act Robert Ferrars performs in the course of the novel. Aside from the trappings of wealth which so entice Lucy, Robert is clearly not good for much – not for anything very important or meaningful. To suggest, as Austen's passage does, an association between the overdressed Ferrars and the toothpicks in the newly ordered, overdecorated case is to summon up other images and associations. It is to suggest something about Ferrars' personal worth and more about his pretensions. Even when ensconced in the bejeweled con-tainer Robert has bespoken, a toothpick is still a mundane and negligible object. Even though exhibiting the appearance of wealth and privilege, a Robert Ferrars is still an inferior specimen, a person of no real signific-ance. And, of course, Austen's point is that Robert does not understand this, that he confuses wealth and social standing with personal worth and merit, that he is as pinheaded as the toothpicks for which he purchases an over-elaborate receptacle, as if to conceal their insignificance.

Literary figures of speech and symbolic representations invite us to grasp one thing *through* or *in terms of* another. The way in which they work is, therefore, rather different from what we get when we attempt to engage in work of a loosely similar sort in philosophical prose by means of carefully deployed analogies. To offer a paraphrase of a passage like the preceding and say that such-and-such a person is dim and useless but unaware of it because his ideas of merit encompass only wealth and class does not capture the whole of the story. To carefully add to this conclu-sion a list of the properties shared by the target and the sample – Robert Ferrars and his toothpicks – (if any philosopher could be expected to do so with a straight face) still seems to miss a great deal of what it is one gets out of reading the passage in the novel. For one thing, there isn't a single target property at issue about which Austen intends us to draw a conclusion. Rather, we see Robert, his concerns and predilections and feelings, through the image of the toothpicks in their pricey case. That image and the associations it invites us to make expose Robert's triviality at the same time as we are shown that he is oblivious of it. We are not directly informed of his mistaking an outward show for interior worth. Rather this is implied by what is said and by the images with which we are presented. In other words, it isn't just that Robert is unaware of Elinor's contempt and of the effect he may have on others in general. It isn't just that ostentation is used to mask insignificance. It is that some people *are* quite successfully blinded by ostentation, that they are quite likely to infer merit from ostentation even, and perhaps especially, when this enables them to deceive themselves about their own importance or worth. Again, this is not something Austen announces. It is something she shows us by letting us see Robert and his pretensions through the lens provided by a particular image with particular associations. The lens is not a forgiving one, of course. The gold, the pearls, the ivory, every ludicrous flamboyance serve to skewer Robert more firmly before Austen's ironic gaze, serve to call up the reader's contempt in tandem with Elinor's. By employing the image of the toothpick case, Austen focuses our attention on particular facets of Robert's character in a particular way. And it is a way that allows us to make the relevant associations and to draw the relevant conclusions ourselves instead of merely being told what they are. There is a kind of active, imaginative participation involved in our response to figures of speech and symbols and imagery that turns reading into a collaboration.

And this, together with our more direct emotional responses to the characters themselves and their respective situations, is what can most often distinguish literary or poetic prose from exposition. Literary devices call for a form of collaboration from the participant. There is often more imaginative engagement in this respect and, just as important, more employment of what Richard Moran would call the dramatic rather than the hypothetical imagination.[7] In other words, we do not just entertain the thought *that* something is the case in imagination. We imagine *events*, and do so seriously, investedly, emotionally. Louise Rosenblatt spoke of the nature of reader engagement in just this way even before Moran did, pointing out that each sentence in a work of literature "will signal certain possibilities and exclude others, thus limiting . . . expectations. What the reader has elicited from the text up to that point generates a receptivity to certain kinds of ideas . . . or attitudes. Perhaps one can think of this as an alerting of certain areas of memory, a stirring up of certain reservoirs of experience, knowledge, and feeling. As the reading proceeds, attention will be fixed on the reverberations or implications that result from fulfillment or frustration of those expectations."[8] Shakespearean pentameter and

---

[7]   Richard Moran, "The Expression of Feeling in Imagination," *Philosophical Review* 103 (1994): 104–6.
[8]   Louise M. Rosenblatt, *The Reader, the Text, the Poem: The Transactional Theory of the Literary Work* (Carbondale: Southern Illinois University Press, 1978), 54.

other poetic devices may, one assumes, produce still different expectancies based not only on the evaluative apprehension of fictional events but on expectations regarding rhythm, concordance and metrics, perhaps not unlike expectations aroused in the course of listening to music. None of this is exclusive to poetry and fiction, but it is fair to claim that this kind of imaginative and invested reading is characteristic of them in a way that it is not characteristic of standard expository prose.

To return to an initial point of this investigation, it seems clear that there is an interdependence of form and content that makes it unproductive to consider either one in isolation from the other. Literary form will always, as I hope some of the examples canvassed have suggested, inform content, and content cannot be divorced in any meaningful way from mode of presentation. The question becomes, then, what kind of a difference *Austen's* use of form, as exhibited in plot construction, deployment of literary devices and ironic narrative voice, make to her portrayal of character and moral judgment. Some of this has already been canvassed in the preceding chapter. The cursory comparison of Austen's style to the literary style of Henry James shows us a little of what makes Austen distinctive.

More than many writers, certainly more than those who rely on melodrama or exotic locations or other features that Aristotle might consign to the category of spectacle, Austen relies on our recognition of the traits of character and the peculiarities of human interaction that she depicts. That she was fully justified in doing so has already been acknowledged in the introduction, for few works have stood the test of time as well as Austen's novels or have so successfully claimed an acquaintance even without the proper introductions. It isn't that Austen offers us stock characters that represent some particular type with which everyone is acquainted. Her people are entirely individual and particular. But, just like real people with certain prominent traits, they *remind* us of a favorite cousin or difficult colleague. Just as a chance acquaintance with an actual person may make us say "I know someone just like that," so exposure to Austen's characters has a similar effect. Their environs are unremarkable, their lives are for the most part unexciting – neither tragic nor adventurous nor desperate nor fraught with emergencies. All that is there to stand out and capture the attention is their humanity and character – their virtues and vices and dealings with one another. And this is, of course, part of the reason why Austen's work has stood the test of time – its focus is on human constants that transcend any particular time and place or that, at any rate, are to be found in most places during any era. This makes her novels a splendid proving ground for ethical dilemmas, for the identification of hitherto unsuspected targets for moral consideration, for the rehearsal of quandaries having to do with intellectual obligations or standards of taste.

Austen's kind of writing is for this reason perfectly suited to give rise to explicitly normative reactions that have a more than passing connection to our repertoire of normative judgments, as outlined in the preceding chapter. That is, where we can imagine the permissibility of a certain kind of act, we can be taken to believe that acts of that kind (perhaps only in the limited set of circumstances presented in the novel) *can* be permissible, that the permissibility of such an act is possible. Where we are led to imagine that one character's belief is woefully unjustified, some core conviction about what constitutes adequate justification is in play. While this need involve no alteration whatsoever in our judgments, it *can* do so – when, for instance, the event endorsed as permissible represents a counterexample to a universal assertion to which we subscribe, or when the unreliability of some particular belief-forming process is brought to our attention and thereby serves to refine our judgments about epistemic warrant. Austen's novels are unusual in that our normative investment, as described above, is almost constant. The whole of our attention is directed toward how people are, toward how they negotiate their relationships and their prospects. Almost every normative judgment that underwrites our imaginative response to Austen's novels is one that we take personally, one that applies to our own lives and dealings. It is not the case, as with Dickens, that our judgments about large-scale social issues are brought into play by reading Austen – judgments about the horrors of poverty or the obligation to ameliorate the condition of the oppressed. Rather, our judgments about how seriously we should take an agent's good intentions in assessing his action (Austen doesn't think much of them in some contexts) or about the feeling of certainty as a potential guarantor of truth (Austen ditto) underwrite and may even be informed by imaginative engagement in Austen's work. This may be one of the reasons why so many find Austen accessible, perhaps more so than they do writers like Dickens. Social conditions change (not enough, of course), but relations among individuals and questions about how they ought to treat one another do not alter as radically.

Because this isn't a book about literary form, but merely a chapter intended to provide some idea of the connection between literary style and content, and between literary style and our normative engagement with fiction, my examples cannot be exhaustive. I've tried to show some of the ways in which mere paraphrases or summaries of Austen fail to produce the same effects as the original. I have also tried to explain how it is that her selection and deployment of subject matter set her apart from other literary figures. As a final example, it seems most appropriate to address Austen's unique narrative voice and the acerbic humor that cannot help but color everything she writes. The preceding chapter has already outlined some of the effects of this stance in rejecting the idea that Austen can be considered a romantic or that her books can be considered sentimental in the pejorative sense. Here, we will consider some others.

"In Love with Jane" was the title of an article that appeared a few years ago in the *New York Review of Books*. Diane Johnson contends, in this review of works about Austen, that "the narrator, she who contributes the aphorisms and asides, and the tone of mockery, has widely been assumed to be Austen herself, as close as any writer can come to speaking in her own voice; and the acerbic charm of that voice is one reason people have tried to look behind the narrator to Austen herself."[9] For some of us, even those of us who write about Austen and the normative, her wit has always been the primary attraction. And so I will finish by considering what it is that humor and ironic distance can contribute, both in establishing the uniqueness of Austen's approach and by reflecting a little on its similarity to a genre that has an established connection to our moral judgments and attitudes.

Thinking first in terms of plot construction, it is readily apparent that much of Austen's humor turns on reversals. Whether or not we are inclined to accept incongruity theories of humor[10] as definitive, no one would contest that much humor does turn on a perception of incongruity and reversal of expectations (provided that there is some added stipulation about our regarding the incongruity or reversal as somewhat benign). Indeed, incongruity approaches to humor echo Aristotle's account of tragedy and the preferred form of tragic plots, in the insistence on reversal and recognition. These are staples in Austen's plot structure. In his *A Fine Brush on Ivory*, for instance, Richard Jenkyns draws our attention to the fact that "Lady Catherine's very attempt to prevent Darcy's engagement to Elizabeth is what precipitates his proposal"[11] and prompts Elizabeth's

<hr>

[9]   Diane Johnson, "In Love with Jane," *New York Review of Books* 6/23/05, p. 23.

[10]   P. Keith Spiegel, "Early Conceptions of Humor: Varieties and Issues," in *The Psychology of Humor: Theoretical Perspectives and Empirical Issues*, ed. J.H. Goldstein and P.E. McGhee (New York: Academic Press, 1972). Spiegel lists twenty-four supporters of the incongruity approach. One of the most philosophically adept contemporary proponents of an incongruity theory of humor is John Morreall, *The Philosophy of Laughter and Humor* (Albany: SUNY Press, 1987).

[11]   Richard Jenkyns, *A Fine Brush on Ivory: An Appreciation of Jane Austen* (Oxford: Oxford University Press, 2004), p. 17.

recognition of her true feelings. We have already explored the myriad reversals to be found in the conclusion of *Persuasion*, where each act or intention, whether Anne's conversation, or Wentworth's letter writing, or Mr. Elliot's plans, turns out to be very different from what it seems. *Sense and Sensibility* ends with an outright reversal of Marianne's romanticism and *Emma* is replete with reversals of almost all of its heroine's matrimonial speculations. *Mansfield Park* concludes with a reversal of Fanny's former subordination and a reversal of the family's estimation of her worth (some of which is funny, and some of which is not). A key element in *Northanger Abbey* turns on the reversal of General Tilney's expectations, and the entire story is designed to foil the expectations of those who favor gothic novels. I realize that the term "reversal" is being used too broadly here to warrant much further speculation along Aristotelian lines, but it is at least evident that Austen's humor is supported by classic plot configurations that have a ready explanation in incongruity accounts of humor.

What Johnson calls the mocking tone and the acerbic charm of Austen's narration are taken by D.A. Miller to be a kind of paradigm of the faceless, enforcedly neutral third person omniscient. According to his jacket blurb, "What does appear is a ghostly No One, a narrative voice unmarked by age, gender, marital status, all the particulars that make a person – and might make a person peculiar." I want to take issue with this claim. I concur that there is sometimes a distancing effect in the very mocking quality of the tone that Austen employs. I also agree that the narration seems for the most part gender neutral, though some (not I, in fact) might detect a gender bias in the subject matter on which our attention seems inevitably to be focused: feelings, relationships, personal reactions to perceived slights or deprivations. Despite this, it seems necessary vehemently to contest the proposal that age, gender and marital status are the central particulars that make a person, peculiar or otherwise. Surely a disinclination to suffer fools, a cheerful cynicism, an ability (borrowed from Hume, perhaps) to detect the tendencies of a character in circumstances where their exercise is impossible, contribute to a distinct personality. Surely these qualities and aptitudes can be thought constitutive of a person's peculiar particularity in a way that age or marital status is not. This seems most obviously the case because no alteration in the latter is generally thought to herald a seismic shift in personality or particularity or identity. I acknowledge that a case can more easily be made for gender as a criterion determinative of personal peculiarities, but even this category is debatable. Nor is it at all clear how it is that all those other third-person omniscient narrations, the ones from which Austen's narration is deemed so different (Henry Fielding's, for instance), *do* convey to us the gender, age, and marital status of their creators in some indisputable way. One cannot help but wonder which tone or which narrative approach could possibly convey that the man behind the curtain was forty-three, say, instead of fifty-four, without the fact being directly stated.

My point is that such features as Miller invokes in association with "making a person peculiar" can be entirely irrelevant to the tinge of personality or peculiarity in a narrative voice. And indeed, as Johnson claims, Austen's narrative voice is distinctive enough to give the lie to these claims of a "ghostly no one" without resorting to further argument. I will certainly not go so far as to ascribe that narrative voice to Austen herself, but it would be pointless to deny that ridicule and irony are the lenses through which Austen shows us the world. These exhibit a kind of neutrality insofar as no character, not even the protagonist, has immunity. But a neutrality of that kind is neither wholly value-free nor wholly impersonal. Because of that, it may prove worthwhile to investigate how, exactly, the overarching humorous perspective affects content and the way it is we take that content.

The neutrality of Austen's ironic narrative voice sometimes allows a kind of detachment. On occasion, Austen permits us to step back even from the moral qualms of her characters. Anne Elliot may look askance at Sunday driving and Fanny Price may be distressed by amateur theatricals (a pastime in which we know Austen participated) but if we do come to share the moral judgments these characters make, Austen is sure to have provided us with better reasons. Anne distrusts Mr. Elliot not principally because of suspected Sunday driving but because of a fundamental dishonesty, an agreeableness so invincible that even those of whom he avowedly disapproves find him charming. Fanny thinks amateur theatricals inappropriate for two central reasons, neither of which is directly tied to her suspicion that acting is somehow morally dubious. First, they are conducted at the unwitting expense of someone who certainly would not wish to subsidize them. Second, they produce emotional harm. Part of the effect of Austen's ironic distance is that it lets us step back. It provides a perspective that permits us consider all the reasons for a given character's judgment – those a character has acquired through reflection and observation as well as those he or she has been taught and holds more or less unreflectively. It is up to the reader to invest in the ones he or she finds convincing. Austen will sometimes choose for us, but not always.

The humor with which everything is presented, the focus on absurdities in reasoning and behavior, splendidly subverts most inclinations toward righteous indignation at the prospect of conduct that is deemed inappropriate. Austen doesn't just make us see how it is that people can come to behave in such a way, and how their reasons might be reasons a lot of us would find compelling in certain circumstances. She also allows us to see the absurdity of those reasons, the way in which people come to justify their actions to themselves, the way in which they can be unaware of acting from vanity or avarice. This is the choicest trick in her repertoire: to show at once how easy it is to act from the motives on offer and how absurd it is to do so. Austen's blackest villains, if we can even call them that, are never entirely alien. Just as humor undercuts the possibility of perfect, virtuous characters, it undercuts the possibility of perfectly bad ones. Austen's people, even the bad ones, are too much like us not to engage at least a modicum of understanding. But instead of using this resonance and comprehension to force reflection on the grimmer facets of the human lot, Austen uses it to make us laugh. I would like to emphasize here that such laughter requires just as much understanding of human nature and the human condition as may the tears elicited by tragedy. Possibly, the laughter is just more perverse. I prefer to think that the inclination to laugh at such things involves a low tolerance for self-pity that is not unlike Austen's, however global and encompassing of one's fellows such self-pity proves to be. Thus, in this respect as well as in her plot reversals, Austen uses some of the same material as the tragedian: for instance, material which presents us with an accessibly imperfect and human protagonist and material that fosters familiarity with some of the sources of paradigmatic errors in judgment. She then uses it to engender understanding just as the tragedian does, to foster a deeper comprehension of human situations and interactions. It is only here that the paths part, for Austen lingers on the everyday absurdity of these things rather than showing them to be intolerable.

So it appears that Austen's particular kind of comedy has not a little in common with tragedy, with one further distinction. There is a kind of reversal of attention at work in Austen as well. While tragedy often shifts focus from a single and singular event to a kind of panoramic depiction of the human lot, Austen's comedy insists on the intimate and the personal. We acquire any understanding of broader human truths by recognizing ourselves and the people we know in the traits and foibles under review. That is, we and the people we know are made representatives of humanity, in a manner of speaking, rather than having a representation of what it is to be human made applicable to ourselves and our lives. This is partly the consequence of the kinds of experiences upon which Austen's comedy, as opposed to most tragedies, invites us to reflect. As has already been indicated, Austen's work does not dwell on the extremes of human emotion or endurance, on disasters and emergencies. It dwells on the everyday, benign incongruities we confront, the kind we recognize. But this shows us that, in Austen, the personal is never trivial, but a reflection, an instantiation, of human constants. In Austen, apparent trivialities are seldom what they seem.

3
Kantian and Aristotelian Accounts of Austen

The purpose of this chapter is to rule out principal contenders for the role which I assign to David Hume. While Kantian and Aristotelian approaches to Austen focus our attention on interesting aspects of her work, neither one of these accounts for all or even most aspects of the ethical life that are clearly important in Austen's depictions, many of which I will attempt to delineate in succeeding chapters that will explore correlations between Hume and Austen. Aristotelian approaches to Austen are by far the more rewarding of the two under review here. These offer a distinct advantage in that they allow us to see Austen as we should: as a virtue ethicist. It is not surprising that Aristotelian readings of Austen should be so prominent among philosophers. Yet, having said that, it is worth noting that Hume offers us a species of virtue ethics as well, tempered by a sentimentalist approach and concerns about utility that resonate more closely with Austen's writing. The response, therefore, to the two primary challenges to my account is to reject the first and incorporate the second. I will try to show that Austen makes an implausible Kantian, a plausible Aristotelian, and a much more plausible Humean.

I

I will begin here by criticizing an approach aligning Austen's normative stance with Kantian deontology. Kantian interpretations of Austen will be reviewed, though I will reserve those interpretations focusing on aesthetic sensibility in particular for the chapter on aesthetic norms. There is a case to be made for Kant, though I will argue that it is ultimately unconvincing. Kantian interpretations of Austen are not the only, or the best, alternatives available, but they have appeared in the literature and are alluded to in work that addresses this topic – the kind that tries to mine Austen's novels for philosophical and, more particularly, for ethical insights. It is necessary, therefore, to establish that Kantian interpretations of Austen's perspective are for the most part mistaken. That this is not immediately apparent suggests a need for some investigation.

It could be argued, mainly by those who use *Mansfield Park's* rule-abiding Fanny Price as their example, that the normative standpoint of Austen's work may coincide with a Kantian deontological perspective. On a typical conservative interpretation, this perspective is based on the assumption that absolute adherence to a set of duties is morally mandatory and that reason rather than emotion is the source of our moral insights. Consider that, toward the end of *Mansfield Park*, Sir Thomas reflects on the defective morals of his daughters (as opposed to those of the upright Fanny) in what could be regarded as a characteristically Kantian way, or at the very least in a way that would gladden the heart of any deontologist: "he feared that principle, active principle, had been wanting, that they had never been properly taught to govern their inclinations and tempers, by that sense of duty which can alone suffice" (MP 463).

Before we reflect further on Kantian readings of *Mansfield Park*, it is important to isolate one line of argument and reserve it for future discussion in a later chapter. *Mansfield Park* has been cited as a source of resemblance between Austen and Kant by Anne Crippen Ruderman, who maintains that "Fanny's taste for natural beauty is presented as a sign of her moral disposition,"[1] something that can clearly be linked to Kant's belief that "to take an immediate interest in the beauty of nature . . . is always a mark of a good soul."[2] There is enough of a case to be made here to warrant separate treatment. A chapter has been devoted in its entirety to Humean and Kantian perspectives on aesthetics (as these may be taken to compare to that of Jane Austen) and to the connection between aesthetics and ethics. So this particular argument for a Kantian reading of Austen will be reserved for an independent discussion. At present, we will focus on the purely ethical questions.

The first of these involves Kant's categorical imperative, which states that we should act only on that maxim which we can at the same time will to be a universal law. This is a test of one's prospective actions: first, a rule that permits the action is universalized; it is then tested for consistency in conception and consistency with the will of the agent (to see if it would

---

[1] Anne Crippen Ruderman, *The Pleasures of Virtue: Political Thought in the Novels of Jane Austen* (Lanham, MD: Rowman & Littlefield, 1995), 82.
[2] Immanuel Kant, *Critique of Judgment*, trans. J.H. Bernard (New York: Hafner Press, 1951), pp. 42: 141, 143.

be consistent with the agent's will if the action were done to him or her, something that universalization would legitimate). There are ways in which the categorical imperative may be made applicable to the moral quandaries of Austen's characters. It is not enough to point out that "steadiness" and "consistency" are always regarded as desirable character traits in Austen. Particular cases should be placed under review. Take Fanny Price, for instance, who is Austen's most priggish and conservative heroine. She is the conscience of Mansfield Park. Her principled opposition to such activities as amateur theatricals is inevitably echoed in the endorsements and condemnations made by the work as a whole. In regard to a play in whose production family members and friends are wholly immersed, Fanny Price has serious moral qualms: "For her own gratification she could have wished that something might be acted, for she had never seen even half a play, but everything of higher consequence was against it" (MP 131). Edmund Bertram, soon to become a member of the clergy, concurs with her every objection. So, when Edmund begs Fanny to approve of his own participation in the play (something allegedly forced on him by a need to keep the cast of players more or less within the family), Fanny cannot give it, even though she understands his reasons. She is particularly distressed by Edmund's inconsistency, something that fits quite effectively into a Kantian analysis: "After all his objections – objections so just and so public! After all that she had heard him say and seen him look, and known him to be feeling. Could it be possible? Edmund so inconsistent. Was he not deceiving himself? Was he not wrong? Alas!" (MP 156).

Edmund's inconsistency may be more disturbing to Fanny than any outright violation of rules. He wishes to make an exception of himself. His own participation in the play is seen as being forced on him by circumstances, whereas the actions of other participants (with the possible exception of Mary Crawford) are still regarded by him as wrong. Edmund's proposed participation would certainly fail any consistency test imposed in the course of applying the categorical imperative, which requires him to will the maxim of his action to be a universal law. He cannot (according to Kant and, it seems, according to Fanny as well) will one thing for himself and another for others.

David Kaufman compares the ethical stance taken in some of Austen's novels to that of Kant, citing an example from *Sense and Sensibility*. The case involves Elinor Dashwood's keeping a secret, and thereby a promise, at great emotional cost. Presumably, Kaufman intends an allusion to Kant's edict about adherence to perfect duties.[3] Perfect duties, like the duty to

---

[3] David Kaufman, "Law and Propriety, Sense and Sensibility: Austen on the Cusp of Modernity," *ELH* 59 (1992): 385–408.

keep promises, may never be violated. Elinor has not violated her duty to keep the promise she has made to Lucy, but Elinor's sister Marianne believes that she has kept that promise at the expense of her peace of mind. Upon discovering that the man Elinor loves has been engaged to another, Marianne demands to know how long Elinor has been aware of this engagement. Elinor responds that she has known of it for four months. Marianne is shocked at the length of time and asks how Elinor has been supported in such a difficult endeavor. Elinor's response would gladden the heart of any Kantian:

> "By feeling that I was doing my duty. – My promise to Lucy, obliged me to be secret. I owed it to her, therefore, to avoid giving any hint of the truth; and I owed it to my family and friends, not to create in them a solicitude about me, which it could not be in my power to satisfy". (SS 262)

Here, Elinor may be said to be acting from a good will – she acts as she does just because she believes she ought to do it, *despite* a natural inclination to confide in her sister and mother. Kant indicates that "the good will is not good because of what it effects or accomplishes or because of its adequacy to achieve some proposed end; it is good only because of its willing, i.e., it is good of itself."[4] It is more obviously evident to a third party that Elinor acts from a good will just because duty prompts her to act *against* her inclination. It is, in other words, easier or safer to ascribe moral merit to those who act against their own desires, since only duty is left to motivate their action. This may have inspired Kaufman's references to Elinor Dashwood's masochism.

In fact, this kind of example raises a classic contrast for classroom ethics, pitting Aristotelian (and in some respects Humean) virtue ethics, in which ease and inclination are allied with virtue, against Kantian deontology, in which (at least according to conservative readings) moral merit is most readily ascribable in cases where the subject's pursuit of duty is at odds with her inclination. As Frederick Copleston puts it in order to simplify matters, "the class of actions performed in accordance with duty is much wider than the class of actions performed for the sake of duty. According to Kant, only those actions which are performed for the sake of duty have moral worth." The matter is complicated, Copleston indicates, by Kant's giving some support to a less than flattering interpretation which proposes that the more loathsome our duty seems to us, the more moral

---

[4] Immanuel Kant, *Foundations of the Metaphysics of Morals*, ed. Robert Paul Wolff (Indianapolis: Bobbs-Merrill, 1969), p. 12.

we'll be when we do it. So people who always hate doing their duty seem to have a clear moral advantage. Those for whom doing their duty is always a struggle will, provided they do it anyway, always be regarded as having better characters than those to whom it comes naturally, with the odd result that the grudging and resentful take moral precedence over the cheerfully generous.[5]

However, Copleston stresses that Kant's central point in the relevant passages "is simply that when a man performs his duty contrary to his inclinations, the fact that he acts for the sake of duty . . . is clearer than it would be if he had a natural attraction to the action." There is, of course, nothing wrong with naturally sympathetic and philanthropic people. They just get no special moral credit, since "the action of doing good to others has no moral worth if it is simply the effect of a natural inclination."[6] Christine Korsgaard, elaborates on these issues in the following way.

> Kant's complaint about the naturally sympathetic person is not that he *wants* to help others only because it *pleases* him to do so. It is rather that he *chooses* to help others only because he *wants* to. This is indeed a reason to help others . . . but there is a better one available, which the sympathetic person would have encountered, if he had only taken thought about whether he could universalize his maxims. Kant condemns the naturally sympathetic person not for the content of his incentive, but rather for making an insufficiently reflective choice.[7]

The question we must ask at present is this. Do the endorsements and moral criticisms made in Jane Austen's novels suggest a Kantian stance *vis-a-vis* the kind of decision-making and reflectiveness that is requisite for moral judgment? As we turn back to Austen with this question in mind, it worth noting that, in accordance with the preceding, characters like *Northanger Abbey*'s Catherine Morland and *Mansfield Park*'s Fanny Price distrust the morality of their actions most when those actions are in fact in accord with their own inclinations. In other words, there are occasions on which both consider that the moral worth of their actions is suspect just because those actions are also instrumental in the achievement of some private good. At one stage in the tale of *Northanger Abbey*,

[5] Frederick Copleston, S.J., "Kant (5): Morality and Religion," in *Modern Philosophy: From the French Enlightenment to Kant*, volume 4 of *A History of Philosophy* (New York: Doubleday, 1994), pp. 316–17.

[6] Copleston, "Kant (5): Morality and Religion," p. 317.

[7] Christine M. Korsgaard, *The Sources of Normativity* (Cambridge: Cambridge University Press, 1998), p. 244.

Catherine Morland insists on keeping an engagement with the Tilneys against the urging of the Thorpes and her brother. Yet, even though keeping this engagement accords with the standards of promise-keeping and truth telling (our heroine counters the lies Thorpe tells in an attempt to cancel the arrangement), Catherine begins to doubt herself when she considers that she greatly prefers the company of the Tilneys to that of the Thorpes. "A sacrifice was always noble," Catherine reflected, and, clearly, keeping company with John Thorpe would constitute a penance for anyone. Would it not have been better to sacrifice her own inclination to enjoy the company of the Tilneys? "If she had given way to [the Thorpes'] . . . entreaties, she should have been spared the distressing idea of a friend displeased, a brother angry, and a scheme of great happiness to both destroyed, perhaps through her means" (NA 103). That is, Catherine's acting from motives in addition to that of duty make her action appear suspect in her own eyes.

Fanny Price expresses similar concerns over refusing to take part in the play which her cousins insist on performing and the production of which they press her to facilitate by taking on a role. Her refusal (like Catherine's action above) has a dual motive. First, she believes that participation in the play is improper (as Catherine believes breaking a promise to be improper). But she is also perfectly terrified of acting and the kind of humiliation that attempts at thespian virtuosity might involve. Just as Catherine worries that her selfish preference for the Tilneys' company has led her astray, so Fanny is concerned that her fear of performing has influenced her decision:

> was she *right* in refusing what was so warmly asked, so strongly wished for
> – what might be so essential to a scheme on which some of those to whom
> she owed the greatest complaisance had set their hearts? Was it not ill-nature,
> selfishness, and a fear of exposing herself? And would Edmund's judgment,
> would his persuasion of Sir Thomas's disapprobation of the whole, be enough
> to justify her in a determined denial in spite of all the rest? It would be so
> horrible to her to act that she was inclined to suspect the truth and purity
> of her own scruples; and as she looked around her, the claims of her cousins
> to being obliged were strengthened by the sight of present upon present
> that she had received from them. (MP 153)

Does Austen, in the above passages and elsewhere, espouse a Kantian ethic? Is there an effective response to such a claim? Frankly, any number of objections and counterexamples come to mind. Consider, for instance, the principled, absolutist judgments of Fanny Price. Let us first review her condemnation of the play and her distress at Edmund's inconsistency.

It isn't clear how distinctively Kantian these reactions are. Her distress at Edmund Bertram's inconsistency is prompted to a great extent by jealousy of Mary Crawford's influence on him. And Edmund's inconsistency is, after all, nothing more than hypocrisy. This is the kind of failing that proves blameworthy from any number of ethical perspectives quite distinct from that of the Kantian.

Moreover, Fanny's objections to the family's engaging in amateur theatricals are based on a number of considerations, none of which seems *exclusively* recognizable from the perspective of a Kantian ethical system. The content of the play, for instance, is seen as sexually improper, especially where the female characters are concerned, so that acting out those parts would involve the actors in suggestive conduct. But there is much more to Fanny's objection. First, any such performance would be strongly condemned by the stern Sir Thomas Bertram, the owner and authority of Mansfield, who is conveniently absent while the plans are being made. Second, the project is expensive, and it is at Sir Thomas's expense (the very person who would most disapprove) that the production is mounted. Moreover, the conduct that the content of the play encourages exacerbates vulnerabilities in such a way as to bring about fairly disastrous results in the long run for at least one person. Fanny's disapproval isn't based only on some single principle (adherence to the known preferences of the *paterfamilias*, say) or tied to some explicit violation of the categorical imperative. There is a general sense of trouble brewing that Fanny finds distressing: prospective anger and disapproval from Sir Thomas, mounting expenses, annoying visitors, importunate amateur thespians, Edmund's attraction to Mary, increasingly desperate flirtations, people caring less and less about one another's feelings. It does not bode well for the future, and Fanny knows it. Of course she doesn't approve. But that need not make her a full-fledged Kantian.

Neither is it clear that Elinor Dashwood acts exclusively from a good will in keeping Lucy's engagement to Edward secret and thereby keeping her own promise. Ruderman, a strong supporter of an Aristotelian interpretation of Austen, argues that "real virtue is never masochistic in the novels, and . . . Austen, unlike Kant, goes out of her way to show how virtue benefits the doer."[8] Elinor is, in many respects, better off if she doesn't spill the beans. Her mother and sister are not notable for their emotional restraint, and the end result of any confidences would saddle Elinor with their distress (at the news of the secret engagement) as well as her own to tranquilize and to cope with. Elinor is glad to have spared

[8]   Ruderman, *The Pleasures of Virtue*, p. 6.

those dear to her "from knowing how much . . . [she] felt" (SS 263) and thus from feeling distress on that account. She is also glad to prevent a situation in which her own unhappiness is exacerbated by the misery of those she loves. Likewise, Catherine Moreland does right by doing what she wants, and it seems unlikely that a little insecurity about having rectitude dovetail so conveniently with one's desires is enough to convict her of a Kantian attitude.

Even Fanny Price, whose self-doubt and second-guessing are fairly constant, seems less a Kantian than an individual who intermittently lacks self-confidence. More to the point, let us consider the single decision which on the face of it would appear the *most* likely to lead Fanny to ponder whether her choice is genuinely in accord with duty. This is the decision which brings down the greatest moral criticism on Fanny's head: her refusal of Henry Crawford's proposal of marriage. It is a decision concerning which the advice and intuition of all others (including the beloved Edmund) goes against her. Sir Thomas actually subjects Fanny to a moral diatribe, and he is at his most hateful and bullying as he does so: "I will, therefore, only add, as thinking it my duty to mark my opinion of your conduct, that you have disappointed every expectation I had formed, and proved yourself of a character the very reverse of what I had supposed" (MP 318). He accuses Fanny of what amounts to a virtual catalog of moral failings. She is willful, conceited, and – most dreadful of all – *independent*, a flaw which makes her also offensive and disgusting. She is perverse, inconsiderate, and disrespectful (for not following the advice of those who clearly know better than she). She is particularly inconsiderate in flinging away the advantages her marriage to a wealthy man would have for her less than wealthy family. She is disloyal. She is ungrateful. Sir Thomas goes on and on, driving Fanny to tears, accusing her of a multitude of sins.

One would think that an individual as sensitive and as insecure as Fanny would for at least a moment have wondered about the propriety of deciding in favor of inclination and acting in opposition to all of the upright authority figures of her acquaintance. She does not. She is horribly pained at being considered ungrateful and is miserable under Sir Thomas' displeasure. But none of that leads her to consider accepting Crawford when it is Edmund she loves. There is a kind of moral principle supporting her decision, of course (it is wrong to marry where one does not love), but the point is that the principle in question is more a dictum of romance than a rule of ethics derivable via application of the categorical imperative. Moreover, Fanny does not act from commitment to that principle alone, since she is motivated by a very strong personal preference. And her action's being entirely in accord with that preference does not lead her to reconsider it. Indeed, further investigations of Fanny's intellectual development in the forthcoming chapter on epistemic norms will suggest that her single intellectual failing is a kind of compulsive under-estimation of her own capacities and deserts, something that this surprisingly firm decision in favor of her own happiness begins to set right.

Furthermore, a passage in *Mansfield Park* tends to militate *against* the notion that more moral merit accrues (or at least that more moral merit is legitimately ascribable) to someone who does her duty in opposition to her inclination. Austen paints a remarkably vivid and convincing por-trait of Julia Bertram's character flaws, a portrait all the more convincing because many of us are not as unfamiliar with Julia's foibles as we might perhaps wish to be. Julia is obliged to keep pace and company with the tedious Mrs. Rushworth out of politeness, while everyone else runs off to be happy: "The politeness which she had been brought up to practise as a duty made it impossible for her to escape; while the want of that higher species of self-command, that just consideration of others, that know-ledge of her own heart, that principle of right, which had not formed any essential part of her education, made her miserable under it" (MP 91). Here is someone doing her duty against all possible inclination. Yet Austen quite obviously takes her misery as a sign that something is lack-ing in her character, not as a kind of proof of merit in that she acts from duty alone and therefore acts from duty indisputably. Clearly, compassion and fellow feeling constitute for Austen a part of what it is to act from principle, as much as does any determination of doing one's duty.

Moreover, there are several examples in Austen in which it is clear that virtuous activity is just that activity which accords with happiness and inclination. Again in *Mansfield Park*, Henry Crawford (for once) does his duty by his tenants in an effort to please Fanny. He becomes "a friend of the poor and oppressed" and finds that virtuous activity is pleasant: "He had gone, had done even more good than he had foreseen, had been useful to more than his first plan had comprehended, and was now able to congratulate himself upon it, and to feel that in performing a duty, he had secured agreeable recollections for his own mind" (MP 404). It is evident that Austen (and her character Fanny Price) regard this action with approval. Henry's character is not redeemed by it, but we are led to see by means of the action the things of which Henry might have been capable if other flaws had not overwhelmed his more promising traits. On the other hand, the consequence of the action would not be enough to render it virtuous, as far as Kant was concerned. Its having been prompted almost entirely by Henry's desire to insinuate himself into Fanny's good graces means that it was not done for the sake of duty. Any agreeable feeling resulting from the performance of a duty for the sake of which one did not act (or an agreeable feeling resulting from the performance of any duty at all) would simply be irrelevant to the question of the moral worth of the action. And while we cannot be sure, we might venture the suggestion that this does not seem to be the case for Austen. If anything, Henry's agreeable feelings appear to suggest that he is not dead to the warmer sensations of compassion and benevolence. This is something that suggests views like those of David Hume rather than those of Kant.

There is also a surprising utilitarian strain running through the whole of *Mansfield Park*, one that seems every bit as strong as the novel's deontological flavor. There is, in fact, just as much talk of "usefulness" and "utility" and being "of use" as there is of "duty" or "principle" in *Mansfield Park*. The focus is naturally on the assessment of character and of particular dispositions rather than particular actions. It is evident, however, that Fanny's and later Susan's *usefulness* sets them above their friends and relations in more than one respect, and does so on moral grounds. An entire chapter will later be devoted to this underlying concern with utility that seems to lie at the heart of Austen's and of Hume's account of virtue. For now, it is enough to note that such a concern is inimical to any Kantian interpretation.

There are further examples of the same felicitous union of duty and happiness that has been noted in *Mansfield Park* in *Emma*. Emma resolves, for instance, "equally as a duty and a pleasure," to call on Jane Fairfax, a connection which both Knightley and Austen approve (E 452). Similarly, Emma "could now look forward to giving [her future husband] . . . that full and perfect confidence which her disposition was most ready to welcome as a duty" (E 475). True virtue in Austen comes naturally and is more often than not conducive to happiness. It is not clear that this is the case for Kant, even if we eschew a conservative interpretation of his conception of acting out of a good will. There is too much in Austen that resists the kind of estrangement of choosing from desiring, or of choice from emotion, on which the Kantian distinction depends.

In the end, one must conclude that critics and philosophers who attempt to promote a *mésalliance* between Austen and Kant are simply mistaken. Happily, this clears the way for a more compatible, propitious union.

II

Most frequently, ethical analyses of Jane Austen's novels, analyses of the ethical insights and positions those works endorse, maintain that Austen's

writing embodies an Aristotelian ethic. Anne Crippen Ruderman,[9] Alisdair
MacIntyre,[10] Gilbert Ryle,[11] Thomas Williams,[12] David Gallop,[13] and others
have offered Aristotelian interpretations of Austen. It is worth noting, however, that most of the evidence brought forward to support an Aristotelian
analysis serves equally well – and sometimes better – to substantiate a
Humean account of Austen's ethical insights. Both Aristotle and Hume
recognize important connections between happiness and virtue, and
between reason and sentiment. Both concern themselves with the tendencies of a character as well as its actual effects. Both associate correct
emotion with virtue. Each centers his ethics on the assessment of character and disposition rather than the evaluation of individual actions or
the prescription of rules. That is, each offers us a virtue ethics, and a virtue
ethics, moreover, that has at its basis the important matter of human
happiness. These are not minor points of resemblance. They place both
philosophers at odds with Kantian deontological approaches to ethics. They
also clearly involve the kinds of normative endorsements and commitments
and assessments with which Austen's work is most plausibly associated.
The claim in this chapter is simply that Austen's ethical stance has a good
deal more in common with the philosophy of David Hume than that of
Aristotle, though this is not to deny a compatibility with both.

There is one important and obviously unbridgeable gulf between Austen
and Aristotle, and between Aristotle and Hume, on subjects related to
women and their potentialities. Such subjects are central to the plots of
Austen's novels, and so should not be ignored or treated as irrelevant.
Indeed, I believe they should predispose us at least a little toward a Humean
reading of Austen. They will be addressed, in part, in a later chapter on
marriage and fidelity. The purpose of the present project, however, is to
survey and evaluate arguments which ally Austen's normative perspective
with Aristotelian insights.

The strongest arguments in the literature at present for Austen's
affiliation with a particular philosophical stance are those which make
comparisons between her ethical intuitions and those of Aristotle. Anne

[9] Ruderman, *The Pleasures of Virtue*, p. 2.
[10] Alisdair MacIntyre, *After Virtue: A Study in Moral Theory* (Indiana: University of Notre
Dame, 1981), p. 223.
[11] Gilbert Ryle, "Jane Austen and the Moralists," in *Critical Essays on Jane Austen*, ed.
B.C. Southam (London: Routledge & Kegan Paul, 1968), p. 122.
[12] Thomas Williams, "Moral Vice, Cognitive Virtue: Austen on Jealousy and Envy," *Philosophy
and Literature* 27.1 (2003): 223–30, at 223.
[13] David Gallop, "Jane Austen and the Aristotelian Ethic," *Philosophy and Literature*
23.1 (1999): 96–109.

Crippen Ruderman, who has devoted a book to her argument, quotes Alisdair MacIntyre's pronouncement that "when Jane Austen speaks of 'happiness' she does so as an Aristotelian."[14] Gilbert Ryle argues that familiarity with Shaftesbury may have exposed Austen to Aristotelian ideas.[15] Recent work on the general topic of Austen and Aristotelian conceptions of virtue and vice has been done by David Gallop and Thomas Williams. Indeed, Gallop has pointed out that the Aristotelian flavor in Austen's novels was detected as early as 1821 by a perceptive reviewer, and happily provides us with the quotation: "We know not whether Miss Austen ever had access to the precepts of Aristotle, but there are few, if any, writers of fiction who have illustrated them more successfully."[16]

Before delving into the claims of these philosophers, however, it might be useful to survey in very general terms the kinds of Aristotelian themes that emerge repeatedly in Austen's novels, and that make an Aristotelian interpretation of Austen come naturally to mind. For instance, each novel addresses to some extent the subject of moderation, the Aristotelian doctrine of the mean. *Sense and Sensibility* offers one of the most telling examples. Marianne Dashwood's "sorrows, her joys, could have no moderation. She was generous, amiable, interesting: she was everything but prudent" (SS 6). Elinor Dashwood is concerned about "the excess of her sister's sensibility" (SS 7). Marianne's excess is contrasted with her half-brother's deficiency, as well as that of his spouse. John Dashwood is "rather cold hearted and rather selfish" and is made even less amiable by his wholly unamiable wife (SS 5). More tellingly, Marianne's excess is contrasted with Elinor's moderation, while her sister-law's greed and selfishness (as well as those of John Ferrars and Willoughby) are contrasted with Edward Ferrars' aspirations, which "are all moderate" (SS 91). Indeed, even Marianne's initial attempts to reform her habits involve resorting to extremes, as she plans to rise at six every morning, practice her music continually, and read six hours a day: "Elinor honoured her for a plan which originated so nobly as this; though smiling to see the same eager fancy which had been leading her to the extreme of languid indolence and selfish repining now at work in introducing excess into a scheme of such rational employment and virtuous self-control" (SS 343).

---

[14]   Alisdair MacIntyre, *After Virtue: A Study in Moral Theory*, p. 223. Cited in Ruderman, *The Pleasures of Virtue*, p. 6.
[15]   Ryle, "Jane Austen and the Moralists," pp. 118–19.
[16]   R. Whately, "Modern Novels," *Quarterly Review* 47 (1821): 352–63. Cited in Gallop, "Jane Austen and the Aristotelian Ethic," 96.

Mansfield Park offers a contrast between excess and deficiency in chronicling Mrs. Norris' compulsive interference and contrasting it with Lady Bertram's indolence. Mrs. Norris always tries to take charge of everyone else's business while her sister "never [thinks] . . . of being useful to any body" (MP 219). Both dispositions are presented as vices, though Lady Bertram's is clearly the easiest to live with. Indeed, Sir Thomas announces that "there should be moderation in every thing" when trying to counteract the cheeseparing policies of Mrs. Norris, which have deprived Fanny of a fire (MP 313). Fanny attempts to conquer her own tendency to excess insofar as she feels it her duty "to try to overcome all that was excessive, all that bordered on selfishness, in her affection for Edmund" (MP 264). We hear in *Persuasion* of another contrast between excess and moderation. We are told that "While Lady Elliot lived, there had been method, moderation, and economy . . . but with her had died all such right-mindedness" (P 9). And, in *Pride and Prejudice*, Elizabeth's uncle Gardiner can "not avoid recommending moderation to . . . [Mrs. Bennet], as well in her hopes as her fears" as he begins his search for Lydia and Wickham (PP 288). The same novel makes it clear that there can be too much of a good thing even in regard to the most estimable traits. Mr. Bennet says of Bingley and Jane that "You are each of you so complying, that nothing will ever be resolved on; so easy, that every servant will cheat you; and so generous, that you will always exceed your income" (PP 348).

Gilbert Ryle has pointed out that "in *Persuasion* Jane Austen gives us what she would have been surprised to hear was a good rendering of Aristotle's doctrine of the Mean."[17] Anne Elliot wonders, for instance, whether Wentworth ever reconsidered his position "as to the universal felicity and advantage of firmness of character; and whether it might not strike him that, like all other qualities of the mind, it should have its proportions and limits" (P 116). Ryle believes that Austen employs what he calls a "wine-taster's technique of comparative character delineation," in the course of which she surveys excesses and deficiencies of particular character traits, observes these traits in combination with others, deploys them to good and ill effect in different circumstances.[18] For Ryle, and with this I entirely concur, Austen falls into the Aristotelian rather than the Calvinist camp, and into the secular rather than the religious camp, with respect to her ethical ideas.

I begin to disagree with Ryle only when he puts "forward the historical hypothesis that Jane Austen's specific moral ideas derived, directly or

---

[17] Ryle, "Jane Austen and the Moralists," p. 117.
[18] Ryle, "Jane Austen and the Moralists," pp. 108–9.

indirectly, knowingly or unknowingly, from Shaftesbury."[19] Or at any rate, since we cannot know with any degree of certainty whether Jane Austen ever read Shaftesbury, I disagree to the extent that Ryle seems to believe that the ethical ideas in Austen's work more clearly resemble those of Shaftesbury (thereby finding their connection to Aristotle) than they do those of any other philosopher. This seems clearly false, and Ryle's arguments for the position are not convincing. First, he maintains that the orthodox ethic for the period was Calvinistic (though he acknowledges that Hume and several others were not disposed in that direction) and that the secular-aesthetic Aristotelianism of Shaftesbury was not in vogue. He takes this to suggest that Jane Austen is unlikely to have absorbed her ethical ideas from the atmosphere in which she lived, since it was noticeably bereft of ideas of that general kind. Yet neither Butler nor Hume was inclined toward a Calvinist ethic, and neither was obscure enough to leave Austen's atmosphere wholly free of trace effects, any more than was Shaftesbury. That Ryle finds no echoes in Austen from Butler or Hume does not convince someone who has found many such echoes herself. But that is a subject to which the rest of this book is devoted and which we can wait to address.

Sharing a "secular-aesthetic Aristotelianism" with Shaftesbury isn't enough to demonstrate that Austen does not share important ideas with other philosophers as well. Certainly, both Hume and Austen seem to share ideas very similar to the ones that Ryle describes. When Hume examines the passions of pride and humility he advises us to consider "the vice or virtue that lies in their excesses or just proportion" and reflects on the connection between vice and excess, echoing just the kind of Aristotelian approach that Ryle notes in Austen and attributes exclusively to the influence of Shaftesbury (T 592).

Ryle's second reason in support of the Shaftesbury hypothesis involves Austen's failure to employ "the flat, generic antithesis of Virtue and Vice, Reason and Passion, Thought and Desire, Soul and Body . . . Duty and Pleasure . . . in her novels. Instead we get an ample . . . and many-dimensional vocabulary."[20] Of course, Hume fails to employ such a bipolar vocabulary and refrains from adhering to such bipolar conceptions as well, so this evidence again fails to establish Austen as a Shaftesburian *rather* than a Humean. In his third line of argument, Ryle claims that Austen uses the word "mind" in a way that Shaftesbury does and Hume does not. As Ryle does not sufficiently inform us about the uniqueness

---

[19]   Ryle, "Jane Austen and the Moralists," p. 118.
[20]   Ryle, "Jane Austen and the Moralists," p. 120.

of this usage (the term is said to be more closely affiliated with Aristotle's "psyche" than with contemporary, often religious, uses of "soul," but it is entirely unclear how this would rule Hume out) we may safely conclude that the arguments which purport to establish Austen as a Shaftesburian do not militate against the claim that she may be more of a Humean. Most of the evidence mustered in support of the Aristotelian and Shaftesburian analyses is equally compatible with similar claims about a Humean flavor in Austen's work.

As indicated earlier, I do not intend to contest the claim that Austen's works embrace an Aristotelian conception of happiness and of virtue as it is thought to relate to happiness. Much of the effectiveness of Austen's novels rests on her depiction of distinctive behavioral dispositions which can naturally be linked to an Aristotelian account of virtue. Harold Bloom once said that, "like Shakespeare, [Austen] gives us figures, major and minor, utterly distinct each in his or her own mode of speech and being, and utterly different from one another."[21] In other words, one of Austen's real gifts, the one most closely related to her reputation for ethical perspicacity, involves her ability to describe behavioral dispositions and habits of response so as to make them wholly believable and wholly accessible to us as the virtues and vices that they are. This grasp of the data of Aristotle's central ethical doctrine, especially of the conception of virtue as a product of habit or practice, is emphasized by David Gallop, whose Aristotelian analysis of Austen is one of the most philosophically convincing of those on offer.

Gallop indicates that, like Aristotle, Austen regards happiness as "rational activity in practicing the . . . human excellences of character and intellect,"[22] something for the achievement of which both Austen and Aristotle believe "moderate resources" are required. What Aristotle says in the *Nicomachean Ethics* is that happiness and virtue cannot be achieved without some external goods. However, the goods in question are such as will be accessible to most of us, most of the time, and so the absence of wealth will not constitute an insuperable obstacle to virtue or contentment in most cases: "we can do fine actions even if we do not rule earth and sea . . . even from moderate resources we can do the actions expressing virtue. . . . It is enough if moderate resources are provided."[23] Gallop draws our attention to the fact that something very similar is

---

[21] Tyler, *The Friendly Jane Austen*, p. 1.
[22] Gallop, "Jane Austen and the Aristotelian Ethic," p. 98.
[23] Aristotle, *Nicomachean Ethics*, trans. Terence Irwin (Indianapolis: Hackett, 1985), p. 290 (1179a1–9).

perfectly illustrated in an interchange between Elinor and Marianne Dashwood of *Sense and Sensibility*. When Marianne demands to know what grandeur and wealth have to do with happiness, Elinor replies that grandeur has little to do with it, but wealth has much, quickly quelling Marianne's outraged claim that only a competence is required for happiness by showing her that "*your* competence and *my* wealth are very much alike . . . and without them, as the world goes now, every kind of external comfort must be wanting" (SS 91). It turns out, in fact, that Marianne's competence exceeds Elinor's wealth at the rate of a thousand pounds per annum.

Gallop convincingly juxtaposes passages from the *Nicomachean Ethics* about the practical intellect and about the importance to virtue of practice and habituation with passages from Austen which illustrate those very points, or which contrast characters' theoretical professions with their actual performance. The former is most aptly illustrated by a selection from *Pride and Prejudice* in which Darcy's avowed lack of talent "in conversing easily with those [he] . . . has never seen before" is wittily compared by Elizabeth to her limited musical talent, for the limitations of which she holds herself liable, because she hasn't taken the trouble to practice (PP 175).[24] Emma suffers from a very similar failing, though she is less inclined openly to admit it. Contrasts between avowed adherence to precepts and actual performance, between self-description and actual habits of action, are everywhere in Austen. "I have been a selfish being all my life," Darcy tells Elizabeth Bennet, "in practice, though not in principle" (PP 369).

It would be fair to say that Austen is at her most devastating when entertaining herself and her readers at the expense of hypocrites, in other words, at the expense of the very people whose voiced ethical stance is never extended to practice. Just prior to our considering the importance of practice to the development of musical and social skills in *Pride and Prejudice*, Austen has Lady Catherine announce that if she had ever learned to play, she "should have been a great proficient" (PP 173), deftly taking credit for the skill without putting herself to *any* of the trouble of having to achieve it.[25]

The novels are filled with descriptions of vicious and virtuous dispositions that are explicitly discussed in terms of habit and practice. Willoughby

---

[24]   Gallop, "Jane Austen and the Aristotelian Ethic," pp. 99–100.
[25]   This is not analogous to a case that Hume would refer to as one of "virtue in rags," of course, (a virtue which we may still credit someone with having) since the opportunity of practice was constantly available to Lady Catherine.

of *Sense and Sensibility* speaks of "giving way to feelings which I had always been too much in the habit of indulging" (SS 320) and Edmund speaks of Dr. Grant's "faulty habit of self-indulgence" in *Mansfield Park* (MP 111). Again in *Mansfield Park*, the difference between the virtuous Fanny and the less virtuous Mary Crawford is in part ascribable to habit: "What was tranquillity and comfort to Fanny was tediousness and vexation to Mary. Something arose from difference of disposition and habit: one so easily satisfied, the other so unused to endure" (MP 285). Edmund's final repudiation of Mary is the result of her inability to step outside established and habitual patterns of response. Despite what Edmund chooses to consider "half a wish of yielding to truths," he maintains that "habit, habit carried it" for Mary, exposing forever the difference between what she really was and what he had imagined her to be (MP 458). Even if one is disinclined to sympathize with Edmund and his estimation of Mary's habits as vicious, there is a distinctly Aristotelian feel to this way of delineating character. Virtues are described in terms of habit and practice just as vices are: Emma advocates "a habit of self-command" (E 268), for instance, and habits of self-examination and reflection are advocated in *Mansfield Park* (MP 114–15).

But, of course, Aristotle's is not the only moral system which provides insights into distinctions between professed moral positions and actual practice, or which advocates a mean between extremes. I believe that Gallop is correct in claiming that Austen's perspective is in many respects Aristotelian. I just want to argue that such a perspective in itself has not a little in common with that of David Hume, and that acknowledging an Aristotelian flavor in Austen's work is not to deny an even more distinctive Humean quality, since any normative system of ethics associated with Hume would have to be a system of virtue ethics as well.

Gallop also calls our attention to a conception of rational emotion which he regards as characteristically Aristotelian and which is evident in all of Austen's novels. Instead of treating emotions as non-rational involuntary responses, Aristotle treats them as something susceptible to rational assessment, and indicates that virtue may often be a matter of feeling the right thing to the right extent at the proper time. Our habits of emotional response can and should be molded so that we have the correct kinds of responses to the right kinds of objects.[26] "Emotional response

---

[26] Relevant passages in Aristotle appear in any edition of the *Rhetoric* 1378a20–1380a4, *On the Soul* 403a2–403b19, *Nicomachean Ethics* 1125b26–1126b9. For an excellent discussion and excerpts, see Cheshire Calhoun and Robert C. Solomon, *What Is an Emotion? Classic Readings in Philosophical Psychology* (New York: Oxford University Press: 1984), pp. 42–52.

and cognitive judgment are closely interwoven" in both Aristotle and Austen, according to Gallop.[27] For instance, just as anger should be aimed at the right person to the right degree at the proper time, so humor and amusement have proper and improper targets and suitable as well as unsuitable conditions for deployment. This is very clear in Aristotle, who criticizes "people who stop at nothing to raise a laugh"[28] and is made equally clear in *Emma*, in a scene in which Knightley reprimands her for being funny at the expense of the wrong person, in the wrong way, in the wrong circumstances. "Miss Bates' age and character, her relationship to Emma, and the company present" (some of whom will take their lead from Emma) all make Emma's jest inexcusable (even though it might not be inexcusable if it involved a different person or were made in different circumstances), and that for characteristically Aristotelian reasons.[29]

I think that Gallop has it exactly right when he aligns a kind of cognitivism about emotion with Austen's ethical perspective. The references in Austen to "proper feeling," the dependence of character judgments on emotional reactions to vice and virtue, add evidence to the broad parallel Gallop draws.[30] But, of course, none of this diminishes parallels which might be drawn between Austen and Hume. While Hume maintains that emotions are unanalyzable sensations, he affiliates the indirect passions with cognitions. In fact, the passions bridge the gap between ideas – those ideas which excite them, and those other ideas which occur on account of them. Moreover, Hume maintains that morality arises from sentiment, describing a role for the moral passions in character assessment that is echoed in Austen. So Gallop is right, but we can still maintain that an even stronger comparison can be made between Hume and Austen.

Ruderman, also, is entirely correct in her contentions about the intrinsic pleasantness of moral conduct in Austen,[31] about the usual compatibility of prudence with the other virtues, about happiness as an aim of virtuous individuals. As has already been indicated, Alasdair MacIntyre says that "when Jane Austen speaks of 'happiness,' she does so as an Aristotelian."[32] He sees her as restoring a teleological perspective: "Her heroines seek the good through seeking their own good in marriage,"

---

[27] Gallop, "Jane Austen and the Aristotelian Ethic," p. 106.
[28] Aristotle, *Nicomachean Ethics*, p. 112 (1128a5–10).
[29] Gallop, "Jane Austen and the Aristotelian Ethic," p. 103.
[30] More examples of and conjectures about Austen's perspective on emotion will be offered in Chapter 4.
[31] See, for instance, Ruderman, *The Pleasures of Virtue*, pp. 37, 71.
[32] MacIntyre, *After Virtue: A Study in Moral Theory*, p. 223.

given the restricted opportunities for women in the eighteenth century.[33] We see these things as often in Austen as we do in Aristotle. We see them when her heroines choose respect and affection over rank and prestige, as when Anne Elliot chooses Captain Wentworth over Mr. Elliot. We see them when Austen's heroines choose for themselves the lives they believe will make them happiest rather than lives of self-sacrifice which will relegate them to caretaker status. Anne Elliot doesn't remain at her needy sister's beck and call. Fanny will not care for Lady Bertram's pugs in perpetuity. Emma Woodhouse does not continue as the sole companion of her querulous father. But all three choose their own ultimate good without thereby depriving others. Anne's sister Mary Musgrove has recourse to her immediate family. Lady Bertram is contented by the arrival of Fanny's sister, who is pleased to become a denizen of Mansfield. A fortuitous poultry-house robbery leads the timid Mr. Woodhouse to develop a keen "sense of his son-in-law's protection" that makes him amenable to Emma's marriage, without which "he would have been under wretched alarm every night of his life" (E 484). These are all compromises, per-haps even the mean between extremes of which Aristotle speaks, but they are not compromises in happiness. Indeed, in the latter two cases, concern for the well-being of additional persons ensures an increase of happiness in that of others, as well as a mitigation of guilt.

However, the observation of a connection between pleasure and virtue does not present us with something that is uniquely Aristotelian. The fore-grounding of such a connection is equally characteristic of both utilitarian and Humean ethics. Hume's affiliation of the moral sentiments with plea-sure and pain, for instance, enables us to make double use of the evidence adduced in favor of the Aristotelian analysis.

Finally, an important comparison between Aristotle and Austen has been touched on by both Gallop and MacIntyre. "Jane Austen's moral point of view and the narrative form of her novels coincide," according to MacIntyre, who maintains that

> she sees the *telos* of human life implicit in its everyday form. . . . she makes her characters and her readers see and say more and other than they intended to, so that they and we correct ourselves. The virtues and harms and evils which the virtues alone will overcome provide the structure both of a life in which the *telos* can be achieved and of a narrative in which the story of such a life can be unfolded.[34]

[33] MacIntyre, *After Virtue: A Study in Moral Theory*, p. 224.
[34] MacIntyre, *After Virtue: A Study in Moral Theory*, pp. 225–6.

Gallop sees Austen's fiction as embodying an Aristotelian aesthetic: all of Austen's novels "achieve . . . exactly the purpose that Aristotle assigned to fiction. . . . Through the causally structured nexus of events that we call a plot, fiction illustrates generalizations about human character and conduct. . . . It speaks to us . . . as practical and moral agents."[35] That is, as Stephen Halliwell has suggested, narratives provide an avenue for the rehearsal of our moral dispositions, and may even modify our future capacities for response.[36]

Yet a very similar view may be ascribed to Hume. At the end of the Essay "Of the Standard of Taste," Hume speaks of our tendency to disengage emotionally from works which endorse conduct that we regard as blameworthy,[37] and goes on to stress the difficulty of altering our sentiments of approbation and disapprobation simply to suit the imaginative moment.[38] This passage has given rise to some controversy, but it certainly makes clear that Hume believes fictions can and do engage us on a moral level, and that they present moral perspectives which can be adopted or resisted, which brings to the fore a further similarity between Hume and Aristotle. Indeed, the kind of narrow circle to which Austen's novels constantly draw our attention is precisely the arena to which Hume believes we are conditioned to respond morally. Fiction removes personal bias by allowing us to stand back from the action. It provides information about the mental states and tendencies of characters. Both this removal of bias and this review of internal states are featured in the description of the process of moral judgment in Hume. Austen's particular brand of fiction proves eminently suitable for the rehearsal of our moral responses in a distinctively Humean way, by engaging our sympathy and by considering the effects of someone's traits of character on those in his or her vicinity. This particular topic will be taken up in later chapters, particularly that which concerns the adoption of what Hume calls the general point of view.

I will maintain that Austen adopts a view of virtue, vice, and human nature remarkably similar to that held by David Hume. As to the present topic, it is granted that there are Aristotelian elements in Austen's writing, but Hume's own work is not devoid of the occasional Aristotelian element. Treating virtue as a disposition and a mean between extremes

---

[35]   Gallop, "Jane Austen and the Aristotelian Ethic," p. 96.
[36]   Stephen Halliwell, *Aristotle's Poetics* (Chicago: Chicago University Press, 1998), p. 352.
[37]   David Hume, "Of the Standard of Taste," in *Essays Moral, Political, and Literary*, ed. Eugene F. Miller (Indianapolis: Liberty Classics, 1987), p. 246.
[38]   David Hume, "Of the Standard of Taste," p. 247.

is only Aristotelian because Aristotle thought of these things first, not because no one followed his example. As we have seen, Hume did not neglect either point in the *Treatise*. The association and interdependence of virtue with happiness and pleasure can be found in the writings of both philosophers, though in Aristotle pleasure is less an end than it is in Hume. But beyond this, there is also considerable evidence of commonality between Hume and Austen in which Aristotelian insights play no part. Their views on how particular vices can manifest in real life, on marriage, on moral feeling and the assessment of character, all tip the balance in favor of the hypothesis that Austen's novels embrace a Humean ethic.

4
Hume and Austen on Pleasure, Sentiment, and Virtue

As was indicated in the preceding chapter, we see in Austen, Hume, and Aristotle a connection between pleasure and virtue. In Aristotle, of course, pleasure is simply a byproduct of virtuous activity whereas happiness or human flourishing is the ultimate end toward which such conduct is directed. We do not find a distinction of precisely this kind in Hume, who uses the term "pleasure" in a broad and all-encompassing way throughout the *Treatise*. There are pleasurable sentiments, such as those of moral approbation or aesthetic appreciation or love or pride. The gratification of curiosity is pleasant also. And just as we may experience pleasures of diverse sorts, their sources can differ: utility gives us pleasure, as does the exercise of the understanding, as does discovering something new. Some of these sources and kinds of pleasure are clearly implicated in human flourishing. Others are not. In this regard, Hume tends to use the term indiscriminately. Austen's conception of happiness seems rather closer to a Humean or modern one than to an Aristotelian one: it includes pleasure as more than a byproduct of activity, and deploys that term in a manner broad enough to include some conceptions of human flourishing. We will begin by considering several of these diverse sources of pleasure, as they are related to virtue, and gradually focus our attention on the (pleasurable) moral sentiment of approbation and its unique connection to the virtuous life.

Anne Crippen Ruderman (who does not make as many distinctions between pleasure and happiness as one would expect of an Aristotelian) argues forcefully and effectively that pleasure is a friend of virtue in Austen, and that pain is an adjunct of vice. "Austen shows," says Ruderman, "how her best characters can achieve happiness, not by deliberately pursuing it or insisting on their right to it, but rather by acting in a way that benefits others *and* perfects themselves."[1] I will agree to some extent with this statement, though I think that it is too strong when we consider Elizabeth Bennet's bold pronouncement to Lady Catherine of a right to her own life plans: "I am only resolved to act in that manner, which will, in my own opinion, constitute my happiness" (PP 358). *Pace* Professor Ruderman, this sounds as deliberate a pursuit as one could hope to see.

It is not, of course, the kind of bullheaded pursuit of one's own interests at the expense of others that both Ruderman and I would argue is incompatible with Austen's ethical stance. Happiness, for Elizabeth, has a rational basis, and a basis in the character of those who experience it. For instance, Elizabeth expects the married felicity of Bingley and Jane to stem from character and intelligence. Their prospects for happiness were "rationally founded, because they had for basis the excellent understanding, and super–excellent disposition of Jane" (PP 347–8). There is, moreover, a clear distinction in Austen between outright egoism and simple prudence. Hume makes a similar distinction. Even if prudence is regarded as a natural ability akin to sagacity rather than a voluntary habit of action, Hume indicates that "all moralists, whose judgment is not perverted by a strict adherence to a system, enter into the same way of thinking; and . . . the antient moralists in particular made no scruple of placing prudence at the head of the cardinal virtues" (T 609). It is people's usefulness to others in their circle, to society, and to *themselves* that makes them virtuous, where that usefulness is determined in terms of the happiness and misery they produce (EPM 5.43, p. 230). Clearly, one's own happiness is part of the equation. In any case, acting with an eye to self-preservation and one's eventual happiness is not comparable to sacrificing the good of others in pursuit of one's own. One can approve the first and condemn the second with no inconsistency. Since that is exactly what most people do, I only bring the point forward as a defense against the various critics whose all-or-nothing stance on self-interest in Austen is justly criticized by Ruderman. Ruderman's point about Austen is, in essence, correct. As the preceding quotation from *Pride and Prejudice* suggests, real fulfillment in Austen's fictional worlds is probably unobtainable without virtue and intelligence. The former term would encompass such dispositions as benevolence and generosity, and would presumably rule out the single-minded pursuit of personal interests, at least when it involved the harm or neglect of others or was undertaken at their expense.

[1] Anne Crippen Ruderman, *The Pleasures of Virtue: Political Thought in the Novels of Jane Austen* (Lanham, MD: Rowman & Littlefield, 1995), p. 14.

The latter would suggest a bar against the indiscriminate gratification of every appetite. Austen's more clearly villainous characters are usually either calculatingly selfish (Lady Susan, Mr. Elliot, Mrs. John Dashwood, General Tilney, Lucy Steele) or undone by the impulse to immediate gratification (Henry Crawford, Willoughby). Neither motivation can be attributed to Elizabeth Bennet's pursuit of happiness. It is clear, at least, that in Austen and in Hume virtue can involve finding the best means to one's own happiness.

It is not just that the most virtuous characters in Austen end by being happiest, however, but that virtue rewards its possessor in the short run by making her more adaptable and less vulnerable to sensations of loss and feelings of ill-use. In *Sense and Sensibility*, the virtues of self-control and forbearance make Elinor Dashwood more capable of coping with the loss of her father and her family's reduced circumstances than do her mother's and sister's self-indulgence. "They encouraged each other in the violence of their affliction," while Elinor "was deeply afflicted; but still she could struggle, she could exert herself" (SS 7). It is very clear that Elinor suffers less, not because she loved her father any less, but because she exercises self-restraint. In *Mansfield Park*, Fanny Price's humility and patience and unselfishness serve her better than the vanity and greed of Maria Bertram serve Maria, both in terms of the friends and lovers that they attract and the courses their lives eventually take. Emma Woodhouse alleviates her pain and wretchedness over having behaved unkindly toward Miss Bates by performing an act of kindness in the course of which she tends to the amusement of her sickly father: "A whole evening of backgammon with her father was a felicity [compared to the party of alleged pleasure that has just taken place at Box Hill]. . . . *There*, indeed, lay real pleasure, for there she was giving up the sweetest hours of the twenty-four to his comfort" (E 377). Cases of this particular kind, although the actions of the protagonists are endorsed, are, I think, more a reflection of Austen's naturalism than they are a reflection of some effort on her part to depict how things ought to be. There is no inevitable straining here to reward virtue, to deliver an endorsement of conduct by depicting that conduct as having a payoff. There is just a depiction of how nicely things can sometimes work out when the right dispositions are exercised in the right way. We get just as many depictions of the wrong dispositions ascendant in Austen without inevitable bad consequences, even though the conduct is clearly not endorsed. I absolutely concede that in some contexts this whole question of endorsement (roughly, its being true in the fictional world that the conduct under scrutiny is right) is ambiguous and involves a complication of factors which may, but do not necessarily, involve a depiction of positive consequences. In the three examples above, we can at least agree that Austen draws our attention to a fairly subtle connection between virtuous conduct and its useful or satisfying (and therefore pleasurable) consequences for the agent.

There are even more examples of the pleasures of virtuous action and the pleasure of virtuous agents in Austen. This is unmistakable in *Pride and Prejudice*. Once she has received Bingley's proposal, Jane cries that she wishes Elizabeth to be as happy as she. Elizabeth's reply is very much to the point: "If you were to give me forty such men, I never could be so happy as you. Till I have your disposition, your goodness, I never can have your happiness" (PP 350). Pleasure and virtue are also linked to self-approbation on the part of Austen's characters. Emma Woodhouse experiences a "twofold complacency" when giving Jane Fairfax her due, in which "the sense of pleasure and the sense of rendering justice" combine (E 167). She later calls on Jane "equally as a duty and a pleasure" (E 452). Marianne Dashwood at her most self-serving proposes that pleasure cannot accompany blameworthy conduct, when defending herself from Elinor's criticism:

> "I am afraid," replied Elinor, "that the pleasantness of an employment does not always evince its propriety."
> "On the contrary, nothing can be a stronger proof of it, Elinor; for if there had been any real impropriety in what I did, I should have been sensible of it at the time, for we always know when we are acting wrong, and with such a conviction I could have had no pleasure". (SS 68)

This is Hume's account as it would appear *without* the imposition of the general point of view to redress bias, but the connection between pleasure and virtue, even if self-interested, could not be clearer. Moreover, Hume chronicles the very inability to correct for the effects of one's personal interests and preferences that afflicts Marianne.

Happiness and pleasure are salient for Austen's characters, not just as life goals but as everyday concerns, and these are often concerns involving the happiness of others. Austen's heroines seek to bring pleasure to those they love and take pleasure in their happiness. Emma, for instance, "cannot allow herself to feel so much pain as pleasure" at the marriage of Mrs. Weston, because that marriage is so much to Mrs. Weston's advantage (E 11). Hume indicates not only that qualities are "approv'd of in proportion to the advantage, which results from them" (T 612) but that our approval is elicited by actions and events which benefit both individual acquaintances and society as a whole (T 533–4). Elizabeth Bennet is described as feeling her sister Jane's pleasure on several occasions. Such occasions of shared pleasure, and of happiness in the happiness of another, are also described in the course of Hume's articulation of his principle of sympathy, a subject which is reserved for the next chapter. It is worth noting at this stage, however, that both Hume and Austen present us with an account of pleasure that shows our investment in the happiness of others.

Ruderman believes that examples such as some of the preceding show that "Austen's indication that noble conduct is intrinsically pleasant is more Aristotelian than modern."[2] In this she is mistaken, either for believing that no modern philosopher made such assumptions or for believing that Aristotle necessarily places greater emphasis on the connection between pleasure and virtue than would any modern philosopher. Pain and pleasure, according to David Hume, are inextricably entwined with vice and virtue. We are so constituted that "certain characters and passions, by the very view and contemplation, produce a pain, and others in like manner excite a pleasure. The uneasiness and satisfaction are not only inseparable from vice and virtue but constitute their very nature and essence" (T 296). Pleasure and pain are held to be "the chief spring or actuating principle of the human mind" (T 574). For Hume, the source of morality itself is to be found in sentiment, and sentiments can be pleasant or painful: "whatever mental quality in ourselves or others gives us a satisfaction, by the survey or reflection, is of course virtuous; as everything of this nature, that gives uneasiness, is vicious" (T 574–5). In other words, "the distinguishing impressions, by which moral good and evil is known, are nothing but *particular* pains and pleasures" (T 471). It is evident that the connection between pleasure and virtue noted by Austen scholars is a central tenet in Hume's ethical philosophy.

For the work of someone who is not exactly celebrated for her unbridled hedonism, Austen's novels contain very frequent references to pleasure. The advent of the full-text database permits us to note the sheer frequency with which she employs the term. For instance, the word "pleasure" and its cognates appear over two hundred times in *Emma*, with comparable results for the other novels. There is nothing unique in this, of course. Other works from the same era and from later periods sometimes refer to pleasure with equal frequency. The point is that, in the course of novels the specialty of which is an intimate focus on the vagaries of human nature and human habit, the kind of constant awareness of pleasure that we see in Austen takes on a certain significance.

[2]   Ruderman, *The Pleasures of Virtue*, p. 37.

Hume and Austen both indicate that we take pleasure in the virtues of others, as well as their happiness. "To have the sense of virtue," says Hume, "is nothing but to feel a satisfaction of a particular kind from the contemplation of a character," though "'tis only when a character is considered in general, without reference to our particular interest, that it causes such a feeling or sentiment as denominates it morally good or evil" (T 471). Pleasure as a reaction to the observation of virtue is everywhere in Austen. When Emma Woodhouse behaves well toward Jane Fairfax, for instance, Knightley, who "had been used to think her unjust to Jane . . . had now great pleasure in marking an improvement" (E 170). This is a subject on which most of the rest of this chapter will turn, since the pleasure we take in the virtues of others involves the moral sentiment of approbation.

It is clear from the preceding cases that one can take pleasure in or derive pleasure from one's own virtue or that of others, that pleasure can prove the consequence or concomitant of virtuous activity and sometimes even be its aim. So far, the interest has been in surveying the sheer diversity of relations between pleasure and virtue that are on display both in Austen's fiction and in Hume's philosophy. But now, the discussion must turn to the sentiment of moral approbation, which is itself the source of some (though not all) of the pleasures that have been placed under review. Moral distinctions are not derived from reason, Hume informs us at the beginning of Book III of the *Treatise*. They are discoverable, rather, "by means of some impression or sentiment they occasion" (T 470). In fact, morality "is more properly felt than judg'd of" (T 470). Thus, says Hume, "when you pronounce any action or character to be vicious, you mean nothing, but that from the constitution of your nature you have a feeling or sentiment of blame from the contemplation of it." Here, he compares virtue and vice to secondary qualities like color or heat and cold, qualities which depend more on perceivers than the objects perceived. What, after all, could be more immediate and pressing to us than our own feelings of pleasure and pain? "And if these be favourable to virtue, and unfavourable to vice, no more can be requisite to the regulation of our conduct and behaviour" (T 469).

Before exploring these Humean hypotheses in detail and going on to find similarly detailed parallels in Austen, it would be helpful to investigate Austen's basic allegiance to this sentimentalist approach, given that morality so clearly arises from sentiment for Hume. So without delving further into approbation and disapprobation as such, let us first investigate what Austen has to say about sentiment in general. Austen speaks of proper and improper feelings, of good feelings (P 87, MP 351) and evil feelings (E 332), of better feelings (P 30) and bad feelings (MP 367). Feelings can be honorable, worthy, upright, delicate and benevolent (PP 80, MP 328, SS 183, MP 348) or selfish and coarse (SS 350–1, PP 220). Such feelings lie at the basis of judgments concerning the character and actions of others, as quotations from preceding passages have demonstrated. Approbation and disapprobation can accompany and ought to precede one's judgment about another's character, but the extent to which and the circumstances under which one *experiences* feelings of approval or disapproval can reveal important things about one's own character. That is, one's moral perspicacity and motivation are inextricably bound up with sentiment.

Consider as well Austen's alliance of good character with "strong," "acute," and "quick" feelings. These terms are, on the face of it, neutral. Yet they usually amount to character recommendations in Austen. One possible exception here involves Maria Bertram's sexuality, which is put down to her "strong feelings" (MP 468). However, it is usually the case that characters in Austen with whom we are expected to sympathize, or of whom we are clearly expected to approve, feel strong emotions. Elinor Dashwood's "feelings were strong" (SS 6). The feelings of Fanny Price "were very acute, and too little understood to be properly attended to" (MP 14). Mrs. Weston is lauded for her "good sense and quick feelings" in *Emma* (E 149). A superior nature, it is also said in *Emma*, is the "sort in which the feelings are most acute and retentive" (E 138). Jane Bennet's feelings are described as "fervent" (PP 208), and she is said to unite composure and cheerfulness with "great strength of feeling" (PP 21). "Jane Fairfax has feeling," according to Mr. Knightley, and this is intended as a compliment (E 289). Fanny Price cannot be won by gallantry and wit "without the assistance of sentiment and feeling" (MP 340), admiring as she does Edmund's "genuine strength of feeling" (MP 442). Anne Elliot is said to have "gentleness, modesty, taste and feeling" (P 26). There is Mr. Knightley, "always so kind, so feeling" (E 450), and the heroic Captain Wentworth, who "could not be unfeeling" (P 91). In *The Watsons*, "Poverty is a great evil; but to a woman of education and feeling it ought not, it cannot be the greatest" (MW 318).

None of this is a recommendation of unrestrained or unregulated feeling, of course, as will become clear in succeeding chapters on sympathy and the general point of view. That the preceding recommendations of emotion do not constitute advocacy of the wholesale abandonment of emotional restraint is also readily apparent in any survey of Austen's treatment of such characters as Willoughby, who describes himself as "giving way to feelings which I had always been too much in the habit of indulging"

(SS 320) and Henry Crawford, "whose *feelings*," says Edmund, "have . . . been too much his guides" (MP 351). Even the emotionally excessive Marianne Dashwood is shown to be in need of amendment. But it is significant that all of these characters are treated far more sympathetically and shown to be far more attractive than the ones described as *resistant* to the effects of emotion.

Mr. Elliot is "unfeeling in his conduct towards" poor Mrs. Smith – she states that he has "no feeling for others" and is "totally beyond the reach of any sentiment of justice or compassion" (P 208, 199). Elizabeth Bennet reflects bitterly on Mr. Bingley's "two unfeeling sisters" (PP 129). Mrs. Dashwood and her daughters suffer "under the cold and unfeeling behavior of her nearer connections" (SS 23). Both Maria Bertram and John Dashwood, who are clearly somewhat wanting in the moral arena, are described as having feelings which are not strong. "Mr. John Dashwood had not the strong feelings of the rest of the family," it is said (SS 5), and Maria's marrying a wealthy dolt is seen (by relatives who are oblivious to her real inclinations) as something that will not discommode her, since "her feelings are not strong" and "probably . . . not acute" (MP 116, 201). The death of a "thick-headed, unfeeling, unprofitable Dick Musgrove" is no great loss to his relations (P 51).

Bad or suspect behavior in otherwise good characters is often characterized as unfeeling. Distressed by the matrimonial compromises of Charlotte Lucas, Elizabeth Bennet "could not have supposed it possible that, when called into action, she would have sacrificed every better feeling to worldly advantage" (PP 125). "How could you be so unfeeling to Miss Bates?" Knightley asks Emma about her cavalier treatment of that lady, and Emma guiltily reflects, "How inconsiderate, how indelicate, how irrational, how unfeeling had been her conduct!" (E 374, 408).

A cardinal vice in Austen appears to involve being careless of or immune to the feelings of others. This is something that will strengthen later claims of similarity between Hume's and Austen's views concerning sympathy and fellow feeling. For the present, it will simply be noted that a sensitivity to the feelings of others, a prerequisite for Humean sympathy, is almost always recommended in Austen, and an insensitivity is almost always condemned. Leading men like *Sense and Sensibility*'s Colonel Brandon, for instance, are "on every occasion mindful of the feelings of others" (SS 62). Such mindfulness is valued throughout the novels. So discomposed is Fanny by her sojourn at Portsmouth, that her picture of Mansfield Park acquires a kind of beatific glow by comparison, enhanced, she believes, by consideration which is paid at Mansfield to the feelings of others: "At Mansfield . . . every body had their due importance; every body's feelings were consulted" (MP 391–2). This isn't exactly true (Fanny's feelings were seldom attended to at Mansfield) but it shows the value placed on paying attention to the feelings of others. It also shows the role that something akin to Hume's principle of comparison has in altering Fanny's attitude. As Hume says, "Every thing in this world is judg'd of by comparison. . . . When a man has either been acustom'd to a more splendid way of living, or thinks himself intitled to it by his birth and quality, every thing below is disagreeable and even shameful" (T 323). Such a principle of comparison is also involved in Fanny's new estimation of the merits of Henry Crawford, whom comparison to her immediate family considerably enhances, and whose sensitivity to her feelings is made to shine by contrast (and not entirely, as Fanny naively believes, in contrast to his former conduct at Mansfield): "he was much more gentle, obliging, and attentive to other people's feelings" (MP 406).

Inattentiveness to such feelings, on the other hand, is roundly condemned. *Emma*'s repellent Mr. Elton is found to be "conceited; very full of his own claims, and little concerned about the feelings of others" (E 35). Mr. Knightley, in speaking with disapproval of Frank Churchill, states that "he can have no English delicacy towards the feelings of other people" (E 149). Emma states, when considering Mr. Dixon's preferring another woman's musical abilities to those of his own fiancée, that she herself could not "excuse a man's having more music than love . . . a more acute sensibility to fine sounds than to my feelings" (E 202). Elizabeth Bennet's rejection of Darcy's first proposal is based largely on such grounds: "From the very beginning, from the first moment . . . of my acquaintance with you, your manners, impressing me with the fullest belief of your arrogance, your conceit, and your selfish disdain of the feelings of others, were such as to form that ground-work of disapprobation" (PP 193). Earlier, Elizabeth reflects on inattention to others' feelings as a source of human unhappiness: "without scheming to do wrong, or to make others unhappy, there may be error. . . . Thoughtlessness, want of attention to other people's feelings . . . will do the business" (PP 136).

So it isn't only in Hume that sentiment proves the source of morality. But now it is time to ask a few questions about how this works. Being told that "virtue is distinguished by the pleasure, and vice by the pain, that any action, sentiment, or character gives us by the mere view and contemplation" (T 475) requires some explanation of what distinguishes morally significant producers of pleasure and pain from others of no apparent ethical import. Recollect, however, that Hume speaks of "*particular* pains and pleasures. . . . An action, or sentiment, or character is virtuous or vicious; why? because its view causes a pleasure or uneasiness of a particular kind" (T 471). There are unique moral sentiments – approbation and disapprobation – that can be readily distinguished from other pleasurable or painful responses. Pleasure produced by contemplating someone's conduct or motives is quite distinct from that produced by listening to music, say, or eating a good dinner. And pleasure is only *necessary* for the recognition of virtue. It is not in itself sufficient. More discussion of what is required for these distinctively moral sentiments will take place in succeeding chapters on Hume's principle of sympathy, and on the general point of view that he indicates is requisite for their production. At present, however, we can at least consider the structure of the indirect passions, to which moral approbation and disapprobation belong as variants of love and hatred.

As indicated, moral approval and disapproval are said to be indirect passions, which Hume calls "impressions of reflection," and which are caused by and occasion distinct ideas. Hume differentiates between ideas and impressions by associating impressions with experience (e.g., sensation) and ideas with thinking rather than direct experience, though he often makes it seem that degree of "liveliness" is the primary way of distinguishing between the two. The indirect passions of approbation and disapprobation are said to be caused by an idea about a positive or negative quality in something (the subject) associated with an agent (the object) and then to occasion another idea concerning that agent. Hume says we must "make a distinction betwixt the cause and the object of . . . passions; betwixt that idea, which excites them, and that to which they direct their view, when excited" (T 278). It is only the second idea which targets the object of the passion: in approbation and disapprobation this is another person, to whom virtue or vice is ascribed. The initial idea, which causes the passion, is about a positive or negative quality in something associated with the individual toward whom the approval or disapproval is then directed. This initial idea arouses the approval or disapproval, from which a moral judgment concerning the object of the passion proceeds. Let us for a moment assume that we can characterize the initial idea as a thought or belief about some state of affairs, say the belief that General Tilney has placed Catherine Morland at risk and distressed her (this is a belief about the pain-inflicting quality ascribable to behavior exhibited by the agent). Such a belief produces indignation and disapproval (on the part of Henry Tilney and the reader), which give rise to a negative evaluation of the General – the judgment that he is an inconsiderate and vindictive creep, say. Notice that it is the sentiment of disapprobation that precedes and is the progenitor of the moral judgment, that the moral evaluation springs from the sentiment. We will see that some of this is echoed in Austen.

Attention has already been drawn to Austen's emphasis on sensibility and emotion, and the connection of these to the apprehension of vice and virtue. Consider, for instance, Anne Elliot's telling distrust of Mr. Elliot, to which we will return again at the end of this chapter: "Mr. Elliot was rational, discreet, polished – but he was not open. There was never any burst of feeling, any warmth of indignation or delight, at the evil or good of others. This, to Anne, was a decided imperfection" (P 161). The preceding clearly does not signify some blanket condemnation of reserve which retroactively censures both Mr. Darcy of *Pride and Prejudice* and Mr. Knightley of *Emma*.[3] First, the reserve of each cannot be taken to reflect an attitude that disapproves or opposes openness and warmth, given that each of these gentlemen falls in love with a warm, open, and out-spoken woman. But openness is not the point in any case, at least not if we understand it to imply some form of extroversion. Only two of Austen's heroines could be described as extroverts: Emma Woodhouse and Elizabeth Bennet. Anne Elliot and Fanny Price fall decidedly into the introverted camp.

What is really at issue is "indignation or delight *at the evil or good of others.*" That is, the cited passage seems to concern spontaneous moral emotions and a willingness to make judgments on their basis. Even Darcy and Knightley, the most reserved characters, experience no difficulty whatsoever in voicing their indignation about the behavior of those whom they take to be their rivals, Wickham and Churchill. Characters are found wanting in Austen, not for reserve, but for a failure to respond emotionally to virtue and vice – that is, a failure to respond with moral approbation or disapprobation. Many such responses are private, of course, and characters can also be deceived about the events to which they do respond, so misunderstandings are always possible. Indeed, a series of such mistakes is what initially separates Elizabeth Bennet and Mr. Darcy. But even though misunderstandings of this kind occur, the virtuous char-acters are always found to have had "proper feelings."[4] And even though heroines like Anne Elliot and Fanny Price are usually restrained in their public expression of emotion, they experience strong emotions nonethe-less, and when these involve moral approbation and disapprobation they do not trouble to conceal them.

---

[3]   See Ruderman, *The Pleasures of Virtue*, p. 105 and Tony Tanner, *Jane Austen* (Cambridge: Harvard University Press, 1986), p. 231.
[4]   See Ruderman, *The Pleasures of Virtue*, p. 63, on Austen's use of this phrase.

It is, in fact, Mary Crawford's failure to feel any genuine moral disapproval about her brother's adulterous liaison with Maria Rushworth that leads Edmund to make a final break with her: "she saw it only as folly, and that folly stamped only by exposure. . . . it was the detection, not the offence, which she reprobated." More significant still is Edmund's reference to Mary's lack of appropriate emotion in the course of the same passage: "so voluntarily, so freely, so coolly to canvas it! – No reluctance, no horror . . . no modest loathings!" (MP 454–5). Indeed, Mary has already aroused a similar response from Fanny Price. Fanny refuses Mary's offer to convey her to Mansfield Park, even though she very much wants to go, because the offer is made in the course of a letter which is a veritable masterpiece of self-exposure. In it, Mary laments Tom Bertram's ill health, but comforts herself and Fanny with the thought of Edmund (whom she hopes to marry) succeeding to Tom's honors. In refusing the favor, Fanny believes that "it would have been a material drawback to be owing such felicity to persons in whose feelings . . . she saw so much to condemn" (MP 435–6).

A failure to respond to events with proper moral feeling is a genuine failure of character. Such a stance seems to require an account of morality which allies it with emotion. For David Hume, of course, morality arises not from reason (T 455), but from sentiment (T 470). To be literally impervious to the moral sentiments, or to be able to quell or ignore them, shows that there is something seriously wrong: "these sentiments are so rooted in our constitution and temper," says Hume, "that without entirely confounding the human mind by disease or madness, 'tis impossible to extirpate and destroy them" (T 474). In accordance with just such an insight, Edmund's real horror at Mary Crawford's failure to respond as he thinks she ought (i.e., with distress and disapproval) lies "in her total ignorance, unsuspiciousness of there being such feelings" (MP 456). Only an ethical stance like Hume's, a stance that allies morality with sentiment, can make full sense of the references to "proper feeling" that we find in Austen, whether or not Hume and Austen would assess a particular case in precisely the same way.

The last point deserves a brief digression. It has been held by readers of both Hume and Austen that the Austen who wrote *Mansfield Park* must be far more puritanical than Hume. I would like to argue that this isn't entirely the case, and that the difference between Hume and Austen in this regard is not so great as it initially appears. First, as I hope the chapter on marriage will later demonstrate, Hume's and Austen's positions on adultery and fidelity are really quite similar, though differently motivated. They both even take note of the double standard in conventions governing the conduct of men and women. Next, as I hope the preceding discussion of Kant has already demonstrated, there is insufficient reason to ascribe a full-blown Kantian absolutism to Austen or to her protagonists.

Consider, now, the vexed question of Mary Crawford, whom many readers prefer to Fanny Price. Mary, as we have seen, is finally spurned by Edmund as her lack of virtue is revealed in her lack of proper feeling. But she is not spurned, it seems evident, *just* because she doesn't take it very seriously that her brother is sleeping with a married woman. That is part of the reason, of course, but there is more to it. Maria Rushworth (whose adultery is in question) has, after all, married someone whom she holds in contempt, and done so only to enrich herself and escape her father's authority. She finds his wealth insufficient to compensate for the tedium of his and his mother's company, injures and insults them both as a return for their initial affection, and runs off with Henry more or less to prove the power of her influence. While one can sympathize with Maria in some respects, she has clearly been stupid, selfish, and very unkind. That is, there are many reasons for disapproval that have nothing to do with sex, even given Edmund's expectation of modest loathings. Mary finds all such considerations irrelevant. She doesn't very often care about the pain of other people except insofar as it will influence behavior which will affect her life or that of her brother. She can hope for Tom Bertram's death without a twinge of guilt, even though it will break Edmund's heart, provided she and Edmund will materially profit by it. This is a classic depiction of a very charming, witty, and talented egoist. She isn't precisely vicious, in that she doesn't typically produce misery among her acquaintance. But she seldom cares about other people (the only counterexample involves a genuine act of kindness toward Fanny, in which her "really good feelings" are applauded, MP 147), and she seldom has a reaction of moral disapprobation to someone causing another's pain. She probably does not have many such reactions mainly because she prefers not to attend to something so unpleasant as pain, but whatever the reason, it is this, more than anything else, that alienates Edmund. As Hume puts it, someone who from "insensibility, or narrow selfishness of temper, is unaffected with . . . human happiness and misery . . . must be equally indifferent to vice and virtue" (EPM 5.39, p. 225).

What Hume calls the moral sentiments – approbation and disapprobation – are constantly in play in Austen. In Austen, of course, these are *sentiments* rather than judgments or emotionless attitudes, just as they are in Hume. "I feel no sentiment of approbation inferior to love," declares Marianne Dashwood of *Sense and Sensibility* (SS 16). Though this makes it sound as if love is a particular species of approbation rather than (more or less as Hume would have it) the other way around, Austen shows us the same close associations that Hume does among pleasure, love, virtue, and approbation. Hume says, after all, that "The pain or pleasure, which arises from the general survey or view of any action or quality of the *mind*, constitutes its vice or virtue, and gives rise to our approbation or blame, which is nothing but a fainter and more imperceptible love or hatred" (T 614). Conduct itself is to be regarded as virtuous or vicious only insofar as it reflects the tendencies of a character and the qualities of mind that individual possesses:

> If any action be either virtuous or vicious, 'tis only as a sign of some quality or character. It must depend upon durable principles of the mind, which extend over the whole conduct, and enter into the personal character. Actions themselves, not proceeding from any constant principle, have no influence on love or hatred, pride or humility; and consequently are never consider'd in morality. (T 575)

In Austen likewise, the objects of approbation and disapprobation are most often persons or the traits or conduct of persons, where conduct serves as a reflection of relevant traits. (Relationships between persons are also frequent objects of approbation and disapprobation, but as these cases involve the interaction of the aforesaid traits, the primary consideration is preserved.) Most examples of approbation and disapprobation that Austen's novels afford involve a given character approving or disapproving of another. At the end of *Mansfield Park*, Fanny acquires the "perfect approbation and increased regard" of Sir Thomas (MP 461), in contrast to the unhappy Yates, someone whom Sir Thomas feels "sure of disapproving" before they have even become acquainted (MP 183). Fanny's having been proved correct in her determined refusal of Crawford, insofar as this establishes her capacity to make correct ethical assessments of the character of others, demonstrates her worth, as does her continual care for the Bertram family. It is Yates' involvement in the early acting debacle, on the other hand – his inability to discern its impropriety even when Sir Thomas walks in upon him as he melodramatically recites his lines in Sir Thomas' radically and unfortunately altered study – that immediately invites disapproval.

Self-approbation is something that both Hume and Austen consider. Hume at one point characterizes virtue as "the power of producing love or pride" (T 575), and without preempting the whole of Chapter 11, we can at least consider Hume's contention that "vice and virtue . . . are the most obvious causes" of humility and pride (T 295). The self is always the object of pride and shame (T 277), just as another person is always the object of love. Self-approbation marks a distinction between Emma and Mr. Knightley, for instance: "She did not always feel so absolutely satisfied with herself, so entirely convinced that her opinions were right and her adversary's wrong, as Mr Knightley. He walked off in more complete self-approbation than he left for her" (E 67). Notice that, here, approbation involves *both* a feeling of satisfaction *and* a conviction, just as they do in Hume, for whom an indirect passion like pride has both a necessary connection to pleasure and a connection to relevant cognitions. As was indicated earlier, an indirect passion acts as a kind of bridge between two ideas: "that idea which excites [the passions] . . . and that to which they direct their view when excited" (T 278). Pride can be excited by an idea about a positive quality in something associated with that emotion's object – namely, oneself. The quality is one which "naturally operates on the mind" (T 281) and which is productive of pleasure for the agent. The idea causes the emotion, which in turn leads to the formation of a different idea. This second idea can sometimes (not always, clearly) be a moral judgment arising from our own approbation of our character or conduct. Hume would tell us that humility follows the same pattern as pride, and that shame and guilt would follow on one's awareness of having erred, in this instance taking the form of a kind of disapprobation of the self. We see this when we observe Emma's shame once her unkindness to Miss Bates is brought to her attention and Elizabeth Bennet's guilt at having misjudged Darcy and having treated him unfairly. Each assesses her own character and finds it wanting.

Finally, both Hume and Austen acknowledge that we experience the disapprobation of others as an injury, and their approbation as an advantage. Thus, according to Hume, "nothing more readily produces kindness and affection to any person, than his approbation of our conduct and character: as on the other hand, nothing inspires us with a stronger hatred, than his blame or contempt," unless, presumably, we find ourselves entering into that contempt (T 346). One of the best examples of this in Austen is the picture given in several of the novels of love's being reciprocated at least in part out of recognition of and gratitude for the excellence of the lover's taste, on account of his or her love for and admiration of one's own character. Henry Tilney, for instance, "though he felt and delighted in all the excellencies of . . . [Catherine Morland's] character" has an affection which has "originated in gratitude," its initial source being "a persuasion of her partiality for him" (NA 243). Edmund Bertram tells Fanny Price (in a brief and wrongheaded pressing of Crawford's suit) that she must have the "natural wish of gratitude" to return Crawford's affection (MP 348). Elizabeth's feelings toward Darcy are improved by evidence of his "valuable qualities," but

> above all, above respect and esteem, there was a motive within her of good will which could not be overlooked. It was gratitude. – Gratitude, not merely for having once loved her, but for loving her still well enough to forgive all the petulance and acrimony of her manner in rejecting him, and all the unjust accusations accompanying her rejection. He who, she had been persuaded, would avoid her as his greatest enemy, seemed . . . most eager to preserve the acquaintance. . . . Such a change . . . excited . . . gratitude – for to love, ardent love, it must be attributed; and as such, its impression on her was of a sort to be encouraged, as by no means unpleasing. . . . She respected, she esteemed, she was grateful to him; she felt a real interest in his welfare. (PP 265–6)

The approbation of another can, and most often will, bring forth one's own, putting Austen and Hume in agreement.

I have maintained at the outset of this book that Austen's novels can sometimes function as thought experiments which not only illustrate some of Hume's contentions, but actually undertake a kind of demonstration of such claims. That is, a thought experiment does more than depict or provide an example of some particular point. It may, for instance, act as a device for discerning possibilities, for determining the alethic status of propositions.[5] Thought experiments have a clarificatory role to play in conceptual analysis. In the following passage from *Persuasion*, a passage which has only been given brief attention thus far, Anne Elliot's assessment of Mr. Elliot makes it clear that adherence to duty, the profession of good opinions, and knowing what is right are in themselves *insufficient* to establish someone's moral character.

> She could not be satisfied that she really knew his character. That he was a sensible man, an agreeable man, that he talked well, professed good opinions, seemed to judge properly and as a man of principle, this was all clear enough. He certainly knew what was right, nor could she fix on any one article of moral duty evidently transgressed; but yet she would have been afraid to answer for his conduct. She distrusted the past, if not the present. . . . She saw . . . that there had been a period of his life (and probably not a short one) when he had been, at least, careless in all serious matters; and,

---

[5] See Simon Blackburn, "Thought Experiment," in *The Oxford Dictionary of Philosophy* (Oxford: Oxford University Press, 1994), p. 377; Roy A. Sorensen, *Thought Experiments* (New York: Oxford University Press, 1992), p. 289.

though he might now think very differently, who could answer for the true sentiments of a clever, cautious man, grown old enough to appreciate a fair character? How could it ever be ascertained that his mind was truly cleansed?

Mr Elliot was rational, discreet, polished, but he was not open. There was never any burst of feeling, any warmth of indignation or delight, at the evil or good of others. This, to Anne, was a decided imperfection. Her early impressions were incurable. She prized the frank, the open-hearted, the eager character beyond all others. . . . She felt that she could so much more depend upon the sincerity of those who sometimes looked or said a careless or a hasty thing, than of those whose presence of mind never varied, whose tongue never slipped.

Mr Elliot was too generally agreeable. Various as were the tempers in her father's house, he pleased them all. He endured too well, stood too well with every body. He had spoken to her with some degree of openness of Mrs Clay; had appeared completely to see what Mrs Clay was about, and to hold her in contempt; and yet Mrs Clay found him as agreeable as any body. (P 160–1)

I will grant at the outset that Anne Elliot's concerns about Mr. Elliot's past (I have excised the reference to Sunday-travelling, but admit to it here) would never have given Hume pause. The point, however, is that Anne Elliot never denies that people can change, but only wonders whether Elliot has in fact changed. Her question is about his present moral character. And in what follows it is very clear that the absence of feeling, the failure to manifest any moral warmth and moral indignation, trump Elliot's rationality and principles and knowledge of what is right. Principles aren't enough to establish an individual's moral perspicacity or his "true sentiments," and it is the true sentiments with which Anne feels she needs to be acquainted before the character of Mr. Elliot is revealed. Moreover, Elliot appears to be invincibly agreeable – even to those of whose character he has informed Anne that he disapproves. Anne's problem, then, is that she cannot trust his feelings even though she has no objection to his judgments. His negative judgment of Mrs. Clay is one with which Anne concurs, but she can detect no *sentiment* of disapprobation. Of course, Anne's suspicions prove entirely correct since, by the close of the novel, Mr. Elliot is driven to the expedient of seducing Mrs. Clay in an effort to keep her from inveigling Sir Walter into a marriage which could produce an heir to usurp Mr. Elliot's place in the line of succession. Even if Mr. Elliot is agreeable to those around him, Anne is not sure about the tendencies of his character, being disinclined to generalize from a limited sample of its actual effects.

As will be discussed in later chapters, Hume indicates that the tendencies of a character are taken into account in the assessment of that character. And as will be discussed in Chapter 7, there is reason to believe we can go beyond this and ascribe a normative stance to Hume. He doesn't simply show us how it is that character is assessed from a third-person perspective, but contends that our approval of useful and agreeable dispositions exhibited by others can motivate us to attempt to acquire by habit and practice those dispositions we lack, partly on account of the self-directed disapproval the recognition of falling short occasions (T 479). In Hume, therefore, defects in the ability to assess character via the moral sentiments and a regulated sympathy appear to rebound on the character of the assessor. He may know via convention, or judicious employment of general ideas, or observation of the judgments of others, what disposition is considered virtuous. But without the sentiment of moral approbation, nothing will motivate him to acquire it.

What the passage from *Persuasion* provides is a species of counterexample. It is a challenge to a universal assertion that functions in more or less the same way as such counterexamples do in ethical thought experiments which appeal to our intuitions. By entering into the perspective endorsed here, which is pretty clearly Anne's, we acknowledge possible exceptions to the universal claim. The challenge is to any contention that someone's moral character is the product exclusively of reason, that it is sufficiently evidenced in his principles and in what he knows rather than what he feels. Anne needs to know Mr. Elliot's true sentiments in order to feel approval of, and then to judge, his character. Knowing that he knows what is right is not enough, for knowledge by itself is not taken to guarantee a motivation to act and so Elliot's knowledge about what is right is not taken by Anne to establish anything conclusive about the tendencies of his character. As Hume puts it, "reason of itself is utterly impotent in this particular" (T 457). "Vice and virtue are not discoverable merely by reason" but "by means of some impression or sentiment they occasion" (T 470).

5

Hume and Austen on Sympathy

Hume maintains that many of our sentiments, the moral sentiments of approbation and disapprobation in particular, depend on the principle of sympathy (T 577). This is a principle whose workings can be seen everywhere in Austen's work. Sometimes it is explicitly mentioned in her novels. More often, its presence and efficacy can be inferred. What is sympathy, in Hume? In the broadest sense, it is a principle of the imagination that makes fellow feeling possible: "as in strings equally wound up; so all the affections readily pass from one person to another and beget correspondent movements in every human creature" (T 576). When we become aware of "the effects of a passion in the voice and gesture of any person," Hume states, our minds will pass "from these effects to their causes," forming such a vivid idea of the emotion that we will, as a consequence, experience it ourselves (T 576).

A belief or idea about the emotional state of another person is transformed or converted into the emotion itself – the idea becomes the very impression (an experience or sensation) that it represents. The idea is converted into an impression by acquiring vivacity from the impression of the self, an impression that gives us so lively a conception of ourselves that "whatever object is related to ourselves must be conceived with a like vivacity of conception" (T 317). That is, the idea of another's passion acquires enough vivacity or force from the impression of the self to be transformed into the passion. Sympathy is not an emotion like pity, but a mechanism that makes this transfer or sharing of emotions possible. In the simplest terms, our awareness of the feelings of another can sometimes lead us to share those feelings.

Hume also points out that when we perceive the causes of any emotion, our minds are conveyed to the effects and are "actuated with a like emotion" (T 576). Observing the medical preparations for a surgery, say – the laying out of scalpels and bandages and instruments upon the purpose of which no one would wish to speculate, the growing anxiety of participants in the procedure – "would excite the strongest sentiments of pity and terror. No passion of another discovers itself immediately to the mind. We are only sensible of its causes or effects. From *these* we infer the passion: And consequently *these* give rise to our sympathy" (T 576). So inferences are made by the sympathizer, based on an awareness of the circumstances (the causes of the passion) and an awareness of the behavior (the effects of that passion) of the individual with whom she sympathizes.

The sympathy mechanism is constantly at work in Austen. First, it is immediately obvious that Austen too often regards sympathy as signifying more than mere pity or kindness. In *Sense and Sensibility*, Marianne (albeit unfairly) denies the possibility that Mrs. Jennings can be sympathetic, on the basis of just such a distinction: "Her heart was hardened against the belief of Mrs Jennings's entering into her sorrows with any compassion. 'No, no, no, it cannot be,' she cried; 'she cannot feel. Her kindness is not sympathy' " (SS 201). That is, pity and concern are not enough in this case. Here, sympathy involves at least a presumed sharing of emotion. Austen will usually employ the term "sympathy" to signify fellow feeling, though sympathy and compassion will sometimes be held to involve pity as well. She does not subscribe to a necessary rather than occasional connection between pity and sympathy, however.

Austen also presents scenarios in which her heroines infer the existence of a passion from its causes and effects, employing just the kind of inferential process which Hume associates with the sympathetic response. In *Persuasion*, we're given a very accurate picture of Anne Elliot's awareness of the effects and causes of an emotion by being shown her awareness of the mental states of others. This occurs when she sees her sister cut Captain Wentworth: "It grieved Anne to observe that Elizabeth would not know him. She saw that he saw Elizabeth, that Elizabeth saw him, that there was complete internal recognition on each side; she was convinced that he was ready to be acknowledged as an acquaintance, expecting it, and she had the pain of seeing her sister turn away with unalterable coldness" (P 176). Anne Elliot shares Wentworth's experience of rejection on account of her careful observation of his behavior and the circumstances.[1] Similarly, Elinor Dashwood of *Sense and Sensibility* sympathizes with Colonel Brandon

---

[1]   It has been suggested by Alex Neill that the pain Anne feels in this context may simply be that quintessentially British emotion: embarrassment. This may be true, of course. Austen is not specific enough to make my reading certain. But if Anne is embarrassed, she is most likely to be embarrassed on *behalf* of her sister (who doesn't have the sense to feel ashamed of herself). That would still be a case of sympathy, of course, since Hume tells us that sympathy often leads us to feel shame on behalf of those who don't have the presence of mind to feel it on their own account, as will be addressed shortly.

when her sister takes obvious steps to avoid him, and feels "particularly hurt that a man so partial to her sister [as Colonel Brandon] should perceive that she experienced nothing but grief and disappointment in seeing him" (SS 162). Each of Austen's heroines attends to the circumstances of another's injury and each subsequently feels hurt on that person's behalf. Distinct from pity, sympathy is both an attunement to and a resonance with the emotional experience of another.

Sometimes, Hume indicates, there may even be cases in which we are led to sympathize with someone who is, in fact, unmoved. We respond to what we believe the general run of people who behave in that way or who find themselves in those circumstances *would* be feeling. Our awareness of someone's misfortune carries our fancy from the cause to the *usual* effect. For example, "when a person of merit falls into . . . a great misfortune, we form a notion of his condition; and . . . conceive a lively idea of his sorrow, and then feel an impression of it," even in cases where we entirely overlook a greatness of mind that makes the individual with whom we sympathize impervious to this emotion (T 370). "From the same principles, we blush," says Hume "for the conduct of those, who behave themselves foolishly before us; and that tho' they show no sense of shame, nor seem in the least conscious of their folly. All this proceeds from sympathy" (T 371).

Austen's characters frequently undergo just such uncomfortable experiences. For instance, Elizabeth Bennet is regularly embarrassed by the conduct of her oblivious parent, and is often described as "blushing for her mother" (PP 43). Similarly, Catherine Morland is said to blush for Isabella Thorpe, who is entirely untroubled by her own conduct (NA 151), and Henry Tilney is said to have "blushed for the narrow-minded counsel [of his unrepentant father] which he was obliged to expose" (NA 247). But, so far, all of these blushes could be explained by a close connection with the individual who *ought* to be, but is not, ashamed. Hume clearly means to imply more than this. We may blush for others even if they are not close friends or family members, and even if there is no way in which we could be held responsible for or implicated in their conduct.

It is true that Hume is speaking here of the imagination's being affected by a general rule, a rule that inclines us to experience an emotion that would *usually* be felt in a given set of circumstances. Foolish conduct usually gives rise to shame in the actor, and our "imagination is affected by the *general rule*, and makes us conceive a lively idea of the passion, or rather feel the passion itself . . . as if the person were really actuated by it" (T 371). However, it is important to remember that the passion under review in Hume's example is shame, which is a species of humility. As Hume also makes very clear, emotions like pride and humility have the same object – oneself: "when self enters not into the consideration, there is no room either for pride or humility" (T 277). It would seem that a self-directed passion like humility could not be sympathetically shared (at least with those for whose conduct one is not responsible and with whom one is not affiliated) unless the sympathizer imaginatively adopted the perspective of another. But such a view suggests an interpretation of sympathy along lines which correspond to current descriptions of empathy – a view more compatible with the claims and proposals of Adam Smith.

Hume never acknowledged the adoption of a view of sympathy comparable to that held by Adam Smith. Smith believed that, in sympathizing with someone who suffers, "by imagination we place ourselves in his situation, we conceive ourselves enduring all the same torments."[2] In other words, we conceive what we ourselves should feel in a particular individual's situation, and this excites "some degree of the same emotion [i.e., the emotion we imagine the other person experiences] in proportion to the vivacity or dulness of the conception."[3] It should at once be acknowledged that some philosophers reject any interpretation of Humean sympathy which affiliates it with Smith's approach. However, other philosophers have maintained both that Smith's discussion of sympathy differs "but little from that of Hume in the *Treatise*," and that the elaboration of this principle in the work of the two philosophers is strikingly similar.[4] Indeed, a contemporary review of Smith's account of sympathy has been convincingly attributed to Hume. In this review, Smith's account is described as both natural and probable.[5]

It might be suggested not that Hume concurred with Smith in all respects, but that he saw Smith's analysis as one possible working out or explanation of the transition from idea to impression that sympathy is said to involve. That is, we could suggest that the impression of the self, which Hume says enlivens our ideas about the experience of another, enlivens them as we imaginatively entertain them from a first-person perspective. To speculate, if we regard the impression of the self (given the view of personal identity in Book I of the *Treatise*) as a kind of perpetually

[2] Adam Smith, *The Theory of Moral Sentiments*, ed. D.D. Raphael and A.L. Macfie (Indianapolis: Liberty Fund, 1984), p. 9.
[3] Smith, *The Theory of Moral Sentiments*, p. 9.
[4] Glenn R. Morrow, "The Significance of the Doctrine of Sympathy in Hume and Adam Smith," *Philosophical Review* 32.1 (1923): [60–78] 69.
[5] David Raynor, "Hume's Abstract of Adam Smith's *Theory of Moral Sentiments*," *Journal of the History of Philosophy* 22 (1984): 67.

shifting mosaic of impressions, then an aspect of this mosaic, captured at a particular moment in time, could be held to incorporate recollections of experiences which resembled those of the individual being contemplated. So there are grounds for thinking that a first-person point of view could have a good deal to do with enlivening our idea of another's passion in such a way as to stimulate that passion in ourselves.

Certainly, a Smithian account of empathy dovetails exceedingly well with much that we find in Austen. Peter Knox-Shaw, whose excellent *Jane Austen and the Enlightenment* suggests for the first time (for the first time, at least, at any length) that Austen's work be considered as an outgrowth of the skeptical traditions of the enlightenment, writes that, in *Sense and Sensibility*, "Austen goes out of her way to build into her text a standard item from the store of contemporary social theory. The idea is from the opening chapters of *The Theory of Moral Sentiments* (1759–90), and represents Adam Smith's particular refinement upon the powerful account of sympathy offered by Hume in the *Treatise* (1739)."[6] Indeed, Knox-Shaw, in a letter to the *Times Literary Supplement*, agrees with his reviewer Michael Caines that Austen may well have been exposed to Adam Smith's *Theory of Moral Sentiments* as a teenager. If one of Maria Edgeworth's heroines is described as having a copy of the *Theory* at her elbow, "it would be rash to deny the same precocity to Jane Austen."[7] Both Smith's and Hume's accounts of sympathy, especially if it is permissible to bring Hume's account a little more into line with that of Smith, are compatible with Austen's treatment of human sympathy.

We should thus consider instances in which Austen's characters project motives and feelings onto to others which *they themselves* would have experienced in similar circumstances, rather than drawing a connection between passion and circumstance according to a general rule alone. For instance, Mrs. Jennings of *Sense and Sensibility* not only feels compassion for Elinor, miserable with worry over her sister Marianne's illness, she also sympathizes with their mother: "when Mrs. Jennings considered that Marianne might probably be to *her* what Charlotte was to herself, her sympathy in *her* sufferings was very sincere" (SS 313). But not all cases of an empathetic kind of sympathy need resemble that of Mrs. Jennings.

It should be remembered that *we*, as sympathizers, may insufficiently resemble those with whom we sympathize. This can provide us with one

---

[6] Peter Knox-Shaw, *Jane Austen and the Enlightenment* (Cambridge: Cambridge University Press, 2004), pp. 139–40.
[7] Peter Knox-Shaw, "Austen's Reading," in Letters to the Editor, *Times Literary Supplement*, March 18, 2005, p. 15.

explanation of a kind of case that Hume describes – one in which we have sympathetic feelings that fail to correspond to those of the individual with whom we sympathize. Jane Bennet of *Pride and Prejudice* feels an agony of shame on behalf of her impervious sister Lydia, whose reputation is in tatters and whom the dissolute Wickham had to be bribed to marry. She gives "Lydia the feelings which would have attended herself, had *she* been the culprit." Jane is "wretched in the thought of what her sister must endure," even though Lydia is perfectly cheerful in her shamelessness (PP 315). When Catherine Morland of *Northanger Abbey* attributes Captain Tilney's wish to dance with Isabella Thorpe to thoughtfulness and good nature (she assumes that he has acted from consideration of Isabella's partnerless state alone) she is disabused by the Captain's brother:

> How very little trouble it can give you to understand the motive of other people's actions. . . . With you, it is not, How is such a one likely to be influenced, What is the inducement most likely to act upon such a person's feelings, age, situation, and probable habits of life considered – but, How should I be influenced, What would be my inducement in acting so and so? (NA 132)

Here, of course, Catherine is accused of drawing an inadequate analogy, of venturing an inference concerning another's mental states that is based on too small or too unrepresentative a sample. Austen also considers other cases in which the identification of the feelings of others via such self-reference goes unambiguously awry. *Emma*'s Mr. Woodhouse and his habit "of being never able to suppose that other people could feel differently from himself," is a comic figure who inadvertently persecutes others by presuming that his own constitutional predilection for quiet evenings and gruel is shared by the whole of his acquaintance (E 8).

But let us suppose that we do not accept the view of Humean sympathy as empathy, and deny a correspondence between Hume and Smith. The phenomenon of shared emotion that is ascertainable under a more limited description which excludes the empathetic is still to be found everywhere in Austen. In fact, Austen's depictions agree with some of Hume's finer points, although many of these points are made in one way or another by other philosophers as well. The claim here is not that Austen's account of sympathy is *more* compatible with that of Hume than that of Smith or Shaftesbury or Hutcheson, though I am inclined to think it at the very least *as* compatible. The first thesis of this book concerns the normative positions endorsed or otherwise supported in her works – it is cumulative rather than specific. It is only necessary, in regard to the issue of sympathy, to establish a strong correspondence. Such a correspondence certainly exists. Hume indicates, for instance, that we tend to "sympathize more with persons contiguous to us, than with persons remote from us: With our acquaintance than with strangers: With our countrymen than with foreigners" (T 581). Such assumptions are evident in Austen's novels.

Most apposite is an example from Austen's *Persuasion*. Anne Elliot realizes that her immediate family's concerns will not engender fellow feeling outside that *very* narrow circle:

> she must now submit to feel that another lesson, in the art of knowing our own nothingness beyond our own circle, was become necessary for her – for certainly, coming as she did, with a heart full of the subject which had been completely occupying both houses in Kellynch for many weeks, she had expected rather more curiosity and sympathy than she found. (P 42)

And Hume's point about our sympathizing more with persons contiguous to us than persons remote from us is beautifully illustrated by a passage from *Mansfield Park* describing Lady Bertram's reaction to her son's illness.

> The sufferings which Lady Bertram did not see had little power over her fancy; and she wrote very comfortably about agitation, and anxiety, and poor invalids, till Tom was actually conveyed to Mansfield, and her own eyes had beheld his altered appearance. Then a letter which she had been previously preparing for Fanny was finished in a different style, in the language of real feeling and alarm. (MP 427)

The most frequent examples in Austen of shared emotion involve the depiction of siblings, another affirmation of Hume's contention that we are naturally inclined to sympathize most with those to whom we are closest. She stresses the importance of fraternal ties, even over conjugal ties: "children of the same family, the same blood, with the same first associations and habits, have some means of enjoyment in their power which no subsequent connexions can supply" (MP 235). A brother or sister is someone with whom "every former united pain and pleasure [can be] retraced" (MP 234). Such a unity of past experience and recollection facilitates a continuing unity of feeling. In *Sense and Sensibility*, even the usually restrained Elinor shares Marianne's distress about Willoughby's desertion and gives way "to a burst of tears, which at first was scarcely less violent than Marianne's" (SS 182). Catherine Morland weeps in sympathy with her brother's disappointment as she reads his account of Isabella Thorpe's perfidy (NA 203). Fanny Price's sister Susan "was always ready to hear [Fanny] and to sympathize" (MP 428). It is said of Jane and Elizabeth Bennet of *Pride and Prejudice* that "each felt for the other" (PP 334).

Sympathy need not involve close ties between siblings, of course. Indeed, sympathy can be felt for persons whom one has never met, but with whose circumstances one has been acquainted, just as Hume indicates. In *Persuasion*, "sympathy . . . [is] excited towards Captain Benwick" among people who have never met him, but who have been informed of the sad circumstance of the death of his fiancée Fanny Harville (P 97). Similarly, the eager amateur thespians of *Mansfield Park* sympathize with the disappointment of the relative stranger Mr. Yates, whose theatrical debut had to be canceled on account of an inconvenient death: " 'It was a hard case, upon my word'; and, 'I do think you were very much to be pitied'; were the kind responses of listening sympathy" (MP 122). Though pity is occasionally united with the compassion of the sympathizer, it is clear in the latter case that it is mainly the frustration of disappointed thespian aspirations that is shared.

Usually, of course, the acquaintance between the sympathizer and the one with whom he or she feels is not so remote. When appraised of Tom's dangerous illness by the Bertrams, Fanny Price "felt truly for them all" (MP 427). On another occasion, Edmund's forgoing pleasure gives Fanny pain, despite the fact that his sacrifice is intended to be advantageous to her. It is also interesting to note that one can share the feeling of another and sympathize with that individual without sharing all of his or her attitudes toward the object of emotion. *Emma*'s Mr. Knightley, when informed that the suit of his protégé Martin had been rejected, "felt the disappointment of the young man," despite being disinclined to regard Harriet (who spurned Martin's proposal) as an object worthy of devotion (E 66). Captain Wentworth of *Persuasion* sympathizes with Mrs. Musgrove over the loss of her son, despite the fact that he probably believes that, all told, she is well rid of him. His sympathy is selective. It shows consideration for "all that was real and unabsurd in the parent's feelings" (P 67–8). It should not be forgotten that we may empathize with those whose beliefs we do not share. All that need be done is to imagine having the beliefs in question, and these may be entertained selectively.

And it should be remembered that the exercise of sympathy can involve pleasure as well as pain. Elizabeth Bennet of *Pride and Prejudice*, for instance, "felt Jane's pleasure," over the friendly attention she received from Bingley and his sister (PP 12). Even sympathy between siblings is itself sympathized with in Austen's work, as when the "sympathetic alacrity" of Edmund and Sir Thomas Bertram leads them to prevent

Mrs. Norris from interrupting and disrupting a joyous reunion between Fanny Price and her brother William (MP 233). Good spirits like those of Catherine Morland can not only prove infectious, but can also reward those who sympathize with her: "Mr. and Mrs. Allen were sorry to lose their young friend, whose good humor and cheerfulness had made her a valuable companion, and in the promotion of whose enjoyment their own had been gently increased" (NA 154). As Hume indicates, the "minds of men are mirrors to one another" (T 365).

Sympathy can sometimes be a comfort to the bereaved or afflicted in Austen's novels, as well as a harbinger of support and assistance. The sympathy of Fanny Price is Lady Bertram's only comfort during her son's illness and her daughter's disgrace: "To be listened to and borne with, and hear the voice of kindness and sympathy in return, was everything that could be done for her" (MP 449). The desperately depressed Marianne of *Sense and Sensibility* feels deprived of the personal sympathy of her mother in her hour of need when she is required to prolong her stay in town (SS 214). Emma Woodhouse enters into the troubles of the poor "with ready sympathy," and gives both comfort and assistance (E 86).

Hume describes sympathy as a "powerful principle in human nature" that is "the chief source of moral distinctions" (T 3.3.6.1; SBN 618). He also believes (as do other philosophers) that an inability or disinclination to sympathize can signal a moral problem. Indeed, it seems this is the case in Austen as well, since a failure to sympathize can sometimes seem to be a moral failure. Fanny Price's relations at *Mansfield Park* are criticized for their lack of sympathy: Fanny "had neither sympathy nor assistance from those who ought to have entered into her feelings and directed her taste; for Lady Bertram never thought of being useful to anybody, and Mrs Norris . . . seemed intent only on lessening her niece's pleasure, both present and future, as much as possible" (MP 219). At another point in the story, Fanny herself feels guilty for her own failure to sympathize with others. She is so happy to be invited back to Mansfield, that the emergency which prompts the invitation is almost forgotten: "The evil which brought such good to her! She dreaded lest she should learn to be insensible of it. To be going so soon. . . . set her heart in a glow, and for a time, seemed to distance every pain, and make her incapable of suitably sharing the distress even of those, whose distress she thought of most" (MP 443). Sympathy can be suitable, appropriate, called for. A lack of sympathy can amount to a moral failing.

Equally interesting is Austen's expectation that her readers will sympathize with her characters. This expectation is unmistakably expressed in *Northanger Abbey*, the only novel in which Austen is at all inclined to address the reader directly. Despite the complicated agenda of this work, which is as much about the nature of novels as it is about the adventures of Catherine Morland, Austen creates a character who engages our sympathy. In the words of Emily Auerbach, "Although Austen still intrudes her narrative voice to tell us whether or not Catherine is leading a heroine's life, she simultaneously has created a character that inspires empathy in her own right."[8] Austen goes so far as to enlist what seems a distinctly Humean sympathy on behalf of her unheroic heroine: "Every young lady may feel for my heroine at this critical moment, for every young lady has at some time or other known the same agitation" (NA 74). For instance, those of us who have "believed . . . [ourselves] in danger from the pursuit of some one whom [we] wished to avoid" (NA 74) share Catherine's anxiety, just as we might share the anxiety of a friend upon this account. Hume says that, even in the case of fiction, our hearts swell "with the tenderest sympathy and compassion" for characters, and that imagining the passions of a character "affects the spectator by sympathy, gives him some touches of the same passions".[9] We recognize the causes of Catherine's agitation, as Hume would put it, because similar circumstances have often elicited just such reactions in ourselves. We recognize the effects of Catherine's anxiety precisely because she is *not* a gothic heroine. That is Austen's entire plan. Catherine is possessed neither of inhuman abilities and acquirements nor of an acute sensibility which leads her to swoon at the drop of a hat. That is, she possesses no traits which ordinary persons might not share, and so the causes and effects of her passion, whose apprehension Hume says is a precursor to sympathy, are easy to ascertain. The ease with which we find ourselves sympathizing with Catherine demonstrates what it is that Austen both enjoins and expects us to do and demonstrates the kind of response to fiction that Hume describes.

To say that Austen's writing can lead us to sympathize with characters in the fully Humean sense is to do more than simply acknowledge that they can move us. To be moved by the plight of a character is not necessarily to sympathize with that character, after all. I may feel pity for an Austen heroine without sharing her distress. There may be further confusion when we consider certain emotions which can be felt for someone else, or on one's own account, or on behalf of another. One can feel fear on one's own behalf, or for a reckless younger sibling who

---

[8] Emily Auerbach, *Searching for Jane Austen* (Madison: University of Wisconsin Press, 2004), p. 75.
[9] David Hume, "Of Tragedy," in Eugene F. Miller, ed., *Essays: Moral, Political, and Literary* (Indianapolis: Liberty Classics, 1987), pp. 216–25, 217.

apprehends no danger, or with a relative awaiting test results. These are all cases of fear, they all have the same feel, and it is easy to confuse them – especially in fictional cases. But confusions of this sort do not plague cases of response to fiction which involve emotions that are prototypically self-directed, as Hume says that pride and humility are self-directed. And I think that the sheer frequency with which Austen's novels can invoke these feelings indicates conclusively that sympathetic reactions to the fictional are neither rare nor peculiar. Consider how often we can be led to feel sympathetic embarrassment or shame on account of the plight of an Austen heroine. Embarrassment, being self-directed, does not constitute something that can be felt *for* or *toward* or *about* a character unless, perhaps, one is an author who is responsible for having created a very bad one. The cognitive consort of an emotion like embarrassment is a consciousness of having personally erred. Thus, it would only make sense to say one was embarrassed for another if that person were someone for whose behavior or upbringing or performance one were personally responsible – one's child or subordinate or student, say. This exception could not, in the ordinary course of events, apply to a fictional being.

Let us consider a scene from Jane Austen's *Emma*. At an alfresco party at Box Hill, Frank Churchill attempts to amuse Emma Woodhouse and other guests by making a proposal:

> "Ladies and gentlemen, I am ordered by Miss Woodhouse to say that she waives her right of knowing exactly what you may all be thinking of and only requires something very entertaining from each of you, in a general way. Here are seven of you, besides myself – who, she is pleased to say, am very entertaining already – and she only demands from each of you either one thing very clever . . . or two things moderately clever; or three things very dull indeed; and she engages to laugh heartily at them all."
>
> "Oh, very well!" exclaimed Miss Bates. "Then I need not be uneasy. Three things very dull indeed. That will just do for me, you know. I shall be sure to say three dull things as soon as ever I open my mouth, shan't I?" (looking around with the most good-humored dependence on everyone's assent). "Do you not all think I shall?"
>
> Emma could not resist.
>
> "Ah! ma'am, but there may be a difficulty. Pardon me, but you will be limited as to number – only three at once."
>
> Miss Bates, deceived by the mock ceremony of her manner, did not immediately catch her meaning; but when it burst on her, it could not anger, though a slight blush showed that it could pain her. (E 370–1)

Here, Emma is guilty of a choice bit of gratuitous cruelty. The precarious economic and social situation of Miss Bates, one which ought properly to invite compassion rather than ridicule, is brought forcibly before Emma by Knightley. And Emma sees the truth of it. "Never had she felt so agitated, so mortified . . . at any circumstance in her life. . . . How could she have been so brutal, so cruel, to Miss Bates! How could she have exposed herself to such ill opinion in any one she valued?" (E 376).

The stance of an onlooker could give us any of several attitudes toward Emma. An onlooker who shared Emma's opinion about the cruelty of her action, an opinion unsoftened by any weakness for a good one-liner, might regard Emma with disapproval. An onlooker concerned with the painfulness of Emma's guilt might regard her with pity. Only an empathetic response could involve shame, a kind of consciousness of culpability. It is only from Emma's perspective that one can feel a twinge of guilt, because this is a point of view that allows one to imaginatively co-opt her actions and assume her responsibility for them. And just as an empirical matter, I'd like to claim that this can be just the sort of uncomfortable feeling one gets when reading the passage – a feeling that begins with a self-congratulatory delight in wit (vanity and pride, as Hume points out, are also passions that take the self as object) and ends with self-dislike. That is, some readers of *Emma* don't feel disapproving or pitying or shocked, they just feel bad, and it's the same kind of bad feeling one has on account of having committed a serious blunder. There could be any number of reasons for having this kind of a reaction to the passage rather than another. Perhaps one has also on occasion been witty at the expense of others. Whatever the reason for responding in this way, the response requires imagining Emma's situation from the inside, not from the perspective of an onlooker. At the very least, it requires feeling it from the inside, if we wish to avoid a Smith-friendly reading of sympathy.

And whichever interpretation is preferred, it seems quite clear that Austen provides the reader not only with illustrations of Humean sympathy, but with a demonstration of how that principle works. She does so by eliciting sympathy for and with her characters from the readers of her novels, as any reader of Austen who has felt inclined to cringe with Elizabeth Bennet at the conduct of her mother should be willing to acknowledge.

6

Hume's General Point of View and the Novels of Jane Austen

Though Hume contends (and Austen appears to concur) that the principle of sympathy is intimately involved in our moral judgments, something beyond sympathy is required for genuinely *moral* sentiments. Hume maintains that sympathy which is unregulated by what he refers to as a general point of view – the proper perspective of morality – will not necessarily lead one to experience moral approbation and disapprobation. A sympathetic response does not always give rise to emotions that dovetail with moral judgments any more than simple love and hatred will always turn out to be specifically moral sentiments. What is required is the adoption of a general point of view that allows us to "correct" our responses, controlling for the effects of distance, intensity, and luck (T 582). In brief, the general point of view is a kind of perspective that we consider in isolation from our ties to the agent whose character is under review. This is the viewpoint (as Elizabeth Radcliffe puts it) "of one who sympathizes with the circle of people most directly affected by the agent's actions."[1] There are two ways in which the general point of view can regulate our sympathy and sentiments.

First, adopting the general point of view has a kind of compensatory effect, counteracting a natural inclination on our part to sympathize more strongly with acquaintances than with strangers in cases where sympathy is unregulated (T 581). Unregulated sympathy may excite a "stronger sentiment of love and kindness" for an unheroic acquaintance than a heroic stranger (T 582). Indeed, stronger sentiments may be roused "even by an eloquent recital of the case" (EPM 5.43, p. 230). In adopting the general point of view, we attempt to correct these sentiments, to observe an individual's traits, and to judge that person's character from within

[1] Elizabeth S. Radcliffe, *On Hume* (Wadsworth, 2000), p. 73.

the perspective of that person's narrow circle, by taking up the attitude of that circle toward him or her. In this way, as Christine Korsgaard indicates, "we view the person not through the eyes of our own interests, but instead through the eyes of our sympathy with the person herself and her friends, family, neighbors, and colleagues. . . . We assess her in terms of the effects of her character on those with whom she usually associates."[2] According to Hume, " 'tis therefore from the influence of characters and qualities, upon those who have an intercourse with any person, that we praise and blame him" (T 582).

Next, unregulated sympathy excites a stronger reaction to the actual effects of traits than to tendencies alone. That is, as Geoffrey Sayre-McCord points out, the initial effects of sympathy sensitize us to the actual effects people have on those around them, so that our first inclination will be to lavish positive sentiments on those who really do benefit people rather than individuals who would do so if they could, but (as luck would have it) cannot.[3] Unregulated sympathy, says Hume, leads us initially to pay "greater regard to one whose station, joined to virtue, renders him really useful to society" (EPM 5.41, n. 1, p. 228). However,

> where a person is possess'd of a character, that in its natural tendency is beneficial to society, we esteem him virtuous, and are delighted with the view of his character, even tho' particular accidents prevent its operation, and incapacitate him from being serviceable to his friends and country. Virtue in rags is still virtue; and the love, which it procures, attends a man into a dungeon or desert, where the virtue can no longer be exerted in action, and is lost to all the world. (T 584)

The general point of view helps us to take into account the tendencies of a character in addition to its actual effects, so as to compensate for circumstances which prevent the exercise of some particular disposition (T 584–5). Thus, the question of moral luck enters our equation. We rely on general rules which supply information about the tendencies of certain traits instead of relying exclusively our observation of the actual effects of those traits in the particular situation in which an individual is placed. "Where a character is, in every respect, fitted to be beneficial to society, the imagination passes easily from the cause to the effect, without considering that there are still some circumstances wanting to render the

---

[2] Christine M. Korsgaard, "The General Point of View: Love and Moral Approval in Hume's Ethics," *Hume Studies* 25 (1999): 3.
[3] Geoffrey Sayre-McCord, "On Why Hume's 'General Point of View' Isn't Ideal – and Shouldn't Be," *Social Philosophy and Policy* 11.1 (1994): 208.

cause a compleat one. *General rules* create a species of probability, which sometimes influences the judgment, and always the imagination" (T 585).

There is some understandable disagreement about whether the general point of view amounts to nothing more than the perspective of an ideal observer, thereby undercutting morality's connection to sentiment. How could the motivating force of morality stem from sentiment when the moral distinctions we make are not the same as and sometimes even at odds with our actual feelings? According to Sayre-McCord, it follows from the preceding considerations that our moral judgments are dictated not by the state of our feelings in a given instance, but by what our feelings *would be* if we were to adopt a general point of view.[4] Similarly, Elizabeth Radcliffe suggests that the source of moral judgments and motivations alike is to be found in our feelings, but that our judgments will correspond to those feelings we *would* have, were we to take up that point of view.[5] Rachel Cohon differs somewhat, arguing that "every time we reflect upon someone's character from the common point of view, we feel an actual sentiment of approbation or disapprobation." This may alter our initial sentiment, merging with it, or the two sentiments toward the same object may remain distinct. She also reminds us that our moral judgments are accompanied by causal judgments about the effects of the trait under consideration, and contends that "we routinely take up the common point of view in order to achieve truth and consistency in our causal judgments."[6]

While rejecting the idea that Hume's general point of view involves the standpoint of an ideal observer, Sayre-McCord nonetheless defends Hume against a charge of wholesale relativism:

> Hume does not take seriously the possibility that two people who *succeed* in taking the general point of view would differ in their responses in any significant way. . . . It might be that one person's heart beats more warmly in the cause of virtue than another's, but as they leave aside their own interests, and control for the distortions of perspective, they will inevitably approve of the same characters to roughly the same degree. . . . Once we take up the general point of view, and focus on the tendency of the character in question, only our humanity comes into play, and that, Hume emphasizes, is the same in everyone.[7]

---

[4]   Sayre-McCord, "On Why Hume's 'General Point of View' Isn't Ideal," 209.

[5]   Elizabeth Radcliffe, "Hume on Motivating Sentiments, the General point of View, and the Inculcation of 'Morality'," *Hume Studies* 20.1 (1994): 52.

[6]   Rachel Cohon, "The Common Point of View in Hume's Ethics," *Philosophy and Phenomenological Research* 57.4 (1977): 827.

[7]   Sayre-McCord, "On Why Hume's 'General Point of View' Isn't Ideal," 226.

Simon Blackburn agrees that we "do not take up a utilitarian, God's eye, ideal observer standpoint and ask for," e.g., the *global* effects of someone's character. Rather, we abstract from our own position and consider the *local* effects of an individual's character – on herself and those close to her.[8] This shift to a common or impartial point of view isn't unique to ethics, Blackburn points out, reminding us that Hume is well aware of it. Just as there are impersonal standards for good fortifications that "describe what anybody who fortifies a city is likely to want," so there is a common point of view we can take with regard to morality that gives us "the capacity to see past the impact" someone's character has on ourselves and enables us impartially to assess it.[9]

It is far from the purpose of this project to recapitulate analyses of Hume's general point of view or to offer a survey of the vast literature on the subject. The preceding accounts have been brought forward as (especially convincing) examples, intended to provide some sense of how apparent conflicts might be resolved without falling back on relativism or severing the connection between morality and sentiment. Let us now turn to our principal project, and consider whether and to what extent Jane Austen's novels reflect the considerations Hume has raised in his discussion of the general point of view.

Especially significant in light of the present topic is the fact that adopting the general point of view involves employing the hypothetical imagination. We imagine how things would seem from the perspective of someone's narrow circle, how things would be if the opportunity to exercise a given trait were afforded. This is distinctly similar to the way in which fiction in general functions. Novels can lessen our remoteness from historical or unfamiliar situations by presenting specific cases. Fiction brings us into the narrow circle of the *dramatis personae* and shows us the effects of their traits and of their overall character on that circle. Fiction also enables us to observe an individual's traits and character, not just by informing us of their actual effects, but also by acquainting us with the individual's thoughts and impulses and private feelings. These are, of course, readily available in literary descriptions. To imaginatively engage with fiction is, in fact, to adopt an ethically charged perspective toward hypothetical events. Literature provides an opportunity, much as Aristotle once said it did, to rehearse our moral dispositions. Fiction elicits moral insights because of the very way in which it engages the imagination. The manner in which fiction can regulate our sentiments about the

---

[8] Simon Blackburn, *Ruling Passions* (Oxford: Clarendon Press, 1998): 210.
[9] Blackburn, *Ruling Passions*, pp. 201–2.

particular kinds of people it represents – i.e., by narrowing the extent of our focus to their effects on a limited circle and by making us intimately familiar with the tendencies of their characters – is more than reminiscent of the kind of regulation Hume associates with one's adoption of the general point of view.

If fictions can sometimes play the role of thought experiments, especially ethical thought experiments, then it must be at least in part because the same mechanism governs our reactions to fiction and to the world. In this context, Martha Nussbaum, Eileen John, and others have, just as Hume has done, stressed the connection between ethical salience and emotional response.[10] If the purpose of fiction is to elicit emotion, and emotional engagement proves in many respects to be a moral engagement, then our response to fiction reflects something about our attitudes to the world. Recollect that most fiction is designed to place us in just such a point of view as Hume says will elicit specifically moral reactions, dwelling on the effects of the protagonist's character and making us aware of his or her inner states and therefore of the tendencies of that character. In fact, as has already been indicated in the first chapter, fiction presents something of an advantage over real life in eliciting sympathetic responses and moral insights. In the case of fiction, we need not make imperfect inferences about the mental states of individuals (as we do when sympathizing with actual people), since such information can be directly presented in the text by an omniscient narrator.

But something may yet be said about why Austen's kind of fiction is particularly well suited to rehearsing just the regulatory function that Hume's general point of view entails. Robert Alter regards Austen's novels as an example of the "worldly literature of the quotidian." Unlike, for instance, tragedy, such writing addresses "the web of social institutions . . . and the spectrum of types of character, with their sundry foibles and virtues, who can be seen colliding and interacting within these social contexts. Intelligence and observation is encouraged by such texts and is essential to the pleasure of reading them."[11] Austen's kind of fiction has a purposely intimate focus on personal and emotional interactions within a small group. It does not reflect on global matters or make sweeping

[10]   See, for instance, Martha C. Nussbaum, *Love's Knowledge: Essays on Philosophy and Literature* (New York: Oxford University Press, 1990), p. 110. See also Eileen John, "Literary Fiction and the Philosophical Value of Detail," in *Imagination, Philosophy, and the Arts*, ed. Matthew Kieran and Dominic McIver Lopes (London: Routledge, 2003), pp. 152–4.
[11]   Robert Alter, "Introduction," in Frank Kermode, *Pleasure and Change: The Aesthetics of Canon* (New York: Oxford University Press, 2004), p. 9.

generalizations about the human condition. It reflects instead on particular character traits and the impact that these can have on one's circle of acquaintance, inviting us to make judgments about character on the basis of these effects. By being drawn into the narrow circle depicted in *Mansfield Park*, for instance, we see the combined effects of Sir Thomas Bertram's sternness and Mrs. Norris' indulgence on Maria and Julia Bertram. We are shown how it could be to have a father who makes one so ill at ease that one's first reaction to his return after a prolonged absence is the contemplation of escape, how the quashing of opportunity for independence could make the inclination for liberty urgent and undiscriminating and ultimately self-destructive. Obviously, Austen's is not the only work that is suited to eliciting insights about specific traits and their effects. But it is a kind of writing that is especially well adapted to evoke from us the focus and perspective that Hume describes.

It is not enough, however, to claim that we as readers adopt a Humean perspective when contemplating stories such as those Austen has given us. Austen's characters themselves engage in the assessment of character. They also are subject to and often acknowledge the very susceptibilities to which Hume refers. Eleanor Tilney of *Northanger Abbey*, for instance, acknowledges a variation of sentiments according to distance and contiguity. Hume notes that one cannot "feel the same lively pleasure from the virtues of a person, who liv'd in *Greece* two thousand years ago, than . . . [one] feel[s] from the virtues of a familiar friend and acquaintance" (T 581). Miss Tilney confesses a very similar tendency with respect to the enjoyment of historical writing: "If a speech be well made, I read it with pleasure, by whomsoever it may be made – and probably much greater, if the production of Mr. Hume or Mr. Robertson, than if the genuine words of Caractatus, Agricola, or Alfred the Great" (NA 109). Here we have a description of the very tendency which Hume ascribes to us.

The manner in which characters in Austen's novels regulate (or neglect to regulate) their sentiments when evaluating someone's character provides a startlingly apt illustration of exactly the issues Hume raises when he discusses the general point of view and its adoption. Marianne Dashwood, for instance, provides a perfect example of the drawbacks contingent on failure to adopt a general point of view: "She expected from other people the same opinions and feelings as her own, and she judged of their motives by the immediate effect of their actions on herself" (SS 201–2). That is, Marianne does not "over-look . . . [her] own interest in those general judgments" of character that she makes (T 582). "Reason requires such an impartial conduct," Hume concedes, but " 'tis seldom we can bring ourselves to it" (T 583). Marianne certainly finds it hard to bring herself to any attitude of the kind.

Proper moral feeling does not depend on a surrender to spontaneous emotion, but requires instead an adjustment and regulation of initial sentiments. This is an adjustment which Austen's heroines frequently make, or at least learn to make as they become cognizant of mistakes. The most telling examples, however, lie in Austen's survey of the diverse modes of character assessment that can be employed by different people. Austen compares different methods used in the evaluation of an individual's character. In some, the evaluator's sentiments are unregulated. In others, they are regulated by adoption of the very point of view Hume advocates.

This is evident in any comparison of assessments of character made by Elizabeth Bennet and by her mother. Mrs. Bennet's assessment of Darcy, based on initial and hasty resentment, remains impervious to evidence or observation until she discovers that he will marry Elizabeth, at which point she executes a complete *volte-face*. The only effects of character that enter into her sudden approbation involve the probable effects of Darcy's wealth. Elizabeth's disapproval of Darcy begins with his slighting her and with Wickham's lies, but slowly changes as she hears from Colonel Fitzwilliam and from Darcy's housekeeper Mrs. Reynolds of (what Hume would call) his effects on his immediate circle. She discovers his kindness to his tenants, his care for his sister, and his loyalty to his friends. Mrs. Reynolds avers that she has "never had a cross word from him in . . . [her] life," that "he is the best landlord and the best master . . . that ever lived," that "there is not one of his tenants or servants but what will give him a good name," and that "whatever can give his sister pleasure is soon to be done in a moment" (PP 248–9). Of course, the effects of Darcy's character are soon felt in Elizabeth's own circle, and she later learns from her uncle Gardiner of Darcy's rescue of Lydia. Both of Elizabeth's opinions about Darcy's character are to some extent governed by her sympathy with (different) occupants of Darcy's narrow circle: at first she mistakenly sympathizes with Wickham; then, she sympathizes with Darcy's tenants, his sister, Fitzwilliam, and Mrs. Reynolds. The evidence about Darcy's actual effects on these people (especially the exposure of Wickham) eventually helps to sway Elizabeth in his favor.

We see another contrast in the evaluation of character when we consider the different assessments of Mr. Rushworth made by the denizens of Mansfield Park. Mrs. Norris and Maria Bertram concern themselves only with Rushworth's income and property, both of which will benefit Maria when she marries him. Edmund's assessment is based on inhabiting Rushworth's narrow circle and observing the tendencies of his character:

> no representation of his aunt's could induce him to find Mr. Rushworth a desirable companion. He could allow his sister to be the best judge of her own happiness, but he was not pleased that her happiness should centre in a large income; nor could he refrain from often saying to himself, in Mr. Rushworth's company, "If this man had not twelve thousand a year, he would be a very stupid fellow." (MP 40)

The impact of an individual's traits and character on his narrow circle can be clearly seen when we consider the effects of General Tilney of *Northanger Abbey* on his acquaintance. Although professing the most benevolent sentiments and kind intentions, although constantly exhibiting a kind of assiduous thoughtfulness toward Catherine Moreland, the General makes everyone in his narrow circle – servants, offspring, and houseguests alike – wretchedly uncomfortable. The General's thoughtfulness is more apparent than real, since it is his habit thoughtfully to infer the preferences of others to be such as will dovetail perfectly with his own. The temporary absence of the General brings universal felicity:

> the happiness with which their time now passed, every employment voluntary, every laugh indulged, every meal a scene of ease and good humour, walking where they liked and when they liked, their hours, pleasure, and fatigues at their own command, made . . . [Catherine] thoroughly sensible of the restraint which the General's presence had imposed, and most thankfully feel their present release from it. (NA 220)

The reaction of General Tilney's narrow circle to his presence is what exposes his true character, despite that gentleman's loud avowals of good will.

Edmund Bertram of *Mansfield Park* provides an example of someone whose moral assessments of another's character are flawed because he cannot help but "consider [at least some] characters and persons, only as they appear from his peculiar point of view" (T 581). Hume advises us to "correct the momentary appearances of things, and overlook our present situation" (T 582), though he acknowledges that " 'Tis seldom men heartily love . . . what no way redounds to their particular benefit; as 'tis no less rare to meet with persons, who can pardon another any opposition he makes to their interest, however justifiable that opposition may be by the general rules of morality. . . . our passions do not readily follow the determination of our judgment" (T 583). Edmund provides a choice case study of this latter difficulty in his continuous (and inadvertently entertaining) insistence that what Mary Crawford says is never really what she means. His attraction to Mary makes him invent explanations for her speech and conduct that will not bear close scrutiny.

Pride and Prejudice affords yet another comparison of character assessments, in addition to those canvassed earlier – those made by Elizabeth Bennet and her far too kind-hearted sister Jane. It is Elizabeth's contention that Jane is incapable of finding fault with anyone, of seeing anybody as other than agreeable. Certainly, Jane seems incapable of criticizing any other person, as Elizabeth observes with some justice (PP 14). When Jane protests, Elizabeth points out that Jane, despite her good sense, is "honestly blind to the follies and nonsense of others," that she takes "the good of every body's character and make[s] it still better, and say[s] nothing of the bad" (PP 14–15). Jane approves of Bingley's sisters, for instance, while Elizabeth, a keener and more objective observer, has reservations: "with a judgment too unassailed by any attention to herself, she was very little disposed to approve them" (PP 15). Elizabeth considers not only the effects of Bingley's sisters on the narrow circle which she has seen them treat contemptuously, but their intention to produce those effects. Jane, on the other hand, prefers to think they had no such intention. In fact, Jane is clearly a person who is strongly disinclined to think of anyone as possessing less laudable traits and tendencies than her own. This is similar to the examples offered in the preceding chapter on sympathy, in which inaccurate inferences are made about the mental states and motivations of others when it is wrongly assumed that others are precisely like oneself. Jane Bennet provides us with an excellent illustration of that particular failing.

When Jane Bennet is presented with evidence of ill effects, as when she is told of Wickham's accusations against Darcy, she defends the conduct and character of all concerned: "they have both . . . been deceived, I dare say, in some way or other, of which we can form no idea. Interested people have perhaps misrepresented one to the other. It is, in short, impossible for us to conjecture the causes or circumstances which may have alienated them, without actual blame on either side" (PP 85). That is, whenever there is an opportunity of interpreting effects in such a way as to infer more praiseworthy causes in the character or traits of any person, Jane will seize it. The contrast between the sisters is at its most pronounced when both interpret a letter and the motivations behind its being written in radically different ways. Elizabeth takes the letter to be the deception of a vain and greedy woman who is distressed to see her brother's affection for the comparatively poor Jane and who hopes to separate Jane and Bingley. Jane takes the letter as a kindly, gentle hint from a friend who knows her brother isn't interested in pursuing Jane's acquaintance, and who wishes to spare Jane disappointment (PP 118). Jane's is a comparatively benign flaw, but it is still a serious flaw in her ability to regulate her sympathy or adopt a general point of view, for she only shares the emotions she *thinks* others are experiencing, and she is often mistaken about what those are. She fails to employ general rules in making inferences from the occasional observable effect to any motivation in someone's character and dispositions, relying instead on an analogy to her own, less typical tendencies. She often overlooks effects altogether. Indeed she presents us with a kind of extreme case of the effects of contiguity on sympathy and benign emotions, since she favors *everyone* of her acquaintance quite indiscriminately.

Austen also provides us with a classic example of muddled character assessment in Lady Russell of *Persuasion*. Lady Russell, it transpires,

> must learn to feel that she had been mistaken with regard to both [Captain Wentworth and Mr. Elliot]; that she had been unfairly influenced by appearances in each; that because Captain Wentworth's manners had not suited her own ideas, she had been too quick in suspecting them to indicate a character of dangerous impetuosity; and that because Mr Elliot's manners had precisely pleased her in their propriety and correctness, their general politeness and suavity, she had been too quick in receiving them as the certain result of the most correct opinions and well-regulated mind. There was nothing less for Lady Russell to do, than to admit that she had been pretty completely wrong, and to take up a new set of opinions and of hopes. (P 249)

Lady Russell has made improper inferences about the existence of traits, and subsequently about the tendencies of traits, on the basis of manners alone – on the basis, that is, of effects that have no necessary connection to the traits in question.

The adoption of Hume's general point of view, as has been indicated, enables us to consider the tendencies as well as the effects of a given character. "The tendencies of actions and characters, not their real accidental consequences, are alone regarded in our moral determinations," Hume claims, despite the fact that a more lively sympathy attends cases in which "the cause is compleat, and a good disposition is attended with good fortune, which renders it really beneficial to society" (EPM 5.41 n. 1, p. 228; T 585). Austen shows an awareness of this distinction, and a corresponding concern with issues involving moral luck, when she considers the respective plights of three sisters, two of very similar character, who have married very differently situated men, and who might have exhibited quite different traits if differently placed:

Of her two sisters, Mrs Price very much more resembled Lady Bertram than Mrs Norris. She was a manager by necessity, without any of Mrs Norris's inclination for it, or any of her activity. Her disposition was naturally easy and indolent, like Lady Bertram's; and a situation of similar affluence and do-nothingness would have been much more suited to her capacity than the exertions and self-denials of the one which her imprudent marriage had placed her in. She might have made just as good a woman of consequence as Lady Bertram, but Mrs Norris would have been a more respectable mother of nine children on a small income. (MP 390)

An even more surprising example is offered by Austen in *Sense and Sensibility*, when Colonel Brandon *without causing offense* compares the character of Marianne to that of a woman who, having been trapped in a miserable marriage, runs off with another man and, in swift succession, falls into debt, is imprisoned, and perishes of a fortuitous consumption probably brought on by regret: "Your sister, I hope, cannot be offended . . . by the resemblance I have fancied between her and my poor disgraced relation. Their fates, their fortunes, cannot be the same; and had the natural sweet disposition of the one been guarded by a firmer mind, or a happier marriage, she might have been all that you will live to see the other be" (SS 208). As in the previous example, we have a comparison of like tendencies paired with different circumstances, where one set of "particular accidents" militates against the operation of the tendency or trait (T 584).

What is especially interesting here is the insight into Hume's approach that Austen's cases may afford. Hume mainly considers instances of "virtue in rags" rather than vice in dishabille. We learn, for instance, that Mrs. Price would have been more respectable and even-tempered, had she been better off. We are informed that Colonel Brandon's poor disgraced relation would not, in other circumstances, have been as susceptible to seduction and self-destructive actions. She would, in other words, have been faithful and well-balanced had she not been forced into an unhappy marriage. We learn, more surprisingly, that the unpleasant Mrs. Norris would have been less so had she possessed a genuine and pressing outlet for her energies. However, as Austen's examples demonstrate, Lady Bertram would undoubtedly have been a perfectly wretched and incompetent mother of nine children on a small income, and Marianne would probably have taken some dreadful risks if forced into an unhappy marriage. If virtue in rags remains virtue, then vice in dishabille seems nonetheless a vice.

Austen also lets us see that Hume's account is equally applicable to cases in which we may be permitted to mitigate blame because of the involvement of circumstances which bring out the worst in more people than we may initially care to acknowledge. Brandon is prepared to forgive Eliza, indeed to love her, on account of extenuating circumstances. Austen clearly sees Mrs. Price, despite her flaws, as not much worse than the more fortunately placed Lady Bertram. That is, vice in dishabille is still vice, but its being a vice which some particular circumstance will elicit from practically everyone should give us pause. The kinds of claims raised on account of the Stanford Prison Experiment, situationist claims about the power of certain circumstances to elicit behavior that wouldn't be exhibited under most other conditions, are not irrelevant to the present point. Consider that the kind of clarification involved in thought experiments is said to enable us to tease out entailments and to expand on the claims under consideration. By looking at the separation of character trait and effect and by considering different sets of hypothetical circumstances in which individuals might be placed, Austen has expanded the arena in which Hume's insights about moral luck can considered relevant. The cases Austen presents make it clear that Hume's general point of view at the very least encourages us to consider them.

So, given its intimate focus on a protagonist and her narrow circle, Austen's writing is especially well adapted to elicit from us the adoption of a perspective very like Hume's general point of view. Further, the very content of that writing offers both illustrations and comparisons of character evaluations. Austen's novels depict such evaluations being made under different circumstances and often under a variety of disadvantages, many of which resemble the disadvantages which Hume's discussion leads us to expect. Hume's particular distinctions between cases that are regulated by adoption of the general point of view and those that are not are amply illustrated in Austen's novels. And since adoption of the general point of view requires us to take into account the tendencies of a character irrespective of its actual effects, the question of moral luck is also of significance in Hume's discussion, and an awareness of that significance is clearly evident in Austen. It therefore seems reasonable to maintain that there is a close correlation between the ethical perspectives of David Hume and Jane Austen, and that the work of one can sometimes lend depth and interest to that of the other.

7

The Useful and the Good in Hume and Austen

One challenge to the present project involves the distinction between normative and meta-ethical considerations. Alex Neill, for instance, has expressed concern about my talk of ethical perspectives and ethical insights. "When Hume does ethics," Alex says, "what he's doing is almost entirely meta-ethics or the metaphysics and epistemology of ethics," offering us "no distinctive normative vision of any richness" apart from his "pretty thin references to utility," whereas what Austen does in the moral arena by way of her novels is almost entirely normative.[1] One of the key words here is "almost" and I absolutely concede that almost all *talk* of Hume's ethics has centered on meta-ethics and much of the writing on ethics in Austen, with the significant exception of the Aristotelian analyses, has centered on the normative. *But*, I will argue, that isn't all there is to talk about.

Questions about the nature of moral reasoning and the source of ethical principles are, of course, conceptually distinct from those concerning what it is that ought to regulate our conduct. Yet it is difficult to raise one set of questions in isolation from the other. There is Hume's discussion of the regulation of sympathy by the general point of view, for instance, which has clear analogs in Austen and which has already been addressed in two previous chapters. This talk of moral sentiments and judgments has obvious meta-ethical aspects, and so establishes the meta-ethical nature of some of the insights on offer in Austen. On the other hand, Hume's focus on correcting sentiments and eschewing personal biases establishes that some of our apparently moral sentiments and judgments

---

[1] These remarks were made in response to one of my papers on Hume and Austen at the 2006 Annual Meeting of the Pacific Division of the American Society for Aesthetics, March 30, 2006.

can be inauthentic or erroneous. This is normative *territory*, surely, even we insist on a distinction between epistemic and moral norms. And the line between those norms can blur in certain contexts, as becomes clear in the discussion of prejudice in the chapter on epistemic normativity. Wherever the line is drawn, we must note that the moral criticism of judgments formed on the basis of general rules and hasty, personally biased, sentiments represents a central theme in *Pride and Prejudice*, which echoes much of what is said in the passage on prejudice in Book I of the *Treatise* (T 146–8).

I am concerned with the implication that Austen's "rich moral vision" will render secondary any "meta-ethical theory that can be seen at work in her writing." I should stress that I am not alone in thinking that there are some very interesting meta-ethical intuitions on offer in Austen's work. Gilbert Ryle and Alasdair MacIntyre and David Gallup think so too. They just think that these are Aristotelian intuitions, while I think that I can make a better case for Hume, especially since Hume has more than a few intuitions in common with Aristotle. Consider, for instance, that *Pride and Prejudice* offers a comparative depiction of the ways in which someone's character can be assessed, with a special focus on the difference that knowing someone's effect on his narrow circle can make to such assessments. Similarly, *Mansfield Park* offers us a case in point of "virtue in rags" by means of the explicit comparison of three sisters (Lady Bertram, Mrs. Price, and Mrs. Norris), two of whom *would* (in other circumstances) have exhibited virtues the exercise of which their present circumstances don't permit. Hume's observations about the source of our moral judgments, the things we bring into consideration when we feel and judge as we do, are often confirmed and brought to life by Austen's fiction. So, as the preceding examples are intended to remind us, evidence of Hume's meta-ethical and epistemic insights in Austen's work has already been provided at some length in earlier chapters. In this chapter, we will attempt to focus on Hume's normative stance and the role of utility within it, and consider whether this too is reflected in the novels of Jane Austen.

While utility plays a significant part in Book III of the *Treatise* and an even more significant one in the second *Enquiry*, it is difficult to classify Hume as a full blown utilitarian, simply because he proposes no maximizing principle or hedonic calculus. Acts are liable to moral assessment only insofar as they prove the outgrowth of vices or virtues, so they cannot be a central unit of evaluation any more than rules. Some have made an interesting case for a Humean brand of disposition-utilitarianism, and argued for important advantages that such an account would have over both act- and rule-utilitarianism.[2] Others have proposed an accommodation of both utilitarian and contractarian concerns within a theory in which "particular evaluations are driven by a concern for specific problems and are determined by what is well-suited to solve" them.[3] However, these approaches tend rather to speculate about the development of a Hume-friendly system than to substantiate anything conclusive about his advocacy of a particular normative stance. There is enough disagreement in the literature to warrant further investigation.

That Hume is at least in some respects a forerunner of the utilitarians seems beyond dispute. Jeremy Bentham held that it was Hume who showed him that "the foundations of all *virtue* are laid in *utility*" and further indicated that Book III of the *Treatise* led him to feel "as if the scales had fallen from" his eyes.[4] Then again, Bentham is critical of the sympathy principle which is so central to the account Hume offers in the *Treatise*, describing it as anti-utilitarian and referring to it as the "principle of caprice."[5] Yet sympathy is defined in a way that makes Bentham's criticism inapplicable to Hume's principle. In Bentham, sympathy "approves or disapproves of certain actions, not on account of their tending to augment . . . nor . . . diminish the happiness of the party whose interest is in question, but merely because a man finds himself disposed to approve or disapprove of them."[6] In Hume, the approval or disapproval to which a regulated sympathy gives rise will *depend* on the happiness or misery which the individual being judged tends to produce within his or her circle. The principle of sympathy which Bentham inveighs against, although it may afflict some less developed philosophical positions, is clearly not Humean fellow-feeling, nor is it regulated by a Humean general point of view. Though Hume never instructs us to maximize utility, it remains the case that the pleasures and pains of other people (and the hypothetical pleasures and pains canvassed when we consider the tendencies of a character apart from its actual effects) are at the heart of a moral response. It is sympathy that shows why we are invested in the happiness and misery of others, why we are inclined to take up moral attitudes. In

---

[2]   Edward S. Shirley, "Hume's Ethics: Acts, Rules, Dispositions, and Utility," *Southwest Philosophy Review* (1991): 129–39.

[3]   Geoffrey Sayre-McCord, "Hume and the Bauhaus Theory of Ethics," *Midwest Studies in Philosophy* 20 (1995): 280–98, 282.

[4]   Jeremy Bentham, *A Fragment on Government*, ed. by J.H. Burns and H.L.A. Hart (London: Oxford, 1977), ch. 1, para. 36, notes 1 and 5, p. 440.

[5]   Bentham, *The Principles of Morals and Legislation* (Darien, CT: Hafner, 1970), ch. II, para. XI (and note 1), pp. 14–15.

[6]   Bentham, *The Principles of Morals and Legislation*, ch. II, para. XI, pp. 15–16.

Hume, sympathy isn't an excuse for doing as one likes or for failing to act (as Bentham sometimes seems to think). Rather, it is the whole reason why the pleasures and pains of others matter: because they are to some extent our own.

This is why I don't believe that Hume's principle of sympathy is at all at odds with his talk of utility, either in the *Treatise* or in the *Enquiry*. Although there is more talk of benevolence than of sympathy in the second *Enquiry*, the section on utility still gives the same role to the sympathy mechanism that was assigned in the *Treatise*: "everything . . . presents us with the view of human happiness or misery, and excites in our breast a sympathetic movement of pleasure or uneasiness" (EPM 5.23, p. 221). From talk of utility and usefulness to society, Hume moves on to discuss our capacity to take up impartial standpoints of assessment and to respond morally to matters of public rather than private interest. He ushers in the principle of sympathy to explain our approval of the useful and our investment in the pleasure and pain of other people. The apprehension of vice and virtue is fundamentally connected to this investment: "If any man . . . is unaffected with the images of human happiness and misery, he must be equally indifferent to the images of vice and virtue" (EPM 5.39, p. 225). He goes on to detail the very correction of sentiments and appearances, adoption of "general views," and abstraction from personal bias described in the *Treatise* (EPM 5.41–2, pp. 228–9). As in the *Treatise*, Hume notes that the tendencies of someone's character are to be considered in evaluation rather than its accidental consequences alone (EPM 5.41 n. 1, p. 228). I will take it, then, that there has been no *fundamental* change in the *Enquiry* from the account offered in the *Treatise*, but only a change of focus. More is said in the *Treatise* about the psychological mechanisms that prompt our response. More, at least comparatively, is said in the *Enquiry* about that *to which* we respond. It is this focus that makes Hume appear to ascribe a kind of utilitarian instinct to human nature:

> If we consider the principles of the human make, such as they appear to daily experience and observation, we must, *a priori*, conclude it impossible for such a creature as man to be totally indifferent to the well or ill-being of his fellow creatures, and not readily . . . to pronounce, where nothing gives him any particular bias, that what promotes their happiness is good, what tends to their misery is evil. . . . Here then are the faint rudiments of a *general* distinction between actions. (EPM 5.43, p. 230)

Of course, none of this is prescriptive in a direct way. Hume is making observations about our moral responses and what it is that prompts them.

But, as suggested at the outset of this chapter, talk of correcting for bias and for the effects of distance, coupled with talk of the hypothetical thinking needed to determine the tendencies of a character, which Hume says are "alone regarded in our moral determinations" despite our initial reactions (EPM 5.41 n. 1, p. 228), suggests that certain procedures are to be followed if our sentiments are to be regarded as genuinely moral ones. The very fact that Hume acknowledges that our sentiments are difficult to correct and our biases are difficult to overcome indicates that he is cataloging a careful procedure for the detection of virtue and vice that will not always sit easily with our inclinations. Where our sentiments are affected by bias of one sort or another, where we have not adopted what Hume calls the general view, our sentiments and the judgments which arise from them will not be moral ones – even, it should follow, if we are under the impression that they are. I am assuming on the basis of what has come before that a false moral judgment could arise from a sentiment superficially akin to approbation which occurred under conditions in which corrections for bias or distance, say, were never made or in which the general view was not adopted. If we can derive from what Hume has had to say some notion of how moral judgments can be correct or incorrect, or at least authentic or inauthentic, then we may well be in what has been previously referred to as normative territory.

Moreover, as Elizabeth Radcliffe indicates, Hume's account has "pinpointed a mechanism in human behavior that accounts for our getting direction or guidance from our moral distinctions and from nature," providing an account "of how a person lacking virtue might be motivated to do the right thing."[7] Self-assessment can arise from the comparison of one's own traits to those the useful and agreeable effects of which are observed in connection with the conduct of other agents. Someone who feels himself to lack a virtuous trait, one which he or she approves and has observed in others, may, according to Hume "hate himself upon that account" and feel compelled to adopt habits of action "in order to acquire by practice" the disposition he does not as yet possess and out of which he cannot as yet act (T 479). The very process of assessment that is described by Hume can provide a basis for self-assessment through comparison and thence a motive for the acquisition of virtues through habituation. Again, we appear to have entered normative territory.

What does that territory have to do with utility? Moral responses are primarily to persons or to their character traits. An apprehension of virtue involves a sentiment of approval (underwritten by a regulated sympathy)

---

[7]   Elizabeth S. Radcliffe, *On Hume* (Belmont, CA: Wadsworth, 2000), p. 76.

toward character traits in persons which are useful and agreeable (i.e., among other things, pleasure-producing and pain-minimizing) to others or to themselves, or (given the concern with tendencies of a character) toward traits which *would* be useful or agreeable in circumstances more typical than those under review. That presents the case for the natural virtues. In the case of the artificial virtues, the traits in question are not necessarily useful and agreeable in their natural effects, but become so collectively within the context of an evolving set of conventions which depend on cooperation (T 490). Our approval depends on the existence of a useful general scheme, one in which respect for property rights, say, is advantageous (T 579). This does not guarantee, of course, that each particular instance of respect for property rights will prove always to be useful and agreeable.

The virtuous, then, are those who prove useful to individuals and to society. Virtues are the traits that make people useful. The focus is first on useful agents (or on agents with useful characteristics) rather than useful actions. The company of such people "is a satisfaction" to us. They elicit both our esteem and our support (T 583). We must infer possession of the relevant traits from actual conduct and also with the help of general rules. Hume does not provide us with a system for determining which people or which traits are better than others, though forms of disposition-utilitarianism have been proposed on his behalf. He does not show us, for instance, how to steer a course that involves our determining to act out of one disposition rather than another. But what he does provide is a virtue-oriented, agent-based system of ethical assessment that is grounded in the usefulness and potential usefulness of agents to themselves, to others, and to society, where that utility has a clear connection to human happiness and misery rather than merely to the "suitability for particular purposes" proposed by some philosophers. This at least establishes Hume's account as one in which utility is an essential component, and further establishes Hume not just as a forerunner but as a progenitor of ethical systems in which utility plays a central role.

Jane Austen's fiction shows a not dissimilar connection between the moral and the useful. The three novels which were written (though not published) last are the ones in which an individual's usefulness to others is unmistakably presented as both a test and a proof of good character. *Mansfield Park* and *Persuasion* in particular offer surprisingly frequent references to utility in the context of character assessment, and even *Emma* provides over a dozen references to usefulness as a crucially desirable character trait. Notice that the connection of utility with dispositions rather than actions in Austen dovetails perfectly with Hume's ethical project.

Neither Austen nor her characters display any but an indirect interest in maximizing utility, nor are they inclined to resort to any overt employ-ment of a utilitarian calculus. However, just as in Hume, the aspect of utility that is given attention is agent- and trait-centered. This is probably why the most popular ethical analyses of Austen cast her as an Aristotelian. Austen's ethical perspective concentrates our attention far more on virtues and vices and the evaluation of character than it does on the ethical assess-ment of particular acts.

In this regard, the perfectly splendid dramatic reversal Austen devises for *Pride and Prejudice* should be considered. Lady Catherine de Bourgh makes a virtue of interfering in the affairs of others by claiming that she is being useful. When she cannot wrest from Elizabeth Bennet a promise *not* to marry Darcy (both for his and her own good, and in order not to pollute the shades of Pemberley), she rushes to inform Darcy of Elizabeth's culpable recalcitrance. Although she hopes by these means to arouse his disgust toward Elizabeth, she instead gives him reason to hope that Elizabeth may respond positively to a second proposal of marriage. This leads to Darcy's making that proposal, and brings about the very event which Lady Catherine had, by her actions, intended to avert. "Lady Catherine's unjustifiable endeavours to separate us," says Darcy to Elizabeth, "were the means of removing all my doubts" (PP 381). Neither Austen nor Elizabeth can resist some fun at Lady Catherine's expense: "Lady Catherine has been of infinite use, which ought to make her happy, for she loves to be of use" (PP 381). The villain of the piece having been of use makes explicit the kind of distinction typical of virtue ethics. Lady Catherine's action, though supremely useful, cannot be virtuous because she did not intend to bring about the consequences in question and because it did not arise from the appropriate kind of disposition. An action's being considered virtuous or vicious "must depend upon durable principles of the mind, which extend over the whole conduct, and enter into the personal character," according to Hume (T 575). What the preceding example makes us understand is that good consequences alone are *insufficient* for estab-lishing either the virtue of the action from which they arose or that of the person who performed it. That is, Austen's depiction of Lady Catherine's inadvertent match-making is, in effect, a virtue-ethics-inspired counter-example designed to deny the possibility of a rigidly act-utilitarian con-ception of virtue in actions or persons.[8] Instead, Austen parallels Hume

---

[8]   This is by no means a criticism of act-utilitarianism in general – it merely establishes that "virtuous" and "right" cannot be treated as synonyms without courting difficulties.

by offering precise depictions of the usefulness of agents to those who inhabit their narrow circle.

There is, of course, talk of duty and principle in Austen, especially in *Mansfield Park*, but there is also considerable advocacy of "useful pursuits" and "useful employment" (sometimes as an anodyne to narcissism). We see an aesthetic based on utility in *Sense and Sensibility* just as we do in the *Treatise*. Anne Elliot of *Persuasion* reflects that "it would be most right, and most wise, and, therefore, must involve least suffering to go" along with a proposed plan (P 33). More to the point, all of the most repellent people in Austen's novels – General Tilney, Lady Catherine de Bourgh, Mrs. Norris, Mrs. Ferrars and her daughter, the Eltons (I want to include Sir Thomas Bertram, but I probably shouldn't) – are law-abiding followers of formal moral rules who produce constant misery in their respective narrow circles. Even the hedonists and adulterers, though they aren't precisely forgiven, are presented in a much more attractive light, in part because they don't make a *habit* of making everyone around them miserable. Hume, of course, says that the natural limitations of people's generosity and our acquaintance with those limitations tend to "confine our view to that narrow circle, in which any person moves, in order to form a judgment of his moral character. When the natural tendency of his passions leads him to be *serviceable and useful* within his sphere, we approve of his character, and love his person, by a sympathy with the sentiments of those, who have a more particular connexion with him" (T 602). And so it usually transpires in our responses to Austen's fictional people and in their responses to one another. Austen certainly was in the habit of depicting just the kind of arena in and to which Hume says we are naturally inclined to respond morally, and within which the usefulness of an individual to herself and to others is usually apparent.

To establish further Austen's normative leanings in regard to utility, we should consider in some detail the three novels in which usefulness as a character trait seems a significant thematic element. *Emma* is a story which, among other things, chronicles the heroine's failed attempts to be "useful" to her friend Harriet, attempts which are described in just those terms (E 26–7, 42). The novel culminates in Emma's eventual discovery of what true usefulness ought in fact to consist. The usefulness of Mrs. Weston and Mr. Knightley, the two most clearly virtuous characters in the story, is often stressed (e.g., E 6, 223). It is even Mr. Knightley's usefulness to Mr. Woodhouse that erodes the latter's objections to Emma's marriage. Emma herself hopes to be useful to the poor (E 29) and is eager to "discover some way of being useful" to Jane Fairfax (E 389–90). Emma's motives are, it should be acknowledged, far more complex than a simple impulse to usefulness can explain. For one thing, her meddling, especially in Harriet's life, often appears to be more of an effort to counteract boredom than a fully thought-out plan of action. Thus, her inferences about people's preferences and desires are often colored by suppositions that owe more to a taste for drama and excitement than solid reasoning.

Emma's interference in the lives of others is not, however, presented in the same light as that of other less attractive Austen busybodies like Mrs. Norris of *Mansfield Park*, Lady Catherine of *Pride and Prejudice*, or even Mrs. Elton of *Emma*. Although these more obviously flawed characters *claim* that usefulness is the aim of their interference, their motives are inevitably proved selfish and any actual usefulness on their part is shown to be inadvertent. Emma, unlike such characters, is ashamed when her attempts to be useful fail and her mistakes cause harm, for she is genuinely well intentioned and her wish to be of use is quite sincere. This may well explain how it is that Emma is so popular a heroine despite her ill-advised meddling. She *intends* to be useful and, by the end of the novel, she has evolved into a person who, having somewhat modified her tactics, is in fact useful to those in her narrow circle, unlike the characters whom Austen has roundly condemned for the same fault. Those characters usually cast a blight on the narrow circle of their acquaintance, as Austen makes entirely clear.

Gilbert Ryle has shown us that solicitude, or a sometimes undue concern in the affairs of others, is a central theme in *Emma*: "Jane Austen's question here was: What makes it sometimes legitimate or even obligatory for one person deliberately to try to modify the course of another person's life, while sometimes such attempts are wrong? Where is the line between Meddling and Helping?"[9] So one of the salient ethical questions raised in *Emma* depends crucially on what constitutes helpfulness and usefulness, and it allows us to judge this in part by looking at the effects of the protagonist's solicitude on her narrow circle, and to make comparisons between the sources and the effects of the solicitude of characters like Knightley and Emma and Mrs. Elton. The novel enables us to investigate circumstances which warrant intervention, i.e., those in which intervention is useful, and compares them to those in which it is harmful. Indeed, some of the final interchanges between Emma and Knightley report Knightley's concern that his "interference [in Emma's early life] was quite as likely to do harm as good," a statement that is followed swiftly

---

[9]   Gilbert Ryle, "Jane Austen and the Moralists," in B.C. Southam, ed., *Critical Essays on Jane Austen* (London: Routledge, 1987), p. 110.

by reassurance from Emma: "I am sure you were of use to me. . . . I was very often influenced rightly by you . . . I am very sure you did me good" (E 462). Knightley, in the proper romantic tradition, states that he owes all his happiness to Emma (E 461), and so the story ends with the union of two people who make themselves useful by making one another happy, a standard ending certainly, but one that makes the goal of happiness and usefulness quite explicit.

Mansfield Park contains literally dozens of references to usefulness. The interfering Mrs. Norris perpetually proclaims her desire to be useful to all and sundry (e.g., MP 9, 30), though signally failing in any endeavor to be so. Lady Bertram, less interfering and quite at ease about her own inertia, "never thought of being useful to anybody" (MP 219). It is Fanny Price who tries relentlessly and quite effectively to be useful to all. She is useful to Lady Bertram (MP 35), who is loathe to part with her when Sir Thomas sends her away. She is more useful than any of the others in practical matters, even to the extent of providing significant help in the staging of a play – a project of which she personally disapproves (MP 166). Fanny's brother William Price is as useful as she. The wealthy and independent Henry Crawford envies the more disadvantaged William this usefulness: "The glory of heroism, of usefulness, of exertion, of endurance, made his own habits of selfish indulgence appear in shameful contrast; and he wished he had been a William Price, distinguishing himself and working his way to fortune and consequence with so much self-respect and happy ardour, instead of what he was!" (MP 236).

But Fanny is at her best when exiled to Portsmouth. There she is "very anxious to be useful" and takes "great pleasure in feeling her usefulness" (MP 390) as she tries to organize the household and institute reforms. She recognizes a similar inclination to usefulness on the part of her sister Susan (MP 383, 397), an inclination which, when added to an awareness of occasions on which she falls short, makes Fanny "understand . . . the worth of her disposition . . . and to entertain the hope of being useful to a mind so much in need of help, and so much deserving of it" (MP 397). Obviously, an inclination to be of use is regarded as a sign of good character. Fanny even makes the idle Henry Crawford useful to his tenants, something he undertakes in the hope of obtaining her approval, as his announcement that he seeks a friend and guide in fomenting "every plan of utility and charity for Everingham" attests (MP 404). The alliance of virtue with a disposition to be of use to others is made absolutely clear when Fanny fears that her seriously ill cousin Tom may go to hell, in part as a result of his lack of usefulness. "Without any particular affection for her eldest cousin, her tenderness of heart made her feel that she could not spare him, and the purity of her principles added yet a keener solicitude, when she considered how little useful, how little self-denying his life had (apparently) been" (MP 428).

Tom's illness and Maria's adulterous liaison prompt the Bertrams to recall Fanny to Mansfield, where "she was useful, she was beloved" (MP 461). Tom Bertram recovers and reforms, becoming "useful to his father . . . and not living merely for himself" (MP 462). Susan was "soon welcome and useful to all" (MP 472). The novel closes, not only with an acknowledgement of the importance to character of early hardship and discipline, but with a paean to Susan's usefulness and the mutual aid and affection of Prices and Bertrams in general: "In [Susan's] usefulness, in Fanny's excellence, in William's continued good conduct and rising fame, and in the general well-doing and success of the other members of the family, all assisting to advance each other . . . Sir Thomas saw repeated . . . reason to rejoice in what he had done for them all" (MP 473). What is valued here is not only discipline, but cooperation, mutual aid, and mutual support, each individual acting so as to be of use to the others. Here is a conception of virtue that is linked at least in part to the usefulness of agents to themselves and to one another.

References to utility in Austen's *Persuasion* are even more pointed. "Austen underscores Anne . . . [Elliot's] utility by contrasting it with other people's futility," according to Emily Auerbach.[10] Sir Walter Elliot is a vain spendthrift, Elizabeth Elliot has "no habits of utility," Mary Musgrove is a hypochondriac prone to the occasional bout of hysterics, and Charles Musgrove is someone who would have had "more usefulness [in] . . . his habits and pursuits" had he married more wisely (P 43). Anne, on the other hand, seems universally useful. She helps to orchestrate the letting of Kellynch Hall to alleviate her father's debts, organizes the family's move to Bath, speaks to the tenants and propitiates the servants, cares for her sister's son when he is injured (P 53), diffuses squabbles, and keeps all the proper people informed of events. She knows herself "to be of the first utility" in these and other circumstances (P 58, 83). She is the person to whom everyone turns in an emergency.

Nowhere is this more evident than at the scene of Louisa Musgrove's accident at Lyme. Louisa falls upon the pavement and lies unconscious while all but Anne prove entirely helpless. Wentworth can only call for help and exclaim in horror. Mary screams repeatedly and clings to her husband, "contributing with his own horror to make him immovable"

[10] Emily Auerbach, *Searching for Jane Austen* (Madison: University of Wisconsin Press, 2004), p. 236.

(P 109). Thus, Charles is entirely incapacitated both by his own distress and by Mary. Henrietta faints. Captain Benwick can only follow orders. Luckily, Anne is there to give them. She makes suggestions to alleviate Louisa's situation and is the only person with the presence of mind to think of summoning a surgeon. She also has a presence of mind that leads her to stop Wentworth and send Benwick for the surgeon instead, since Benwick is the only resident of Lyme, and so the only member of the party who knows where one might be found. A crowd has gathered, of course, "to be useful if wanted," but really only "to enjoy the sight of a dead young lady, nay, two dead young ladies, for it proved twice as fine as the first report" (P 111). It is only Captain Harville who, once he arrives, proves "instantly useful" (P 111) and has Louisa conveyed to his home. Anne is the first choice of most to stay and nurse Louisa, but her sister Mary is affronted at this preference: "why was not she to be as useful as Anne?" (P 115). In the end, since no one can face Mary's recriminations and whining, Anne is sent back to inform the Musgroves of their daughter's plight. Indeed, Wentworth's reaction to her departure makes her fear that "she was valued only as she could be useful to Louisa" (P 115). However, she has "the satisfaction of knowing herself to be extremely useful" to the Musgroves, both as a companion and as an assistant in making arrangements, and their "real affection . . . [is] won by her usefulness when they [are] . . . in distress" (P 121, 220).

Auerbach says it best when she points out that Mary, Elizabeth, and Sir Walter "all feel *ill-used* rather than *of use* because they arrogantly expect one-way devotion and service from those around them."[11] Anne is perceptive enough to be ashamed of her relations. Those for whom she feels genuine affection and admiration – Wentworth (despite his lapse at Lyme), Captain Benwick, the Crofts and Harvilles and elder Musgroves, Lady Russell and Mrs. Smith – are people whose warmth and openness and efforts to be of use to others not only compensate for their lack of wealth and rank, but entirely eclipse it. All try to be helpful, and those who err in this regard admit their error when they fail. Benwick, Croft, and Harville can claim social utility on account of their profession. Lady Russell can claim good intentions and an inclination to reform her opinions once the badness of her advice has been exposed. These are the truly desirable companions, the ones with whom Anne wishes to spend time.

Persuasion ends by reporting Wentworth's reciprocal usefulness to the infirm, impoverished, and widowed Mrs. Smith, who is scorned by Sir Walter and Elizabeth and whose requests for help are spurned by

---

[11]   Auerbach, *Searching for Jane Austen*, p. 238.

Mr. Elliot. Years before, Mrs. Smith "had been useful and good to . . . [Anne] in a way which had considerably lessened her misery" after her mother's death (P 152). Even prior to Wentworth's welcome assistance, Mrs. Smith triumphed over her wretched health and circumstances by means of "elasticity of mind . . . that power of turning readily from evil to good, and of finding employment which carried her out of herself, which was from nature alone. It was the choicest gift of Heaven; and Anne viewed her friend as one of those instances in which, by a merciful appointment, it seems designed to counterbalance almost every other want" (P 154). In the worst of circumstances, Mrs. Smith's happy disposition was of use to her: "she had moments only of languor and depression, to hours of occupation and enjoyment" (P 154). And in those dreadful circumstances she still managed to be useful to others, attempting "to do a little good to one or two very poor families" in her vicinity (P 155). Nor are Mrs. Smith's usefulness and happiness diminished by the improvement in her heath and circumstances wrought by help from Anne and Frederick: "she might have bid defiance to even greater accessions of worldly prosperity. She might have been absolutely rich and perfectly healthy, and yet be happy" (P 252).

Mrs. Smith's felicitous disposition is significant in two respects. First, Austen reserves the final paragraph of her novel, not only for romantic prognostications concerning the happy future of Anne and Captain Wentworth, but for an account of the character and disposition of Anne's ailing friend. It is not unlikely that Austen herself was already ill when she was completing *Persuasion*. It is at least suggestive that she should reserve part of the closing passage of that novel for a minor character. Here, despite William Galperin's calling her a "manipulative and mendacious person whose main goal is to regain her West Indian property, and the slaves that presumably go with it, even if it means encouraging Anne to marry someone . . . whom Mrs. Smith knows to be thoroughly ruthless,"[12] is a woman whom Austen clearly wants us to regard as admirable and even, despite her many misfortunes, as lucky. This is a woman, moreover, whose happiness depends neither on marriage nor even on good health. It depends on her emotional nature and on useful employment. It may be, then, that Austen has not effaced herself from the pages of her work as entirely as some critics appear to think.

It does not seem in any case that the Galperin interpretation of the character of Mrs. Smith should be regarded as preferable to one which

---

[12]   William Galperin, *The Historical Austen* (Philadelphia: University of Pennsylvania Press, 2003), p. 232.

takes Austen's estimation of that character at Austen's word. Mrs. Smith's failure of frankness (and frankness is not always a virtue in Austen) can be seen more as a practical matter of self-preservation in a woman with no friends or protectors and no funds to purchase the services of stand-ins for these. Austen's acute and personal awareness of the limited options available to women of the period, especially women forced to make their way in the world on their own, makes her see Mrs. Smith's alternatives in a light in which Galperin does not see them. But let us return to the question of usefulness. Mrs. Smith's failure to divulge the truth about Elliot's former misdeeds lasts only as long as the conviction that Anne's connection with him is certain. To say such things to a woman in love would, one assumes that she believes, be useless. She would only lose Anne's friendship and any hope of aid thereby. Once she discovers that Anne does not intend to marry Elliot, she immediately tells her the truth, including the truth about her own silence. One might even suppose that Mrs. Smith is carefully setting a course that will minimize harm to all parties.

Austen's commitment to the virtue of those individuals disposed to be of use to themselves, to others, and to society is clear. What is also evident it that Austen's literary focus on interactions among small groups of individuals provides her with precisely the arena in which people's usefulness to their immediate circle is most readily ascertainable, an arena to which Hume says we are conditioned to respond morally. That is, the little bit of ivory and the fine brush with which Austen transmits her ideas are exactly suited to be of use in our formation of judgments of moral character.

8

Aesthetics and Humean Aesthetic Norms in the Novels of Jane Austen

The eighteenth century, Paul Oskar Kristeller tells us, in addition to crys-
tallizing what we now call the fine arts, is also marked by an increased
lay interest both in the arts and in criticism.[1] Amateurs as well as philosophers ventured critical commentary on the arts. Talk concerning taste
or beauty or the sublime was so much a part of general discourse that
even novelists of that era incorporated such subjects in their work. Henry
Fielding "was able to construct a novel on the true and false sublime in
art," according to Samuel Monk, "and to draw an analogy between the
sublime in art and the sublime in character."[2] So we shouldn't find it
surprising that perspectives on aesthetics are sometimes presented in the
novels of Jane Austen. This subject matter ranges from descriptions of
skill in the execution and sensitivity in the appreciation of particular arts
to general observations about beauty and taste and what is requisite for
the apprehension of the former and the possession of the latter.

Consider the following catalog of arts and beauties. *Mansfield Park,
Sense and Sensibility, Pride and Prejudice*, and *Northanger Abbey* contain
many references to the beauties of nature, both cultivated and wild. Taste
in music is a topic in *Persuasion, Mansfield Park, Pride and Prejudice*, and
Lady Susan. A taste for poetry and literature is the lot of heroines of
Persuasion, Northanger Abbey, Mansfield Park, and *Sense and Sensibility*.
Taste and talent for drawing is exhibited by characters in *Sense and
Sensibility, Emma*, and *Northanger Abbey*. Both *Sense and Sensibility* and
Mansfield Park contain discussions of the merits of effective reading, that

---

[1] Paul Oskar Kristeller, "The Modern System of the Arts: A Study in the History of Aesthetics
(II)," *Journal of the History of Ideas* 13 (1952): 17–46, 17.
[2] Samuel H. Monk, *The Sublime: A Study of Critical Theories in XVIII-Century England*
(Ann Arbor: University of Michigan Press, 1960), p. 63.

is, reading well aloud. *Mansfield Park* even comments on acting ability, albeit rather disapprovingly. More general reflections on taste and beauty, as well as their connection to morality, are equally typical.

It is possible to venture several different arguments about the philosophical perspective into which such observations best fit. Kantian analyses have already been ventured in the literature. Anne Crippen Ruderman calls our attention to the Kantian flavor of the connection Austen draws between sensitivity to natural beauty and one's moral disposition, for instance, and David Kaufman compares Austen to Kant, though primarily in regard to ethics.[3] Nonetheless, it will be shown that the strongest correlations and correspondences are between Austen's and Hume's positions on aesthetics. Evidence in support of a Kantian analysis will first be canvassed, and later compared with claims in favor of a Humean alternative.

So I will try to establish that the positions on taste and beauty and delicacy that are explicitly stated in or can be inferred from Austen's novels fit a Humean model and fit it with a fair degree of precision. In doing so, I hope to demonstrate a correspondence strong enough to serve as the staging area for the further speculations that constitute the second thesis of this chapter. A great deal has already been said by philosophers, and by me, about the capacity of literature to elicit moral reactions from the reader. Fictions can present ethical endorsements and invite us to adopt ethical perspectives by making it true in the world of the work that some course of action is right or some character is laudable. They can do this not by *telling* us that an act is right or a person meritorious, but by *showing* us the rightness of the action and the commendability of the individual, by asking us to imagine traits that call forth our own approval and commendation. I will contend that aesthetic norms can be treated in much the same way as moral norms. That is, I will claim that the fiction of Jane Austen, in addition to evidencing the conscription of a Humean aesthetic, so engages us that we are led imaginatively to adopt certain aesthetic perspectives in the course of its contemplation – not just by being told what is aesthetically pleasing or commendable, but by being made to feel pleasure and to experience commendation; not just by being told what constitutes discriminating taste, but by being led to discriminate in a particular way. That the taste in question is distinctively Humean necessitates that we begin with an extended exploration

[3] Anne Crippen Ruderman, *The Pleasures of Virtue: Political Thought in the Novels of Jane Austen* (Lanham, MD: Rowman & Littlefield, 1995), 82; David Kaufmann, "Law and Propriety, *Sense and Sensibility*: Austen on the Cusp of Modernity," *ELH* 59 (1992): 385–408.

of Austen's aesthetic stance, and only then proceed to investigate these further possibilities.

I

Before embarking on any comparisons between Hume and Austen it is important to note that it is aesthetics more than any other subject which invites a Kantian interpretation of Austen's perspective. *Mansfield Park* is the particular work that includes extensive passages in which an aesthetic responsiveness to nature is allied with an individual's moral character.[4] Such an alliance can clearly be linked to Kant's belief that "to take an immediate interest in the beauty of nature . . . is always a mark of a good soul . . . when this interest is habitual, it at least indicates a frame of mind favorable to the moral feeling if it is voluntarily bound up with the contemplation of nature." An interest in the beautiful in nature is held to depend on a prior interest in the morally good, making it permissible to infer a good moral disposition from the aesthetic appreciation of nature.[5]

Austen's heroine Fanny Price has such an interest in the contemplation of nature. Indeed, she has a greater sensitivity to nature than her fellows, something that appears at times to constitute evidence of her greater goodness. For example, the moral superiority of Fanny Price over Mary Crawford is established quite early in the story, when Fanny's interest in the natural landscape is contrasted with Mary's inattention: "Miss Crawford was very unlike her. She had none of Fanny's delicacy of taste, of mind, of feeling; she saw nature, inanimate nature, with little observation" (MP 81). Austen frequently has Fanny rhapsodize over starry skies and sylvan landscapes in a manner reminiscent of Kant's reflections on the sublime:

> Here's harmony. . . . Here's what may leave all painting and all music behind, and what poetry can only attempt to describe. Here's what may . . . lift the heart to rapture! When I look out on such a night as this, I feel as if there could be neither wickedness or sorrow in the world; and there certainly would be less of both if the sublimity of Nature were more attended to, and people were carried more out of themselves by contemplating such a scene. (MP 113)

However, although there are some similarities between Austen's and Kant's thoughts about the appreciation of nature, this mainly shows that both

---

[4]   Anne Ruderman points this out in *The Pleasures of Virtue*, p. 82, as has been indicated.
[5]   Immanuel Kant, *Critique of Judgment*, trans. J.H. Bernard (New York: Hafner Press, 1951) 42: 141, 143.

Austen and Fanny Price are creatures of their era. Philosophers other than Kant, Burke in particular, also wrote about the sublime. Indeed, as Mary Mothersill indicates, the mid-eighteenth century saw sublimity embedded in non-philosophical discourse, until "Every man of taste . . . had at his fingertips a catalogue of examples – volcanos, raging seas, towering cliffs."[6] This was, after all, a time period during which the work of William Wordsworth introduced an attitude toward nature that has been said to amount to "a fresh view of the organic relation between man and the natural world," and to culminate in "metaphors of a wedding between nature and the human mind, and beyond that, in the sweeping metaphor of nature as emblematic of the mind of God."[7] Austen's work could more accurately be said to reflect her exposure to the romantic poets, to whom she refers repeatedly in her novels, than to the thought of Kant. Nor is Kant the only philosopher to draw a connection between aesthetic and moral sensibility. We see such connections in the work of David Hume as well, so this ground for a Kantian reading of Austen is insufficient.

Furthermore, Fanny Price's raptures about the glory of nature are not so typical of the taste of Austen's heroines. Only Marianne Dashwood's enthusiasm for the natural world in *Sense and Sensibility* comes close, and it is represented with an air of restrained cynicism. That is, Marianne's attitude is almost but not quite comic, especially since Marianne quite obviously believes her own taste and sensibility superior to those of almost all her fellows: "Oh . . . with what transporting sensations have I formerly seen . . . [the leaves at Norland] fall. . . . What feelings have they, the season, the air . . . inspired! Now there is no one to regard them. They are seen only as a nuisance . . . and driven as much as possible from the sight." Elinor, the real heroine of the story, responds drily, "It is not every one . . . who has your passion for dead leaves" (SS 87–8).

Instead of a focus on the sublimity of nature, *Sense and Sensibility* offers us a view of beauty as it is allied with utility. Edward Ferrars responds to Marianne's paeans of admiration with something more down to earth: "You must be satisfied with such admiration as I can honestly give. I call it a very fine country, – the hills are steep, the woods seem full of fine timber, and the valley looks comfortable and snug, – with rich meadows and several neat farm houses scattered here and there. It exactly answers my idea of a fine country, because it unites beauty with utility" (SS 97).

---

[6] Mary Mothersill, "Sublime," *A Companion to Aesthetics* (Cambridge: Blackwell, 1995), p. 407.
[7] "Wordsworth, William," *The New Encyclopaedia Britannica* (Chicago: Encyclopaedia Britannica, Inc., 1995), vol. 12, p. 753.

Where Marianne sees hills rising with grandeur, Edward cannot help but notice "a very dirty lane" (SS 88). Marianne is most displeased. Moreover, there is some reason to believe that, of the two, only Marianne is intended to seem a bit ridiculous. The main point is to provide as entertaining a contrast in aesthetic positions as possible, of course, but Edward's judgment in general (with the exception of his getting himself engaged to the conniving Lucy Steele in a disastrous exhibition of youthful impetuosity) is endorsed throughout the novel. He is depicted as morally punctilious and splendidly decent. Moreover, no amusing counterarguments are ventured in opposition to his utilitarian aesthetic positions, nor do events follow them in such a way as makes them retroactively ridiculous. Given that Austen finds such steps extremely difficult to resist when it comes to any position concerning which she has even the faintest qualms, it seems safe to suppose that it is more likely that the utilitarian position is endorsed.

Like Edward Ferrars, Hume maintains that "the conveniency of a house, the fertility of a field . . . form the principal beauty of these several objects" (T 585). Hume adds to this his contention that our pleasure in the contemplation of such things derives from their tendency to produce pleasure in others. We deem something beautiful when it tends to advantage another; it is sympathy with that other person which leads to our pleasure. The principle of sympathy explains "the beauty, which we find in every thing that is useful." Just so "a fertile soil, and a happy climate, delight us by a reflexion on the happiness which they wou'd afford the inhabitants" (T 585). This demonstrates not only a new correspondence between Hume and Austen, but another kind of connection between aesthetic appreciation and moral sensibility. Our apprehension of beauty can be tied to our capacity for fellow feeling – tied, that is, to the principle of sympathy, which is said by Hume to be a chief source of the moral distinctions that we are inclined to make.

This connection between beauty and utility is reflected more frequently in Austen's novels than is the kind of reaction to nature typically associated with Kant's aesthetics. The delightful Admiral Croft of *Persuasion*, for instance, cannot help but be appalled by a particular picture, very much on utilitarian grounds:

> But what a thing here is, by way of a boat . . . What queer fellows your fine painters must be, to think that anybody would venture their lives in such a shapeless old cockleshell as that? And yet here are two gentlemen stuck up in it . . . and looking about them . . . as if they were not to be upset the next moment, which they certainly must be. (P 169)

I do not claim that Austen intends us to consider the Admiral an irrefutable art critic on account of this particular set of objections to the work in question. It is his honesty and straightforwardness that make him a valuable person and companion in the novel. But we are also, I think, intended to take that honesty and straightforwardness to heart in this particular context, for he sees something false and delusory in the picture that spoils his enjoyment and we are expected to sympathize with him in this regard. Moreover, the criticism is not as unsophisticated or simple-minded as one might at first think. Hume, unsurprisingly, is as one with Admiral Croft: "A ship appears more beautiful to an artist, or one moderately skilled in navigation, where its prow is wide and swelling beyond its poop, than if it were framed with a precise geometrical regularity, in contradiction to all the laws of mechanics." This is about naturalism in representational art, something we know that Austen favored on the literary front, at least.

And there are further examples in Austen of a beauty that is related to usefulness. Even *Mansfield Park* permits itself some less than sanguine reflections on the work of the improvers, who can sacrifice comfort and convenience on the altar of the picturesque (MP 57). When admiring Darcy's taste in furniture, Elizabeth Bennet of *Pride and Prejudice* notes approvingly that it is not "uselessly fine" (PP 246). Likewise, Hume observes that convenience and usefulness arouse pleasure and indicates that this observation "extends to tables, chairs, scritoires, . . . ploughs, and indeed to every work of art; it being an universal rule, that their beauty is chiefly deriv'd from their utility, and from their fitness for that purpose, to which they are destined" (T 364).

Austen's Edward Ferrars goes so far as to deny outright an appreciation that is dictated exclusively by picturesque principles: "I do not like crooked, twisted, blasted trees. I admire them much more if they are tall, straight, and flourishing. I do not like ruined, tattered cottages. . . . I have more pleasure in a snug farm-house than a watch-tower, – and a troop of tidy, happy villagers please me better than the finest banditti in the world" (SS 98). Hume clearly believes much the same:

Tis evident, that nothing renders a field more agreeable than its fertility. . . . Tis the same case with particular trees and plants, as with the field on which they grow. I know not but a plain, overgrown with furze and broom, may be, in itself, as beautiful as a hill cover'd with vines or olive-trees; tho' it will never appear so to one, who is acquainted with the value of each. . . . Fertility and value have a plain reference to use; and that to riches, joy, and plenty; in which tho' we have no hope of partaking, yet we enter into them by the vivacity of the fancy, and share them, in some measure, with the proprietor. (T 364)

The superabundance of quotations offered here has a purpose beyond the provision of examples. It should now be entirely clear that a Kantian analysis of positions on aesthetics favored in Austen's novels is untenable. Kant's judgments of beauty cannot be interested judgments, for the pleasure we take in the object must be disinterested pleasure. "We must not be in the least prejudiced in favor of the existence of things, but be quite indifferent in this respect."[8] And, of course, "that which pleases only as a means we call *good for something* (the useful). . . . In . . . [this] there is always involved the concept of a purpose . . . and thus . . . some kind of interest."[9] Utility, when it is a utility attended to by us, disqualifies our judgments from the class of those which can be genuine judgments of taste.

Moreover, the kind of emotional self-indulgence exhibited by a Marianne Dashwood would be looked askance by Kant, who indicates that "taste is always barbaric which needs a mixture of *charms* and *emotions* in order that there may be satisfaction."[10] The sublime (as opposed to the beautiful) is held to involve emotion by Kant, but Kant thinks ideas of the sublime are excited by nature "in its chaos or in its wildest and most irregular disorder and desolation,"[11] where there is an admixture of attraction and repulsion in our response to the object. The satisfaction we take in the sublime involves "admiration and respect" rather than enjoyment.[12] Only Fanny's contemplation of the starry heavens resembles what Kant would call a judgment of the mathematically sublime, and even here we find her rather more sanguine (she feels as if there could be neither wickedness or sorrow in the world) than Kant might think appropriate.

Hume's standard of taste is not absolutely unlike that proposed by Kant. Both accounts indicate that judgments of taste rely on reactions of pleasure. More importantly, both characterize such judgments as *intersubjective* – neither entirely relative to the subject nor wholly independent of her perspective. There is a connection in each, albeit an entirely different one, between the moral and the aesthetic. Hume even requires us to step away from personal biases. Not unlike someone who adopts the general point

---

[8]   Kant, *Critique of Judgment*, 3: 39.
[9]   Kant, *Critique of Judgment*, 4: 41.
[10] Kant, *Critique of Judgment*, 13: 58.
[11] Kant, *Critique of Judgment*, 23: 84.
[12] Kant, *Critique of Judgment*, 23: 83.

of view in regard to moral matters, Hume's appreciator should abstract from his own interests. Adopting a perspective that enables one to put personal prejudices to one side and to assume the point of view of the intended audience is strongly advocated. "A critic of a different age or nation . . . must . . . place himself in the same situation as the audience, in order to form a true judgment." Likewise, such a critic should not allow an acquaintance with author to influence her, but must place herself in "that point of view, which the performance supposes."[13]

Nonetheless, Hume's judgments of taste seem to involve us with moral ideas in a way that is quite distinct from the Kantian conception of "aesthetic ideas" which works of art are said to convey. Kantian aesthetic ideas are said to be intuitions "of the creative imagination for which an adequate concept can never be found," which do not impart knowledge, are not subsumable under concepts, and are said to "provoke more thought than admits of expression in a concept determined by words."[14] That is, such thoughts are typically taken to be aroused by means of symbol and association, in a way that is not at all paraphraseable, as it was indicated in Chapter 2 that Martha Nussbaum said of the work of Henry James. According to Kant, genius and the creative imagination may thus strive past the limitations of experience to give embodiment to rational ideas – moral ideas like those of virtue and vice.[15] Now this should not sound unfamiliar, for such issues were raised in the second chapter, in the course of discussing literary form and the effects of various modes of presentation on content. As was indicated in that chapter, Hume himself was not impervious to such considerations, though he wrote a good deal less about them than Kant. (I would even argue that a more complex position on the impact of literary form can be inferred for Hume).[16] The difference that I want to stress here between Hume and Kant is that while a Kantian appreciation of artworks does attend to content and the moral ideas therein presented,[17] it does not attend to it in precisely the same way as we would attend to experiences of virtue and vice encountered in life, which is how Hume would expect us principally to derive moral insights from literature. The contribution of Kantian aesthetic ideas is more ineffable than practical.

[13]   David Hume, "Of the Standard of Taste," in *Essays: Moral, Political, and Literary*, ed. Eugene F. Miller (Indianapolis: Liberty Classics, 1987), p. 239. Henceforth abbreviated "ST."
[14]   David Whewell, "Kant, Immanuel," *A Companion to Aesthetics*, ed. David Cooper (Cambridge: Blackwell, 1995), p. 250.
[15]   Kant, *Critique of Judgment*, 49: 158.
[16]   I touch on this subject in "Pleased and Afflicted: Hume on the Paradox of Tragic Pleasure," *Hume Studies*, 30.2 (November 2004): 213–36.
[17]   Thanks to Rachel Zuckert for pointing this out to me.

It "diffuses in the mind a multitude of sublime and restful feelings" or "quickens the cognitive faculties."[18] It does not rehearse the moral dispositions employed in everyday living, most of which, I should add, are quite subsumable under concepts. In fact, I believe the Kantian account of how moral ideas can be expressed in the very way in which content is presented is true, and I do not believe Hume would reject it. On the other hand, I do not think this is the only way for a work to express moral ideas, and I do believe that Kant would reject Hume's moral claims about fiction.

Toward the end of his essay on taste, Hume reflects on literary works which depict conduct that is believed immoral by the reader, but that neglect in any way to condemn it (ST 246), suggesting that such works are flawed because they deter a response (e.g., approval) the author aspires to elicit. We cannot (or at least are disinclined to) "enter into such sentiments," or assume an attitude of approbation toward something of which we actually morally disapprove. These claims raise many interesting questions, few of which can be addressed in the course of the discussion of a peripherally related topic.[19] It is important to note, however, that they make it very clear that Hume regards fiction as something which can engage us morally. In other words, our contemplation of fiction is an exercise which can, in an Aristotelian manner, rehearse our moral dispositions and patterns of response. Fiction can invite us to adopt a variety of moral perspectives, and we can acquiesce in or resist that invitation. Such responses to art do not in the least resemble those Kant ascribes to the impact of aesthetic ideas, which seem to provide the principal route (in Kant's account) by means of which moral concerns enter the aesthetic sphere.

While Austen makes use of literary devices in the way that Kant describes (and this is a way that I would argue is not in general terms inimical to Hume's ideas) she also sees fiction as a repository of quite concrete (i.e., subsumable under concepts) information about human capacities. The novel is a "work in which . . . the most thorough knowledge of human nature, the happiest delineation of its varieties," is to be observed (NA 38). When she writes *about* fiction, moreover, her concern is typically less with the ineffable and the associations to which it may give rise than it is with the emotions it arouses and the beliefs or behavior it may sometimes change. Her heroines are moved by fiction, and perusing it can have noticeable effects on the attitudes of the reader. *Northanger*

---

[18] Kant, *Critique of Judgment*, 49: 159–60.
[19] This subject is addressed in my "The Vicious Habits of Entirely Fictive People: Hume on the Moral Evaluation of Art," *Philosophy and Literature* 26 (2002): 38–51.

Abbey makes this clear in a comic way when delineating Catherine More-land's tendency to project ridiculously sinister and extravagantly gothic fictional scenarios onto real-life situations, under the influence of *Udolpho*. Nevertheless, it is in the same work that Austen issues her defense of novels, describing them as works "in which the greatest powers of the mind are displayed" (NA 38). In *Persuasion*, Anne Elliot warns Captain Benwick (described as both intellectual and literary) that "it [is] . . . the misfortune of poetry to be seldom safely enjoyed by those who enjoy . . . it most completely; and that the strong feelings which alone [can] . . . estimate it truly [are] . . . the very feelings which ought to taste it but sparingly," when his obsession with tragic themes exacerbates his distress over the loss of his fiancée (P 100–1). He is thought to enter too deeply into the work of the tragic poets. Hume accounts for this kind of a response, though he might well consider it as excessive as Austen does. Kant would consider the response inappropriate, but for entirely different reasons. For one thing, it sounds as if Benwick has a quite determinate concept of tragic loss and tragic heroes in mind. For another, his response seems to involve not cognitive enrichment derived from contemplating poetic images and their associations, but outright identification and self-pity. In the Humean scheme, of course, we are expected to respond emotionally to fiction, and expected to respond to it as to life, though this doesn't license needless wallowing.

For Hume, good taste involves "the same excellence of faculties which contributes to the improvement of reason, the same clearness of concep-tion, the same exactness of distinction, the same vivacity of apprehension" (ST 240–1). All of these are essential. It is evident that there is no spe-cial aesthetic faculty, but that taste involves the very same faculties that inform our understanding of the world. To improve one's taste is to improve one's capacities in this wider arena. It is notable that the issue of utility now arises in a new context, for taste connotes the rehearsal of faculties which can aid one in the course of one's life, not just in the perusal of works of art. That is, there is a utility to having and exercising one's taste (beyond the capacity of taste to focus attention on utility) insofar as taste will involve the possession of talents that will enhance the ability to conduct one's life and one's projects.

So taste requires sense as well as delicacy and sensitivity. Indeed, "where good sense is wanting," a subject "is not qualified to discern the beauties of design and reasoning, which are the highest and most excellent" (ST 241). For Austen, taste and sense are very often linked as well. In *Emma*, the task of framing a picture properly must be given to "some intelligent person whose taste . . . [can] be depended on" (E 49) and a failure of manners is dismissed as "a mere error of judgment, of knowledge, of taste" (E 134). In *Mansfield Park*, Edmund states that there is "more general observation and taste, a more critical knowledge diffused than formerly" with regard to effectively addressing a congregation (MP 340). None of this is to say that reason and taste cannot be at odds, of course. Austen certainly believes they can. One such conflict arises upon observation of the

> large fat sighings [of Mrs. Musgrove of *Persuasion*] over the destiny of a son, whom alive nobody had cared for. Personal size and mental sorrow have certainly no necessary proportions. A large bulky figure has as good a right to be in deep affliction, as the most graceful set of limbs in the world. But, fair or not fair, there are unbecoming conjunctions, which reason will patronize in vain – which taste cannot tolerate – which ridicule will seize. (P 68)[20]

In Austen, taste often amounts to cultivation and refinement. It requires, or is at least aided by, education, direction, and practice. In *Emma* and *Pride and Prejudice*, the heroines draw a distinction between artistic capacity or potential and the competence that can be conferred only by practice (E 44; PP 175). In *Mansfield Park*, Edmund Bertram "recommended the books which charmed [Fanny's] . . . leisure hours, he encouraged her taste and corrected her judgment; he made reading useful by talking to her of what she read, and heightening its attraction by judicious praise" (MP 22). Such education involves not only the intellect, but delicacy and feeling – the cultivation of sensitivity and discrimination from childhood. Fanny is told that "they are much to be pitied who are not taught to feel" as she does, and whose taste in nature has not been nurtured and developed (MP 113). Similarly, Hume advocates education and practice for the development of taste. Practice is vital to discerning beauty, for Hume, and he believes that we should undertake to peruse works of significance and merit more than once, considering them from different perspectives and taking care not to overlook important facets of both form and content. In fact, Hume believes that superficial and inferior works will not stand up to repeated perusal, and will pall upon the taste with repetition

---

[20] Incidentally, it is worth remembering that Hume himself, often the butt of jokes on account of his girth, wondered "why fat people should be so much the object of mirth, rather than lean." He proposed ascribing this "either to the cowardice or benevolence of mankind. Perhaps we are not so commonly witty as you and, consequently, men think they will have an easy conquest in attacking us. Perhaps we are better natured and men think they run no risk of offending us." David Hume, *Letters*, ed. J.Y.T. Grieg (Oxford: Oxford University Press, 1932), vol. I, p. 112.

(ST 237). Such works can certainly not withstand Hume's test of time, since they cannot even retain their initial charms over repeated readings or viewings. Thus, truly discerning taste requires study and practice and a process of familiarization with what is judged.

Hume's successful critics possess "strong sense, united to delicate sentiment, improved by practice, perfected by comparison, and cleared of all prejudice" (ST 264). Sense, practice, and the elimination of bias have already been addressed. Only delicacy remains. Delicacy of taste is, of course, a sensitivity to beauty, one that allows us to be "sensibly touched with every part of it,"[21] a fineness of perception. It is the ability to discern properties which Hume says are fitted by nature to produce sentiments of beauty or deformity (ST 235). Delicacy of taste is more desirable than a delicacy of passion, for the latter makes us subject to the whims of fate, intensifying our reactions to ill fortune as well as good, while the former is exercised at our own whim, over those works we choose to contemplate. A genuinely refined taste is that which, alike, "enables us to judge of the characters of men, of compositions of genius, and of the productions of the nobler arts" (DTP 6). Indeed, Hume states that fine sense and strong taste are virtually inseparable (DTP 6). He also believes that delicacy of taste is favorable to love and friendship, for it confers the ability, sometimes inaccessible to sense alone, to distinguish among characters and to mark "those insensible differences and gradations which make one man preferable to another" (DTP 7). Recollect that it is only Fanny Price, whose delicacy of taste, mind, and feeling is extolled, who quite acutely notes the impact of Henry Crawford on Julia and Maria, and who even more accurately estimates the things of which he is capable, while all other apparently intelligent characters are entirely oblivious to these things.

An arbiter of taste is one who determines how well something is fitted to attain the end for which it is intended (ST 221). Similarly, a moral arbiter attempts to discern whether people are fitted to attain certain ends, instead of relying exclusively on those dispositions their circumstances have permitted them to exercise. That is, a moral arbiter, or one who adopts Hume's general point of view, will try to observe the *tendencies* of people's characters as well as their actual effects. Delicacy in moral matters permits one to discern virtue in rags – virtue which has had no opportunity of exercise, but exists nonetheless. An individual possessed of one kind of discernment will not necessarily possess the other, it should be noted,

---

[21] David Hume, "Of the Delicacy of Taste and Passion," in *Essays: Moral, Political, and Literary*, ed. Eugene F. Miller (Indianapolis: Liberty Classics, 1987), p. 4. Henceforth abbreviated "DTP."

any more than good taste in music can be expected to confer literary acumen. Much depends on what practice and education contribute and on the varieties of prejudice one finds it easiest to resist. But to point to the possession of one kind of taste is at least to point to the development of faculties which can be directed toward new objects.

Austen's use of words like "delicacy" and "taste" enters the moral as well as the aesthetic sphere, just as it does in Hume's writing. In *Mansfield Park*, true delicacy is repeatedly ascribed to that individual who can make fine moral distinctions (MP 140). A "want of delicacy and regard for others" is clearly a moral failing, whereas the "disinterested-ness and delicacy of [Fanny's] character" is praised (MP 328, 326). Anne Elliot of *Persuasion* is concerned for the well-being of young Charles Hayter: "she had delicacy which must be pained by any lightnesss of conduct in a well-meaning young woman" toward Charles, "and a heart to sympathize in any of the sufferings it occasioned" (P 77). *Sense and Sensibility*'s Lucy is convicted of "want of delicacy, of rectitude, and integrity of mind" (SS 127) while Elinor wonders what kind of a wife she will make Edward, "with his integrity, his delicacy and well-informed mind" (SS 140).

In fact, a great many of Austen's references to taste are to taste in *people*. Henry Crawford has "moral taste enough" to value Fanny's virtues (MP 235) and Mary Crawford, when considering aspirants to her hand, "was long in finding . . . any one who could satisfy the better taste [in character and manners] she had acquired at Mansfield" (MP 469). Good-natured Miss Bates of *Emma* is "very much to the taste of every-body," and Emma cannot believe it possible "that the taste or pride of Miss Fairfax could endure such society" as that which the Eltons can provide (E 85, 285). Harriet is "infinitely to be preferred by any man of sense and taste" to the loathsome Mrs. Elton (E 331). The "fasti-diousness of [Anne Elliot's] taste" prevents her from forming a second attachment (P 28) and Admiral Croft admits that "there is something about Frederick more to [his] . . . taste" when contemplating Louisa's preference for Benwick (P 172).

In fact, similarities in taste are seen as a mark of compatibility, espe-cially in marriage. Fanny and Edmund have "no fears of opposition of taste" (MP 471) at the beginning of their marriage. Elizabeth believes all of Bingley's expectations of happiness with her sister will bear fruit, because they have similar tastes and similar feelings (PP 348). Naturally, this can be carried too far. Marianne Dashwood states categorically, "I could not be happy with a man whose taste did not in every point coincide with my own" (SS 17). Then again, Marianne can tolerate no divergence from her own tastes in anyone, so it is not surprising that she sets the bar so high in the case of romance (SS 127).

Some variations in taste are, of course, permissible. Hume acknowledges that we all have our preferences in the arts. Some of us prefer the comic to the tragic. Some are hypersensitive to flaws while others are happy to overlook them. Provided we do not allow such preferences to limit our appreciation to one genre or one style, there can be no objection. This is simply the way things are (ST 244). The preceding isn't an argument for relativism, as has been made clear in Hume's argument from disproportionate pairs and his appeal to sense, delicacy, practice, and the removal of bias. It does, however, make it clear that some divergences in taste are positively to be expected and perfectly permissible.

In a different context, Austen considers a similar variation in taste, a taste in noises. We begin with Mrs. Musgrove in the middle of Christmas chaos, countless importunate children underfoot, everyone talking at once: "Anne . . . would have deemed such a domestic hurricane a bad restorative. . . . But Mrs Musgrove . . . concluded . . . with a happy glance round the room, that . . . nothing was so likely to do her good as a little quiet cheerfulness at home." Anne's friend Lady Russell is appalled. But Austen observes that we may often see variations in taste, even taste in noises. Sounds can seem pleasant or irritating just because of the kinds of sounds they are. Consider Lady Russell, so allergic to the chaos of a Musgrove celebration:

> When Lady Russell . . . was entering Bath on a wet afternoon . . . amidst the dash of other carriages, the heavy rumble of carts and drays, the bawling of newspapermen, muffin-men and milkmen, and the ceaseless clink of pattens, she made no complaint. No, these were noises which belonged to the winter pleasures; her spirits rose under their influence; and like Mrs Musgrove, she was feeling, though not saying, that after being long in the country, nothing could be so good for her as a little quiet cheerfulness. (P 134–5)

The conclusion to be drawn from these examples and observations, therefore, is that the philosophical perspective into which Jane Austen's reflections on taste and beauty best fit is that espoused by David Hume. This is a perspective in which in which fellow feeling has a central role in the determination of beauties, where aesthetic and moral preferences are determined by employing the same faculties, and where aesthetic sensibilities are not divorced from ordinary human experience.

II

Indeed, we may take a further step and wonder whether, in the words of William Seeley,[22] "Austen's texts embody a meta-analysis of aesthetic practice with a direct effect on how we interpret their meanings." The short answer to this question is in the affirmative, and the name of the meta-analysis is *Northanger Abbey*. I will go so far as to claim that *Northanger Abbey* provides us with a species of thought experiment that demonstrates what it is that novels ought and ought not to do, not just by telling us what it is but by showing us how it's done. Austen's book performs three functions. It is, first, about novels and about that of which they ought properly to consist. Such issues are often discussed in a very direct way. Austen obtrudes herself as author into the narrative, and does so more frequently than in any other work, addressing the reader repeatedly, announcing what will come next, criticizing critics, defending women writers, commenting on and expressing irritation about standard attitudes toward novels and their characters. Use of the first and second person abound. *Northanger Abbey* is, next, a send-up of gothic novels. Even though it is a defense of the novelist's art in general, it nonetheless makes clear that some novelists and some novels are better than others. Austen comments ironically on the turgid melodrama of the gothic and its swooning sentimental heroines, eventually embarking on a demonstration of the absurdity of gothic conventions. Finally, *Northanger Abbey* is the kind of novel that Austen thinks is the best kind – the kind that engages our feelings and our sympathy for the characters because we recognize them as the kinds of people whom we're likely to meet in the course of our lives, and because we can imagine having their experiences. I will argue that Austen offers us not only an aesthetic applicable to her own work, but a kind of thought experiment that demonstrates the silliness of the gothics and the superiority of her own work by making us *respond* to gothic conventions *as* silly, and to her own depictions *as* we would to depictions of real people and real events.

Austen's critical attitude toward gothic melodrama appears to be shared at least in part by Hume in his essay "Of Tragedy," when he complains of the depiction of events which are "too bloody and atrocious,"[23] a practice that he believes can precipitate artistic failure. From the beginning

---

[22]   In his comment on a very abbreviated version of this paper at the Eastern Division meeting of the American Society of Aesthetics in Philadelphia, April 2006.
[23]   David Hume, "Of Tragedy," in *Essays: Moral, Political, and Literary*, ed. Eugene F. Miller (Indianapolis: Liberty Classics, 1987), p. 225.

of her novel, Austen is both directly and indirectly critical of the popular gothics. Her heroine, she announces, falls "miserably short of the true heroic height" attained by the female protagonists of such works (NA 16). None of the vicissitudes which typically afflict a gothic heroine have troubled the early life of Catherine Morland. But Austen introduces just such vicissitudes, in the form of stock gothic conventions, as the story progresses. Initially, Henry Tilney teases Catherine by making lurid predictions about her prospective sojourn at Northanger Abbey, anticipating storms and ancient cabinets with secret compartments, and predicting the appearance of cryptic manuscripts and the distressing occurrence of suddenly extinguished lights (NA 158–60). Shortly thereafter, Austen teases the reader by bringing about a storm with which to usher in Catherine's first night at the abbey and importing into Catherine's room a mysterious chest containing a roll of paper whose perusal is rendered impossible by Catherine's unintentional and hence unnerving extinguishing of a solitary candle (NA 168–71). Upon the following morning, safe in the daylight, Catherine discovers the mystery parchment to be nothing more than an ordinary washing-bill. Catherine's assumptions concerning the chest and the roll of paper, and later concerning General Tilney (assumptions nourished by a steady diet of such deathless works as *The Mysteries of Udolpho*), are ludicrous. But Austen never *tells* us that they are. She simply arranges that we *respond* to those assumptions as ludicrous by making us laugh at them and finally by arranging that we share Catherine's conviction of their absurdity (NA 199). Thus Austen does not merely describe the silliness of gothic literary conventions. She demonstrates it by making us find them funny.

This entire procedure has a conceptual component, in that the shift in emotional response can be linked to a subtle shift in conception. A response of amusement and contempt to the very fictional features to which the general public had hitherto responded with trepidation signals that a kind of conceptual shift has been orchestrated by Austen. Just as imagining events of a kind that we believe dangerous can underlie a fear response, so imagining events whose potential threateningness we find ourselves unable to take seriously will undercut any such response, since we cannot imagine what we cannot conceive. This isn't to say, of course, that Austen's work signals any outright changes in conceptions of danger, for it does not. But it does seem to be the case that the gothic harbingers of dread and terror – the stormy nights and mysterious documents and ancient abbeys and flickering, undependable candles – have been somewhat undermined by Austen's satire. Although he is disinclined to consider fiction a thought experiment, Roy Sorensen indicates that such an experiment

is a "natural test for the clarificatory practices constituting conceptual analysis," which include "drawing distinctions, crafting adequacy conditions,
teasing out entailments," and "mapping inference patterns."[24] If this is
so, then it seems that *Northanger Abbey* has made some small contribution
in this regard, if only in establishing that standard gothic plot contrivances
of the sort canvassed do not represent conditions sufficient for disaster.
It does so by situating them firmly in a more believable world in which
regarding them as sufficient for anything of the kind becomes absurd.
This suggests no immediately significant consequences with regard to reader
attitudes toward the world. However, the recognition of absurdity elicits
a strong inclination toward naturalism in fiction, and naturalistic fiction
is, after all, the kind best suited to influence the attitudes of readers toward
the world.

Emily Auerbach takes note of Austen's anti-gothic, realistic characterization in her *Searching for Jane Austen.*[25] It is Auerbach's contention that
Austen believed "realistic lively novels filled with natural characters are
superior to stilted works by past masters of prose."[26] We should also
recollect that, as has already been indicated, Austen maintains that the
novel can prove a font of information about human nature and its
varieties (NA 38). This applies to humanity's vices as well as its virtues.
Auerbach, Claudia Johnson, Paul Morrison, and others point out that,
in Austen, being a villain does not depend on gothic irrelevancies, on such
characteristics as dueling scars and aristocratic connections to fallen
houses and tendencies to burst into maniacal laughter. Villains can look
and behave like perfectly ordinary people.[27] That is, despite the falsity of
Catherine's darkest suspicions of General Tilney, he still proves a quite
recognizable villain: selfish, greedy, and unkind. No flights of gothic fancy
are required to render his nastiness apparent. Austen elicits our disapproval
of the General even before he mistreats Catherine, by letting us see what
Hume would call his unfortunate effect on his narrow circle – the dis-
comfort and anxiety he produces in his family, servants, and any hapless
visitor. She elicits further disapproval as we respond in sympathy with
Catherine when General Tilney dismisses her from his home without even

---

[24]   Roy A. Sorensen, *Thought Experiments* (New York: Oxford University Press, 1992), p. 15.
[25]   Emily Auerbach, *Searching for Jane Austen* (Madison: University of Wisconsin Press,
2004), p. 75.
[26]   Auerbach, *Searching for Jane Austen*, p. 96.
[27]   Auerbach, *Searching for Jane Austen*, p. 91. Auerbach cites an interview with Claudia
Johnson, author of *Jane Austen and the Courage to Write*, Wisconsin Public Radio, 10/95.
She also quotes Morrison's "Enclosed in Openness: Northanger Abbey and the Domestic
Carceral," *Texas Studies in Literature and Language* 33 (1991): 1–23.

offering an explanation for the incivility. (It is only later Austen tells us that the General, having discovered he'd been misinformed about Catherine's wealth and prospects, was moved to punish her for his own credulity and disappointed greed.) This is the very kind of moral engagement that Hume says we have with fiction. In the *Treatise*, for instance, Hume tells us that "A generous and noble character affords a satisfaction even in the survey; and when presented to us, tho' only in a poem or fable, never fails to charm and delight us" (T 296). We can assume that our survey of an ignoble character like General Tilney will likewise afford dissatisfaction. Hume expects fiction to "excite sentiments of approbation and blame, love and hatred." We should anticipate its doing so, at least, when it doesn't make the error of endorsing conduct which we regard as vicious, as has already been discussed (ST 247). It assuredly does so when we entertain the thought of the despicable General Tilney.

Notice that this excitation of moral sentiments is far more effectively performed by naturalistic fiction like Austen's than by the average gothic. In rehearsing and refining our moral responses to the sorts of characters and situations that we can find in the ordinary world, Austen's kind of fiction has considerably more utility than the standard melodrama. So, in the course of providing a naturalistic argument for the adoption of naturalism, Austen has fulfilled some (not all, of course) of the criteria for aesthetic excellence canvassed in her own work. If aesthetic merit can, in part, depend on utility, and if naturalistic fiction is morally useful, then the methods of aesthetic evaluation that Austen advocates confirm the superiority of her work.

With the advantages of Austen's naturalism in mind, we should also consider her admirable deployment of analogs in *Northanger Abbey*. The most striking example is to be found in the passage describing Catherine Morland's last night at the Abbey. This passage provides the reader with a mirror image of Catherine's first unquiet night at Northanger: the building is ancient, the room is dark, the wild wind produces peculiar noises, Catherine is sleepless, tormented, a prey to agitation.

> Yet how different now the source of her inquietude from what it had been then – how mournfully superior in reality and substance! Her anxiety had foundation in fact, her fears in probability; and with a mind so occupied in the contemplation of actual and natural evil, the solitude of her situation, the darkness of her chamber, the antiquity of the building, were felt and considered without the smallest emotion. (NA 227)

Confronted with real difficulties – that is, her virtual eviction from the Abbey at the behest of General Tilney – Catherine dismisses former susceptibilities. Her anxieties on this occasion are perfectly rational, because the beliefs upon which they are based are rational. Fact and probability rule the day, instead of flights of fancy.

This scene marks the intellectual evolution of the heroine just as it engages the readers' sympathy on Catherine's behalf, instead of their amused contempt. The same scenario is actually presented three times in the course of the novel. First, we see Catherine respond to Henry Tilney's classic gothic story. Then, her response to an actual situation is governed by the conventions of melodrama, to ridiculous effect. Finally, her response to her situation is governed by the apprehension of actual evil – by an accurate estimate of her circumstances. Step by step, Austen moves us from melodrama to naturalism, negotiating an evolution in our reactions and our sympathies as she does so. Both Austen and Hume expect us to respond to characters as to real people. Our attitudes toward fiction are to each but an extension of our attitudes toward the world. Austen demonstrates this point in two ways: by showing us the silliness and general uselessness of gothic contrivances and sensibilities in a naturalistic context and by showing us how more familiar and less melodramatic human interactions may still elicit our emotions while, in addition, arousing our moral interest. And this last point, as has already been indicated, incidentally demonstrates that Austen's fiction has aesthetic merit on the ground of its usefulness in this regard.

Both Hume and Austen also ascribe aesthetic value to more traditional sources – to the formal aspects of works, to excellence in the mode of presentation. Neither lingers much over such observations, perhaps taking them as given. And the aesthetic values canvassed here do not begin to encompass all of the aesthetic merits which may properly be ascribed to Austen's own work, or begin to explain why it is probably a lot more *aesthetically* valuable than Hume's prose (with some considered exceptions for the particularly well-turned phrase). These subjects have been touched on in the second chapter and will be pursued further in the last.

I would like to close this chapter with an afterthought. One final idea to which the investigations in this chapter have given rise concerns an interesting question in the philosophy of art.[28] If fiction can sometimes affect the reader in such a way as to get him or her to adopt or modify some particular moral perspective, then what I have said here suggests that it can alter or modify aesthetic perspectives as well. But that seems counterintuitive to a lot of people. As one colleague said, "even Austen

---

[28]   Thanks to Anne Eaton for raising that question.

could not get me to like Renoir or find haggis appealing, even fictionally!" First (I am replacing haggis with olives in imagination) the point is surely that some Dickensian depiction of the joy of a hungry kilted infant falling upon a steaming Christmas haggis is probably going to cause just the kind of imaginative disengagement that Hume would associate with the fictional endorsement of immoral conduct. My suspicion is that those who hate haggis may be able to imagine *that* someone finds haggis delicious, but find themselves at a loss when it comes to imagining the deliciousness of haggis. At least when it comes to a settled and habitual loathing for certain foods, I would be surprised if fiction could change our minds (even if a character were to exclaim "capers make all the difference!" or the dis-liked food were compared by the author to food one liked). But that is not at all at odds with Hume's claim, which never makes any suggestions about frequency but only seems to acknowledge the possibility. Still, I do believe that the *idea* of eating the despised food could be made more attractive on other grounds. Haggis could be shown as an alternative to starvation, or as the acme of sophistication (tonight we're serving haggis, with a poison thistle vinaigrette reduction), or as something that was very, very good for one's health, or libido, or ability to do philosophy. Coming to believe any of the latter could change one's gustatory habits and thereby perhaps gradually change one's tastes. But such a case is much easier to make for art. I think that a prose description of a real painting, whether fictional or not, could make it seem objectionable, or ugly or sexist, in a way that it had never seemed before, spoiling it forever for a former appreciator. I also think that a negative opinion of an artwork might be altered for the better in much the same way, but that is because I believe that our conception of what makes a painting or a novel good is rather more complicated than our conception of what makes haggis or olives disgusting. In fact, I'm not sure how much of a concept the latter sort of reaction involves. A distaste for haggis or olives seems more a settled reactive aversion than something involving an underlying concept. I will therefore focus on art in the remaining discussion.

The question of interest to me, personally, is whether fiction can achieve a change in our aesthetic reaction to some work or some thing with any more ease and dispatch than could a simple giving of reasons. I think that, as with modifications to moral judgments, the way fiction alters aesthetic reactions will most likely involve the arousal of emotions, though this may simply involve the giving of reasons in fictional dress. First, any moral factor that was thought to affect aesthetic evaluation would enter into a fictional depiction in just the way other moral considerations might. That is, just as a fiction might show us how objectionable a given stereotype was, a fiction that led us to recognize such a stereotype in a famous work – perhaps only indirectly, or by depicting a character's reaction – might lead us to lose our taste or feeling for the work. Could a fiction really change our opinion that something was beautiful, or make us regard as beautiful something that we had not hitherto so considered? It probably goes without saying that the more settled and definite and reflected-upon the opinion, the more difficult it would be to change, just as with moral judgments. But with that said, I do believe that a fiction could alter a belief that something was beautiful. It is usually easier to spoil things, or at least to undermine a taste that was insufficiently reflective. A critic can do it, as Hume points out, by showing flaws (or, in the reverse case, by pointing out merits). Jane Austen could have created at least a mild distaste for the romantic poets if she had been just a little less restrained in her depiction of Marianne Dashwood, or just a little more inclined to rehearse their most saccharine inventions out of context. And novelists can make us see loveliness where we didn't see it before. They can sometimes, for instance, make us more likely to imagine beauty in the physical manifestations of age, and so more likely to look for such things in life. As with moral responses, imagining beauty in the skull beneath the skin and in gray hair acknowledges the possibility that age can be beautiful and so one's concept of beauty has expanded. This is a contention with which I do not think Hume and Austen would be inclined to disagree. I'd be willing to wager that many readers of *Northanger Abbey* acquired a contempt for melodrama and a taste for naturalism, along with altered beliefs about what should be valued in a novel.

9
Hume and Austen on Good People and Good Reasoning

Much has been written about the ability of literature to offer specifically moral insights. In this book, I have more or less jumped on the bandwagon, arguing that fiction can bring the normative repertoire of the reader into play by eliciting moral and emotional responses. In the present chapter, I will argue that a somewhat similar case can be made, if not always for intellectual virtues and vices *simpliciter*, then at least for the role good reasoning is thought to play in the acquisition of virtue and the way in which faulty or defective reasoning is often implicated when we try to account for vice. I will contend that there are interesting parallels between Hume and Austen in the connections each is inclined to draw between virtue and effective reasoning, and between virtue and justified belief.

Recent discussions of intellectual virtue, more than one of which resorts to Jane Austen for examples of the connection between moral goodness and active intelligence, tend first to draw our attention to similarities between the discourse of epistemology and the discourse of ethics. In her *Virtues of the Mind*, Linda Zagzebski points out that "epistemologists have routinely referred to epistemic *duty* and *responsibility*, to epistemic *norms* and *values*, and to intellectual *virtue*."[1] Questions of justification, rationality or proper warrant are inescapably normative, carrying with them the notions of permissibility and of blameworthiness for errors. Such criticism, Zagzebski writes, "is much closer to *moral* criticism than the criticism of bad eyesight or poor blood circulation," despite questions about the voluntariness of belief formation.

---

[1] Linda Trinkaus Zagzebski, *Virtues of the Mind: An Inquiry into the Nature of Virtue and the Ethical Foundations of Knowledge* (Cambridge: Cambridge University Press, 1998), p. 1.

When people call others shortsighted or pigheaded, their criticism is as much like a moral criticism as when they call them offensive or obnoxious; in fact, what is obnoxious about a person can sometimes be limited to a certain pattern of thinking. The same point can be made . . . of a variety of other names people are called for defects that are mostly cognitive: . . . recalcitrant . . . or obstinate; wrong-headed, vacuous, shallow . . . muddle-headed . . . or obtuse.[2]

Zagzebski hopes to show that epistemic evaluation is a form of moral evaluation, but for my purposes it is enough to note philosophers' awareness of similarities between epistemic and moral methods of evaluation and to note the apprehension of an occasional interdependence between epistemic and moral considerations, in particular the more than occasional dependence of virtue on effective reasoning.

The effort here will center on an attempt to show some similarities in the way Hume and Austen address certain questions of epistemic evaluation, in particular those which appear linked to moral concerns. We must keep in mind, after all, that any number of virtues and vices have both moral and intellectual components. Hypocrisy, for instance, is a failure both of integrity and of self-knowledge. And integrity could be taken to depend on an internal consistency between one's values and one's dispositions or, indeed, the knowledge that this consistency or coherence obtains. Prejudice, considered as a vice, brings both moral and epistemic questions to the fore, and is a topic taken up at length in the writings of both Hume and Austen. It seems primarily to be an intellectual failing which, when acted on, has morally significant outcomes. It involves attitudes and assumptions that can have harmful effects both within and outside the narrow circle of the possessor.

Let us begin with this latter vice, focusing on Hume's discussion of prejudice in the first book of the *Treatise*. In order to bring to light some aspects of the connection between epistemic and moral concerns, let us consider this passage as it reflects on Hume's infamous footnote in "Of National Characters." The footnote concerns a subject about which Hume's personal beliefs leave something to be desired, given that he writes such things as "I am apt to suspect the negroes to be naturally inferior to the whites."[3] But, of course, no personal prejudice of Hume's need be taken to support implications about his general philosophical position.

[2]   Zagzebski, *Virtues of the Mind*, pp. 5–6.
[3]   David Hume, "Of National Characters," in *Essays: Moral. Political, and Literary*, ed. Eugene F. Miller (Indianapolis: Liberty Classics, 1985), p. 208.

As even his critics acknowledge,[4] Hume goes to considerable lengths to explore the phenomenon of prejudice. In particular, he finds the source of prejudice in general rules, often formed or maintained in the face of the contrary evidence of "present observation and experience" (T 147). That is, he outlines the various psychological factors involved in our adherence to general rules in the face of counterevidence. And Hume's examples exactly fit the case of his problematic footnote: "An Irishman cannot have wit, and a Frenchman cannot have solidity; for which reason, tho' the conversation of the former in any instance be visibly very agreeable, and of the latter very judicious, we have entertain'd such a prejudice against them, that they must be dunces or fops in spite of sense and reason. Human nature is very subject to errors of this kind" (T 146–7). Customary associations affect the imagination, leading us to "transfer our experience in past instances to objects" which may only bear a faint resemblance to the initial objects of such experiences. The "custom goes beyond the instances from which it is deriv'd, and to which it perfectly corresponds; and influences . . . [an individual's] ideas of such objects as are in some respect resembling, but fall not precisely under the same rule" (T 148). As in repeated conjunctions of cause and effect, "in almost all kinds of causes there is a complication of circumstances, of which some are essential and others superfluous" to the production of the effect. When superfluous circumstances are frequently conjoined with the essential, we may be carried along to a conception of the usual effect by superfluous circumstances alone. This is, of course, perfectly applicable to the problematic footnote. There, Hume notes that "there are no ingenious manufactures among . . . [blacks], no arts, no sciences," completely discounting reports of an educated black man as exaggerations.[5] The superfluous circumstances in the case of the stereotype are, naturally, those of race; the essential, those of bondage, alienation, and lack of opportunity. Hume should have seen it. But he explains why it may be that people sometimes don't. And, more importantly, he provides a remedy for his own error: "We may correct this propensity by a reflection on the nature of those [essential as well as nonessential] circumstances," even if custom "gives a biass to the imagination" (T 148).

Of course, Jane Austen's *Pride and Prejudice* is devoted to an investigation of prejudice, described in terms of the heroine's adherence to assumptions formed on the basis of negative first impressions and retained in

[4] See, e.g., Richard H. Popkin, "Hume's Racism," in *The High Road to Pyrrhonism*, ed. Richard Watson and James Force (San Diego: Austin Hill Press, 1980).
[5] Hume, "Of National Characters," p. 208 f. 10.

the face of counterevidence. Indeed, the novel was originally called *First Impressions*. Customary associations affect the imagination of both Elizabeth and her neighbors when they contemplate the manners of Mr. Darcy as they are initially displayed in the assembly rooms: "Mr. Darcy danced only once with Mrs. Hurst and once with Miss Bingley, declined being intro- duced to any other lady, and spent the rest of the evening in walking about the room, speaking occasionally to one of his own party. His char- acter was decided. He was the proudest, most disagreeable man in the world" (PP 11). This isn't precisely the same as Hume's example of ethnic stereotypes, of course, but certainly seems to involve a not dissimilar class-based stereotype about wealthy snobs: people who think they're too good to associate with us. And this is a class of people into which Darcy's behavior appears to have drafted him. Elizabeth's pride is injured when she overhears Darcy describe her as merely "tolerable" and announce his disinclination to dance with her. On the basis of these brief observations everyone, especially Elizabeth and her mother, had Darcy pegged as "so high and so conceited that there was no enduring him!" (PP 13). This makes all and sundry happy to accept Wickham's corroborative lies and innuendos about Darcy's character and makes them entirely unwilling to attend to evidence which shows it not to be as black as first supposed: "The general prejudice against Mr Darcy is so violent, that it would be the death of half the good people in Meryton to attempt to place him in an amiable light" (PP 226). Darcy's refusing Wickham the living which was promised to him, coupled with Darcy's removal of Bingley from Netherfield, are instantly imputed by Elizabeth to his overweening pride and coldheartedness and a generally defective character.

But Elizabeth is too intelligent to disregard Darcy's own eventual explanations of his treatment of Wickham and of his attempts to separ- ate Bingley and Jane (and too intelligent to ignore character testimonials provided by Darcy's housekeeper and his cousin). These explanations provide an alternative to the conceit, pride, and unfeeling cruelty which she initially believed were the source of his actions. Darcy is certainly proud, and sometimes even proud in the manner of a certain class of privileged people, but pride is a superfluous circumstance in the production of this particular behavior, behavior which is prompted mainly by Darcy's knowledge of Wickham's bad character, by Wickham's having demanded and received cash in lieu of the living, by concern for the well-being of his friend, and by the conviction that Jane will not be injured by a separation. These are the essential factors which prompt Darcy's actions. Just as Hume claims, Elizabeth's propensity to impute Darcy's actions to a defective character, possibly in line with stereotypes which attribute overweening conceit and other vices to the moneyed upper classes, is *corrected* by a reflection on those essentials despite the custom that has given the bias to her imagination (a custom based, as has been suggested, on a view about a particular class of people – rich people who think they are better than we are – that seems to have embedded itself in the imagination of most of the inhabitants of Meryton).

Elizabeth's awakening to the realities of the situation brings with it a consciousness of both moral and epistemic errors:

> Of neither Wickham nor Darcy could she think without feeling that she had been blind, partial, prejudiced, and absurd.
> "How despicably have I acted!" she cried. – "I, who have prided myself on my discernment! – I, who have valued myself on my abilities! who have often disdained the generous candour of my sister, and gratified my vanity, in useless or blameable distrust. – How humiliating is this discovery! – Yet, how just a humiliation! – Had I been in love, I could not have been more wretchedly blind. But vanity, not love, has been my folly. – Pleased with the preference of one, and offended by the neglect of the other, on the very beginning of our acquaintance, I have courted prepossession and ignorance, and driven reason away, where either were concerned. Till this moment, I never knew myself. (PP 208)

She convicts herself both of vanity and of prepossession, of ignorance and of unreasonableness. The moral and the epistemic defects seem to be causally connected, for vanity has led to prepossession and a failure of discernment, which have led to false beliefs, which have salved her pride, which has led her to discount the observations of those who disagree with her initial estimates of Darcy's character (Jane, for instance), because she considers herself the better judge. Elizabeth speaks of herself as having *encouraged* prejudices (PP 226), something she has done out of injured vanity. The change in her beliefs is what prompts her shame, the subjects of that shame including the very faculties which were prior to this episode the subjects of pride. Recollect in this context that Hume provides us with an account of pride, shame, and the moral sentiments that stresses the interdependence of idea and passion and that depicts just this shift in sentiment as a consequence of the transition in idea and subject.

And, of course, vanity *encourages* sloppy or biased thinking. In its simplest form, it involves an overestimation of one's own merits coupled with a perpetual focus of attention on the attitudes of others toward oneself. The more complex account offered in Austen shows us how vanity and the biases or prejudices it produces (to the detriment of those who do not appear to think well of us, for instance, or in favor of those who perceptively recognize our merits) can affect our interpretations of events and the inferences we make about the motives, tendencies and dispositions of others. The failings tied to vices here are largely cognitive failings.

Contra writers like John Casey, however, this does not put Austen at odds with proponents of sentimentalist accounts of morality like Hume.[6] First, Hume's account of the indirect passions has a significant role for ideas, insofar as both the cause and the effect of the passion are concerned. Second, Hume's talk of vices like vanity, particularly in the *Treatise*, dwells as much on beliefs and behavior as it does on unanalyzable sensations, as I hope a perusal of the chapters in this book devoted to the discussion of particular vices will attest. Take for instance this discussion of pride from Book III of the *Treatise*: "Alexander . . . abandon'd by his soldiers, among barbarians, not yet fully subdu'd, felt in himself such a dignity of right and of empire, that he cou'd not believe it possible any one cou'd refuse to obey him. Whether in Europe or in Asia, among Greeks or Persians, all was indifferent to him: Wherever he found men, he fancied he found subjects" (T 599). While one finds oneself perversely hoping that Alexander's beliefs will undergo as sudden a reversal as is compatible with manifestations of unsubjectlike behavior on the part of all who surround him, this example nonetheless shows that a clear connection is made between the disposition of pride and some very noticeable (and perhaps delusional) beliefs. Casey appears to be under the impression that "the sentimentalist tradition [as exemplified by David Hume, apparently] prizes passive states of feeling above the cultivation of active habits, and underplays the need to cultivate a realistic view of the world."[7] He is mistaken, at least as regards Hume. Indeed, since Hume's entire argument for sentiment's being the source of morality is based on the claim that it is sentiment rather than reason which motivates action, it is difficult to believe that Casey is familiar enough with Hume's philosophy to formulate adequate assumptions about what it entails.

On the other hand, to give credit where it is due, both Casey and Marilyn Butler, whom he cites, make interesting and convincing observations about the connection between moral goodness and the intellect in Jane Austen's novels. Butler writes that goodness is "an active, analytical process, not at all the same thing as passive good nature"[8] and Casey states

[6] John Casey, *Pagan Virtues: An Essay in Ethics* (Oxford: Clarendon Press, 1992), pp. 160–1. Casey cites Marilyn Butler here, but Butler herself disaffiliates Hume from aspects of sentimentalist tradition which are relevant to our discussion. Marilyn Butler, *Jane Austen and the War of Ideas* (Oxford: Oxford University Press, 1974), p. 10.
[7] Casey, *Pagan Virtues*, p. 161.
[8] Butler, *Jane Austen and the War of Ideas*, p. 271.

that "stupid characters are not truly good in Jane Austen."[9] I concur with some of this, but I also think the contention that intelligence collaborates in the production of virtue is entirely compatible with Hume's account of virtue. Further, I believe that neither writer (leaving Hume out of the discussion for the moment) uses the word "good" in quite the way Austen uses it. There are a number of superlatively good characters, if we rely entirely on Austen's use of the term and its synonyms, that are a little wanting in intellectual attainments. The goodness of Jane Bennet, meaning by this her kindness and generosity and penchant for excusing people, is perpetually extolled, but she is one of the least discriminating characters in *Pride and Prejudice. Sense and Sensibility*'s Sir John and *Emma*'s Miss Bates are good but a bit on the simple side. *Mansfield Park*'s Sir Thomas and *Persuasion*'s Lady Russell are good people who give very bad advice on the basis of seriously flawed character assessments. It is perfectly possible, in Austen's novels, to be good even when afflicted with any number of cognitive deficits. What is not possible is to be a *good judge of moral character* without the benefit of intelligence. We have only to observe a Mrs. Bennet or Mr. Collins, a Mrs. Elton or Sir Walter Elliot, a John Thorpe or Mrs. Norris or Miss Steele to realize that this is the case in Austen's fictional worlds. And in considering what is required for being or becoming a good judge of moral character, it is clear that we can use some of what Hume has to say about the matter as a model.

Let us rehearse some of the material from the chapter on sentiment. The moral sentiments arise *from* ideas, for Hume, very often ideas about the impact people have on the narrow circle they inhabit or the impact that one has on one's own circle. They also give rise *to* ideas. In some cases these latter are moral judgments. The understanding has an obvious function here, it should be noted. Disapprobation, for instance, like hatred, is produced by an *idea* concerning a negative quality in something (the subject) associated with another person (the object). And this disapprobation can produce, in its turn, a negative moral judgment about the person whose character is being observed. Initially, this delineation might seem to be at odds with the Humean contention that morality arises from sentiment. If moral disapproval springs from an idea, perhaps characterizable (as I have characterized it here) as a belief, then reason seems to take precedence over sentiment. However, such a conclusion is not inevitable. For instance, we need acknowledge no inconsistency if talk of causation is taken to convey claims about conceptual necessity rather than temporal precedence.

---

[9] Casey, *Pagan Virtues*, p. 164.

Moreover, we can regard the idea which is the source of approbation or disapprobation as a belief or thought concerning a matter of fact, for instance that some particular course of action or decision (the subject) performed by a given individual (the object) is such as to inflict pain and suffering (the quality). To give a more specific example, consider Elizabeth Bennet's belief that Darcy's refusing Wickham the living that has been promised to him not only constitutes a case of promise-breaking but also inflicts pain on Wickham himself, since this step deprives him of his preferred vocation (PP 81). Such a belief produces indignation and disapproval, which in turn gives rise to a negative evaluation of the person of whom one disapproves (the second idea): for instance, the belief that Darcy is proud, jealous, immoral, and altogether "abominable" (PP 81). Here, the sentiment of disapproval produces the specifically moral judgment, while the idea or belief said to cause that sentiment is *not* a moral judgment. This preserves Hume's causal story while eliminating the charge of inconsistency, since the idea which produces the passion is not normative, and the normative appraisal still springs from sentiment. Thus, to return to the subject which gave rise to these speculations, the understanding remains subordinate to sentiment in moral response.

Hume might also give reason a part to play in the adjudication of moral disputes, but this would involve getting clear on matters of fact, where different beliefs concerning the facts would give rise to different sentiments. Elizabeth has, in fact, been grossly misinformed. Wickham, having decided against taking orders, advises Darcy that he wishes for "some more immediate pecuniary advantage in lieu of the preferment" (PP 200). Darcy gives Wickham three thousand pounds. Wickham spends it in record time, returns, and demands the living. Darcy refuses. Wickham then attempts to elope with Darcy's fifteen-year-old sister. That is, in the case of this example, disputes about whether the denial of the living is unfair can be settled by calling into question beliefs about the facts, not beliefs which incorporate evaluations. The moral belief would once again spring from sentiment, this time from a changed sentiment in response to a fuller awareness of the facts. However, the factual belief, independent of sentiment, could not by itself provide a motive for action (an action such as Elizabeth's refusing Darcy's proposal of marriage, in the case of the initial false belief).

We should also consider what it takes for someone to become a competent moral judge, a good judge of character, in the Humean scheme of things, beginning with the discussion of Hume's general point of view in preceding chapters and his advocacy of its adoption as a regulator of sympathy and sentiment. Adopting the general point of view enables us to correct initial sentiments by controlling for the effects of distance and intensity. It prompts us, when assessing another, to consider the tendencies of his or her character as well as its actual impact on the world, effectively enabling us to bring questions concerning moral luck to the table. Reason and understanding are necessary insofar as they create the framework within which approbation and disapprobation can most fruitfully give rise to moral judgments. Adopting the general point of view is intended to focus our attention, to eliminate distractions, and to encourage hypothetical and counterfactual thinking. Even sympathy unconnected to moral evaluation calls for inferences about the mental states of others. Reason may not be central, but it is necessary. Hume's meta-ethical concerns seem to range into a territory that requires adequate reasoning as a necessary condition for moral evaluation and, indeed, even for fellow feeling.

Austen often draws incisive comparisons between the kinds of evaluations of character that people can make. These comparisons will not be rehearsed here, since they have already been discussed at length in the chapter devoted to consideration of Hume's general point of view. As for virtue in rags, there are a few excellent examples to be found in Austen, especially in *Mansfield Park* and *Sense and Sensibility* (also discussed earlier), of both virtue in rags and vice in *dishabille*. Even *Pride and Prejudice*, our current font of illustrations, provides a sample case, though of musical proficiency in rags rather than virtue. What Austen does with the case is especially interesting, because she shows us how it is that claims about virtue or talent in rags may prove specious. One need look no farther than the abominable Lady Catherine de Bourgh for a thoroughgoing abuse of counterfactuals: "There are few people in England, I suppose, who have more true enjoyment of music than myself, or a better natural taste. If I had ever learnt, I should have been a great proficient" (PP 173). This is a scene in which Austen mocks Lady Catherine and her pretensions, on logical as well as moral grounds. Evidently, the woman is arrogant and conceited. But her reasoning is just as clearly at fault. Depending on how one defines "proficiency," there is an air of question-begging about the entire formulation. Lady Catherine appears to be claiming that, had she acquired musical skills, she would have been skillful, and then somehow converting this into evidence of "talent in rags." This is a perfectly splendid case of a narrator's inviting us to identify and to disapprove an error of which a character remains ignorant. She does so, not by telling us *that* the character is in error, but merely by allowing us to recognize the faultiness of the character's reasoning because our own methods of epistemic evaluation are engaged.

Jane Austen's novels all have a clear focus on intellectual development. It is probably not incidental that, with the possible exception of

Catherine Morland, all of Austen's heroines are intelligent. Elizabeth Bennet demonstrates her skills in argument with both Darcy and Lady Catherine de Bourgh. Some of Elizabeth's interchanges with Lady Catherine in particular show her to be no stranger to logic. Lady Catherine is the first speaker:

> "A report of a most alarming nature reached me two days ago. I was told that . . . *you* . . . would, in all likelihood, be soon . . . united to my . . . nephew, Mr Darcy. Though I *know* it must be a scandalous falsehood, though I would not injure him so much as to suppose the truth of it possible, I instantly resolved on setting off for this place, that I might make my sentiments known to you."
>
> "If you believed it impossible to be true," said Elizabeth . . . "I wonder you took the trouble of coming so far. What could your ladyship propose by it?"
>
> "At once to insist upon having such a report universally contradicted."
>
> "Your coming to Longbourn, to see me and my family," said Elizabeth coolly, "will be rather a confirmation of it; if, indeed, such a report is in existence." (PP 353–4)

Clearly, Elizabeth comes off best in this, and in other encounters. The heroine of *Emma* is described as clever in the first sentence of the novel. She too engages in argument, and even finds herself "taking the other side of the question from her real opinion, and making use of . . . arguments against herself" (E 145). Surely this alone is a sign of cognitive dexterity. Fanny Price, though too timid to argue, is probably Austen's most intellectual heroine. Every bit as well read and intellectually adept as Elinor and Marianne Dashwood of *Sense and Sensibility* and Anne Elliot of *Persuasion*, she adds to this a propensity for reflection and pondering. It is Fanny who thinks to ask Sir Thomas Bertram about the slave trade, although the only response to her question is dead silence (MP 198). It is Fanny who reflects on ecological diversity at one moment and, like Hume (T 85), on the nature and fallibility of human memory the next (MP 208–9). However, all of these clever heroines are guilty of intellectual errors, many of which have morally significant consequences. It would be fair to say that each of Austen's novels concerns the intellectual growth of the central characters as well as their moral development, and that the two are, more often than not, interdependent.

At the most simple-minded level, getting clear on the facts is something with which the heroines of Austen's novels sometimes struggle. As we have seen, Elizabeth Bennet's initial bias against Darcy, formed partly by deploying a stereotype and partly by considering the effects of Darcy's actions on herself alone rather than on his circle as a whole, makes her particularly susceptible to Wickham's false claims and insinuations. She does not, as Hume advises, "over-look . . . [her] own interest in those general judgments" which she makes about Darcy (T 582). As Elizabeth says, "I could more easily forgive *his* pride, if he had not mortified *mine*" (PP 20). So Elizabeth Bennet accepts false assumptions by accepting Wickham's word. And, as has been indicated, she reacts to these assumptions with disapprobation, a sentiment which leads her to form judgments about Darcy's character, judgments which a clarification of the facts eventually leads her to reject as the evidence dissipates her disapprobation. Likewise, Darcy's initial reaction to Elizabeth undergoes several changes. Even more interesting is the fact that Darcy's pride changes to humility just as Elizabeth's pride in her discernment becomes humiliation when she realizes her errors. Darcy's realization parallels Elizabeth's. She, after all, had been misinformed, whereas he had no such excuse:

> As a child I was taught what was *right*, but I was not taught to correct my temper. I was given good principles, but left to follow them in pride and conceit. . . . my parents . . . encouraged . . . me to be selfish and overbearing; to care for none beyond my own family circle; to think meanly of all the rest of the world; to *wish* at least to think meanly of their sense and worth compared with my own. Such I was, from eight to eight and twenty; and such I might still have been but for you. . . . What do I not owe you! You taught me a lesson, hard indeed at first, but most advantageous. By you, I was properly humbled. I came to you without a doubt of my reception. You shewed me how insufficient were all my pretensions to please a woman worthy of being pleased. (PP 369)

It is Darcy's conviction of his own superiority and worth (a conviction that makes the stereotype applied to him not entirely inapt, though still for the most part unfair) that has undergone a radical change. With the altered assessment, his pride changes to humility, which alters the judgments he is inclined to make concerning both himself and others. The changes in Darcy and in Elizabeth are moral *and* intellectual. Both have moved beyond a biased self-serving way of attending to the world, and both have gained in self-knowledge and self-understanding.

Emma is another novel which expends its art, in the words of Graham Hough, on tracing the heroine's "growth, the dispelling of her illusions and wrong judgments, and the gradual emergence of her character in its fundamental integrity and clear-sightedness."[10] Initially, of course, Emma's

---

[10] Graham Hough, Afterword in *Emma* (New York: Signet, 1980), p. 388.

inventive imagination deludes her about the motives behind Mr. Elton's attendance on Harriet and herself, about the character of Jane Fairfax, and about Harriet's penultimate and ultimate preferences in a mate. Gilbert Ryle is undoubtedly right in proposing that a central theme of *Emma* is solicitude, and that a central focus of the action is on the influence exerted by some characters on others and the question of when this constitutes outright interference in their affairs. Knightley influences Emma, and Emma influences Harriet, but "Mr. Knightley dealt with Emma as a potentially responsible and rational being. Emma dealt with Harriet as a doll."[11] Yet Emma's interference in Harriet's life, and even her unwitting and thankfully temporary interference in Jane's engagement, is prompted by beliefs that she has arrived at illegitimately, beliefs that are more the result of wishful thinking and conjecture arising from injured vanity and boredom than any kind of reasonable inference. Emma's own perception of her assumptions about Elton's interest in Harriet, assumptions that have led her to encourage unrealistic expectations on Harriet's part, casts the error as an epistemic one:

> she would gladly have submitted to feel yet more mistaken – more in error – more disgraced by mis-judgment, than she actually was, could the effects of her blunders have been confined to herself. . . . How she could have been so deceived. . . . She looked back as well as she could; but it was all confusion. She had taken up the idea, she supposed, and made every thing bend to it. (E 134)

Emma resolves "to do such things no more" (E 137). The resolution does not last. Perhaps this is due to boredom, given the limited arena in which a young woman of the period could exercise her abilities. Perhaps her unjustified assumptions and manipulation provide Emma with the pleasure of control as well as a form of entertainment. Whatever the answer, the results of Emma's further mistaken assumptions and meddling are worse than before.

This time Harriet is moved by Emma's encouragement in a direction which the latter never anticipated, presuming that she has captured the interest not of Frank Churchill (as Emma expects), but the rather more unattainable Mr. Knightley. Emma is appalled: "She saw it all with a clearness which had never blessed her before. How improperly had she been acting by Harriet! How inconsiderate, how indelicate, how irrational, how

11 Gilbert Ryle, "Jane Austen and the Moralists," in *Critical Essays on Jane Austen*, ed. B.C. Southam (London: Routledge, 1987), p. 111.

unfeeling had been her conduct! What blindness, what madness, had led her on!" (E 408). Emma describes herself as both irrational and unfeeling – her mistakes are both intellectual and ethical. Here, as in the case of Elton, she has ascribed the symptoms of attraction to the wrong object for the wrong reasons. And the revelation of Harriet's feelings and misconceptions reveals in turn to Emma that she wants Knightley for herself. Self-knowledge and realization, just as they do for Elizabeth Bennet and Mr. Darcy, come only with humility and a recognition of one's own intellectual and moral shortcomings.

Interestingly, it is this last revelation that finally leads Emma to rein in her imagination and adopt instead what we can only call the empirical method:

> It must be her ardent wish that Harriet might be disappointed; and she hoped, that when able to see . . . [Harriet and Knightley] together again, she might at least be able to ascertain what the chances for it were. – She should see them henceforward with the closest observance; and wretchedly as she had hitherto misunderstood even those she was watching, she did not know how to admit that she could be blinded here. – He was expected back every day. The power of observation would be soon given. (E 416)

Only observation will do now. The matter is urgent enough to prompt Emma to abandon her flights of fancy and outright invention in favor of empiricism.

When the engagement of Frank Churchill and Jane Fairfax is disclosed, Emma regrets both her libelous assumptions and her conduct, acknowledging that "envious feeling" kept her from becoming more closely acquainted with Jane. If only such an acquaintance had existed, Emma

> must have been preserved from the abominable suspicions of an improper attachment [of Jane] to Mr Dixon, which she had not only so foolishly fashioned and harboured herself, but had so unpardonably imparted; an idea which she greatly feared had been made a subject of material distress to . . . Jane's feelings, by the levity or carelessness of Frank Churchill's. Of all the sources of evil surrounding the former, since her coming to Highbury, she was persuaded that she must herself have been the worst. (E 421)

Emma admits, and this is no small part of the self-knowledge mentioned earlier, that it was her envy of Jane and Jane's superior abilities that led her to speculate about an inappropriate relationship between Jane and her friend's husband. This is all very much in line with some of Hume's reflections on envy in the *Treatise*, in particular the reflection that resembling impressions are connected in such a way that one gives rise to the other as, for instance, when envy gives rise to malice (T 283). This certainly seems to be true in Emma's case.

Hume further states of "that envy, which arises from a superiority in others, that 'tis not the great disproportion betwixt ourself and another, which produces it; but on the contrary, our proximity" (T 377). If Jane were a professional musician, Emma wouldn't envy her for a moment. But Emma and Jane are fellow residents of Highbury, whom "birth, abilities, and education had been equally marking" out as potential companions (E 421). They have had roughly the same opportunities to develop their skills. In fact Emma has had more opportunities, since she is much better off. Until the engagement, Jane expected to have to work as a governess, whereas Emma is secure in the expectation of perpetual support. Emma could be expected to have had an equal or greater chance to develop her musical abilities, yet Jane's prove far superior. And that, according to Hume, can make things worse. He speaks of the envy people feel when "they perceive their inferiors approaching or overtaking them in the pursuits of glory or happiness" (T 377). Jane, with less money, less opportunity, fewer advisors and, until the engagement, far less to look forward to, nonetheless winds up with more grace and talent. Her disadvantages must have made her achievements even harder to bear. It is really very much to Emma's credit that she acknowledges her envy, regrets it, and tries to make things right. Emma's growth and change occur on both intellectual and ethical levels. Her envy changes to appreciation and admiration, her tendency to invent becomes a tendency to observe, her confusion becomes clarity. Even more than Elizabeth Bennet, this heroine evolves in terms of both intellect and self-understanding.

Northanger Abbey bears some resemblance to *Emma* when we consider the intellectual evolution of the heroine. It should go without saying that there are also differences. *Northanger Abbey* is a satire, the heroine of which is so young and naive at the outset that her intellectual improvements in the course of the story cannot hope to equal those of an Emma Woodhouse, given the starting point. However, there are a number of noteworthy parallels between Emma and Catherine Morland. Both resort to something resembling outright invention in speculating about the motives, tendencies, and dispositions of others. Both experience shame when the degree of their error in speculating as they do is revealed to them. Both vow to reform these tendencies. Both fall a prey to exactly the same error a second time. Both are corrected at some point by the individual in whom they have a romantic interest, though the degree of exposure differs. Let us first address their unwarranted speculations. *Northanger Abbey*, in that it is a satire, describes speculations that are more outrageous and more exaggerated than any in which Emma Woodhouse would indulge. But Emma is described as an "imaginist." She reflects on Harriet's rescue by Frank in the following terms:

> Could a linguist, could a grammarian, could even a mathematician have seen what she did, have witnessed their appearance together, and heard their history of it, without feeling that circumstances had been at work to make them peculiarly interesting to each other? – How much more must an imaginist, like herself, be on fire with speculation and foresight! – especially with such a groundwork of anticipation as her mind had already made. (E 335)

She is, according to Carol Shields, "in short, a novelist."[12] And while Catherine Morland lacks Emma's originality, she makes up for it by borrowing her speculations from the most lurid gothic novels available.

Inspired by Henry Tilney's teasing story of wild storms and flickering lights and hidden manuscripts, she begins to take the possibility of a genuine mystery altogether too seriously. When the following day reveals a laundry bill rather than the thrilling manuscript she expects, "She felt humbled to the dust. . . . Nothing could now be clearer than the absurdity of her recent fancies. . . . How could she have so imposed on herself? – Heaven forbid that Henry Tilney should ever know her folly!" (NA 173). Here again we have the advent of humility, based this time on the apprehension of one's own credulity. Yet despite her shame and her fear of discovery Catherine begins to harbor baseless (though very exciting) suspicions of General Tilney, imagining that he has murdered his wife or, better yet, that the poor woman "yet lived, shut up for causes unknown, and receiv[ed] from the pitiless hands of her husband coarse food" (NA 188). Catherine convinces herself that Mrs. Tilney languishes in the Abbey, a helpless prisoner of her husband. When she enters the suspected prison and sees that it is no such thing, doubt assails her, "and a shortly succeeding ray of common sense added some bitter emotions of shame" (NA 193). But it is not until Henry Tilney challenges her assumptions that she fully realizes her mistake:

> Catherine was completely awakened. Henry's address . . . had more thoroughly opened her eyes to the extravagance of her late fancies than all their several disappointments had done [i.e., events tended always to disconfirm her suspicions]. Most grievously was she humbled. Most bitterly did she

12   Carol Shields, *Jane Austen* (New York: Viking, 2001), p. 160.

cry. It was not only with herself that she was sunk – but with Henry. Her folly, which now seemed even criminal, was all exposed to him, and he must despise her forever. The liberty which her imagination had dared to take with the character of his father – could he ever forgive it? The absurdity of her curiosity and her fears – could they ever be forgotten? She hated herself more than she could express. (NA 199)

This is a more intense repetition of the same regret and shame that accompanied the realization of Catherine's first mistake. This time, Catherine's self-reproaches have some effect, and her reasoning does appear to undergo improvement as the story progresses.

Consider, for instance, the last unquiet night that Catherine spends at the abbey – a night that is as unquiet as the first (most of which Catherine spent hiding beneath the bedcovers in a state of proper gothic terror), but that differs remarkably in other respects. Austen makes the comparison quite explicit. Again, Catherine is sleepless and agitated. But now the source of her sleeplessness and agitation is "superior in reality and substance" and her distress has a "foundation in fact, her fears in probability." So occupied is she with real evils, that all the things which terrified her on former occasions (the dark, the ancient building, the noises made by the wind) have no effect whatsoever (NA 227). Confronted with authentic difficulties, Catherine dismisses former susceptibilities. Her anxieties on this occasion are perfectly rational, because the beliefs upon which they are based are rational. Fact and probability rule the day, instead of flights of fancy. Catherine may be very unhappy, but she has at least the comfort, cold though it may be, of intellectual and emotional improvement.

Marianne Dashwood's excess of sensibility is amply chronicled in *Sense and Sensibility.* She is yet another heroine whose gradual intellectual and moral growth is depicted. The novel does not recommend sense at the *expense* of sensibility, of course. Many of its less attractive characters (John and Fanny Dashwood, for instance) are described as "cold" and "unfeeling" and condemned on that account (SS 5, 23). If the novel can be taken to issue a recommendation, then it would presumably endorse a combination of the two, one which gave neither a complete ascendency. In any case, the first half of the story finds Marianne "neither reasonable nor candid" (SS 202). She is emotionally self-indulgent: "her sorrows, her joys, could have no moderation" (SS 6). Her sentiments are her moral barometer, but she never bothers to be clear on the facts or to consider anyone else's point of view before acting in accordance with her emotional preferences. She is conveniently convinced that her own pleasure

guarantees the moral permissibility of whatever activity happens to produce it (SS 68). She is intelligent, but unreasonable and clearly inclined
to indulge in wishful thinking. Her misery over Willoughby is in part a
result of these tendencies, especially since she makes wholly inaccurate
inferences about Willoughby's motivations and intentions, which she later
acknowledges were "every day implied, but never professedly declared"
(SS 186).

After she almost dies of an illness she believes to have been partly the
result of her own self-indulgence, Marianne is overwhelmed by regret and
self-abhorrence (SS 346). She is sorry for her former selfishness, and for
the contempt that she has exhibited toward well-intentioned people like
Mrs. Jennings. As in the case of some of Austen's other heroines, her
former pride and contempt have become humility. As in the case of all
those heroines, she intends reform:

> I have laid down my plan, and if I am capable of adhering to it, my feelings
> shall be governed and my temper improved. They shall no longer worry
> others, nor torture myself . . . if I do mix in . . . society, it will be only to
> show that my spirit is humbled, my heart amended, and that I can practise
> the civilities, the lesser duties of life, with gentleness and forbearance. As
> for Willoughby . . . his remembrance can be overcome by no change of
> circumstances or opinions. But it shall be regulated, it shall be checked by
> religion, by reason, by constant employment. (SS 347)

Marianne now speaks of the regulation rather than the suppression of
emotionally evocative recollections. At the end of the book, Austen
makes the point about epistemic improvement crystal clear: "Marianne
Dashwood. . . . was born to discover the falsehood of her own opinions,
and to counteract, by her conduct, her most favourite maxims" (SS 378).
This even has a Humean ring in its rejection of dogma. The pattern of
epistemic improvement, the recognition of error followed by an emotional response of humility, then by judgments (often moral ones) about
oneself, and finally by amendment, is evident here as in the other novels,
and certainly not incompatible with much of what Hume has to say in
the *Treatise*.

I will not attempt to force either *Persuasion* or *Mansfield Park* into
the pattern just described, but it should be noted that each still takes up
as central an epistemic evolution of sorts. While *Mansfield Park*'s Fanny
Price is not guilty of the kinds of mistakes that Marianne or Catherine
or Emma make, she is nonetheless responsible for epistemic errors, albeit
for more subtle ones. Though she makes no overt mistakes, Fanny is guilty

of cognitive errors in her nearly constant fearfulness, which can be readily associated both with a tendency to overestimate risks and with a tendency to underestimate her own ability to cope with them. Indeed, Fanny regularly underestimates herself and her own worth. Her perpetual humility is tied to an undervaluing of her own traits and abilities. In all of Austen's novels, the heroines confront intellectual as well as moral challenges, and the error here seems to amount almost to an inability to value oneself, or an to inability to believe that one possesses valuable traits. It is only once she is forced to confront what she most fears – the disapproval of those whom she respects – that Fanny is likewise forced to acknowledge to herself that *she* is correct, while all whom she believes to be her superiors are mistaken. This occurs several times in the novel, but most tellingly when Fanny refuses Henry Crawford's offer of marriage despite the urging and the eventual displeasure of every person whom she regards as an authority. Fanny, like Anne Elliot, might have acceded to authority if it enjoined her to *refrain* from marrying, even where she loved, and especially if this sacrifice were presented as a benefit to the beloved. She cannot, on the other hand, undertake to marry where she doesn't love at all, no matter what the prompting. She cannot make herself find Henry Crawford admirable or lovable and believes everyone else's judgment in this regard to be mistaken.

This is the reverse of the pattern we have seen at work in *Pride and Prejudice* and in *Emma* (and perhaps even in *Sense and Sensibility*). There, an overestimation of one's discrimination and abilities, a confidence in the accuracy of one's inferences, was followed by a humbling recognition of one's errors. Here, it is a lack of confidence that is succeeded by a conviction of the accuracy of one's opinion that withstands even the opposition of those whose opinions matter most. This represents a real change for Fanny. As has already been indicated in the discussion of Kantian interpretations, Fanny is, prior to this character-building refusal, too prone to question herself, as when she torments herself about her own motives when refusing to be bullied into taking part in the play. Since she finds the whole idea of acting absolutely terrifying, she is insecure about her motives in refusing to participate, fearing that they are actually selfish rather than principled (MP 153). Fanny suspects both the truth of her scruples and her motivation for holding them. Yet when it comes to Henry Crawford's proposal, Fanny's timidity gives way to determination and independence, despite the concerted bullying of Sir Thomas Bertram, of whom she is completely terrified. She is told that she is willful, perverse, and ungrateful – inclined "to that independence of spirit, which prevails so much in modern days . . . and which in young women is offensive and disgusting beyond all common offence" (MP 318). Despite this, she neither gives in nor suspects her own motives. She cries, she apologizes for distressing everyone, but she won't budge an inch. In the face of Sir Thomas' speech about independence, her exhibition of such traits makes even those who find Fanny irritating and priggish want to cheer her on.

So instead of finding humility, of which she possesses a surplus, Fanny finds the courage of her own convictions. The shift is from timidity to courage, from insecurity and uncertainty and lack to confidence to certainty. Like Aristotle, Hume speaks of both pride and humility in terms of "the vice or virtue that lies in their excesses or just proportion" (T 592). Clearly, then, an excess of humility is as bad as, or worse than, an excess of pride, and in as urgent a need of rectification. Indeed, where humility is concerned, Hume appears to think that it is merely an out-ward show of humility that is really expected if one is to be credited with a mean between the extremes. He finds it difficult to believe that any humility which "goes beyond the outside" could really be thought our duty, whereas self-esteem, "if well-conceal'd and well-founded" is an indispensible advantage in any number of respects (T 598). As a matter of fact, it is quite apparent that Hume considers pride entirely preferable to humility:

> Courage, intrepidity, ambition, love of glory, magnanimity, and all the other shining virtues of that kind, have plainly a strong mixture of self-esteem in them, and derive a great part of their merit from that origin. Accordingly we find, that many religious declaimers decry those virtues as purely pagan and natural, and represent to us the excellency of the Christian religion, which places humility in the rank of virtues, and corrects the judgment of the world, and even of philosophers, who so generally admire all the efforts of pride and ambition. Whether this virtue of humility has been rightly under-stood, I shall not pretend to determine. I am content with the concession, that the world naturally esteems a well-regulated pride, which secretly animates our conduct, without breaking out into such indecent expressions of vanity, as many offend the vanity of others. (T 600)

One can see that Hume would prefer an Elizabeth Bennet to a Fanny Price. By present lights, of course, Fanny's judgments concerning the Crawfords, whose pride is in a much healthier condition than her own, seem harsh. But her predictions of their tendencies turn out to be quite accurate. It is perhaps an unattractive trait to be as impervious to charm as Fanny is, but one must give her credit both for discerning the effects of Henry Crawford on his narrow circle at Mansfield (effects to which most of the rest of the family seem entirely oblivious), and for discerning the tendencies of his character as well. If she is biased by her jealousy of Mary, she at least makes an effort not to be, just as she is careful to acknowledge Henry's kindness to William. Fanny, it seems, has come closest to adopting a Humean general point of view, and has triumphed as well over the self-doubt and self-distrust and excessive humility that constitute her own particular intellectual and moral foibles.

In considering the particular epistemic quagmire in which Anne Elliot might find herself immersed, a single issue comes immediately to mind. Anne Elliot defers to Lady Russell rather than thinking and deciding for herself. She seems to ascribe a kind of invincible correctness to authority and makes a decision that leads to seven years of misery by allowing Lady Russell to persuade her to break things off with Wentworth. That is, very much against her own inclinations, she comes to believe Lady Russell when Lady Russell tells her that her engagement is wrong.

> It might yet have been possible to withstand her father's ill-will . . . but Lady Russell, whom she had always loved and relied on, could not, with such steadiness of opinion, and such tenderness of manner, be continually advising her in vain. She was persuaded to believe the engagement a wrong thing: indiscreet, improper, hardly capable of success, and not deserving it. But it was not a merely selfish caution, under which she acted, in putting an end to it. Had she not imagined herself consulting his good, even more than her own, she could hardly have given him up. The belief of being prudent, and self-denying, principally for his advantage, was her chief consolation, under the misery of a parting, a final parting; and every consolation was required, for she had to encounter all the additional pain of opinions, on his side, totally unconvinced and unbending. (P 27–8)

Of course, the conviction that the engagement is wrong is one which Anne, in time, repudiates, as she does the belief in its imprudence. Seven years later, Anne

> thought very differently from what she had been made to think at nineteen. She did not blame Lady Russell, she did not blame herself for having been guided by her; but she felt that were any young person, in similar circumstances, to apply to her for counsel, they would never receive any of such certain immediate wretchedness, such uncertain future good. She was persuaded that under every disadvantage of disapprobation at home, and every anxiety attending his profession . . . she should yet have been a happier woman in maintaining the engagement, than she had been in the sacrifice of it; and this, she fully believed, had the usual share, had even more than the usual share of all such solicitudes and suspense been theirs,

without reference to the actual results of their case, which, as it happened, would have bestowed earlier prosperity than could be reasonably calculated on. (P 29)

The facts justify Wentworth's optimism about early success, and show Lady Russell's distrust of these expectations to have been mistaken. Indeed, Anne would have thought her belief about the wrongness of the engagement mistaken even if Wentworth had *not* proved successful, as the preceding passage indicates.

Anne comes to believe that Lady Russell erred in her advice quite completely. Despite this, Anne thinks that she was not wrong in allowing herself to be guided by someone who stood to her in place of a parent. The guilt that would have been brought on her by refusing to listen to Lady Russell would have been severe. Recollect that a lover, in Austen, would not automatically take precedence over a sibling or a parent or (in this case) a mother figure in either one's affections or one's attention. Anne stresses, however, that she "certainly never should, in any circumstance of tolerable similarity, give such advice" (P 246). This is a puzzling passage. Austen is clearly not advising people to follow blindly the advice of those in authority, nor is she advising them to follow their hearts despite the council of beloved family members. To speculate a little, here is what I think may be at issue. Anne is, at nineteen, trapped between two opinionated and adamant advice-givers, both of whom she loves, both of whom (as she is well aware) are much more informed about matters pertinent to the decision she is about to make than she is herself. Anne has no sources of information about the prudence and practicability of the engagement other than these two people. The question really seems to be one about whom to trust, or about whom to trust more. Wentworth is much younger than Lady Russell, not an acquaintance of long standing, and not beloved for nearly so long a time. Moreover, the engagement is presented by Lady Russell as a harm to him as well as to Anne. From the beginning of the story, of course, Anne is aware that her former belief in the wrongness and imprudence of the engagement was false. But, and I think this is the thrust of Anne's final reflection, at the time the belief was formed *it was justified* even if false. Rejecting Lady Russell's reasons would have involved rejecting an authority hitherto entirely reliable and entirely invested in promoting Anne's well-being. What we have here is the classic epistemic distinction between the truth of a belief and its justification. And, as Humean skepticism would have us put it, no justification places these kinds of beliefs and opinions beyond doubt. So Austen has shown us not only that beliefs with plenty of evidence to support them may still turn out to be false. She has also shown us how it is that we may turn out to have been (epistemically) *correct* or *warranted* in believing something that wasn't true.

There are, I think, some almost purely intellectual virtues for Austen, though my suspicion is that these would center more on good sense than on theoretical wisdom. The intelligence of her protagonists is seen as valuable in its own right, and the evolution and refinement of that intelligence is central in every novel. But, of course, such traits do not exist in isolation from others, and the question of how it is that one will live one's life is, in Austen (or, indeed, any virtue ethicist), a question about the interaction of all one's dispositions. The connections here, many of them causal, between dispositions to reason in particular ways and dispositions to behave in particular ways are intricate and convoluted enough to make us pause and wonder whether certain errors in reasoning are more properly to be regarded as moral errors, or whether ethically problematic attitudes can be put down to misconception rather than outright vice. Austen makes us aware of some of these interconnections (we see many of them in Hume as well, especially when he speaks of how it is moral judgments may be made) but does not weigh in with a solution, content simply to show us what there is.

10

"Lovers," "Friends," and other Endearing Appellations: Marriage in Hume and Austen

All of Austen's novels end happily in matrimony. They focus principally on relationships between people, though not inevitably romantic ones. This is, in fact, what makes them such a fruitful source of observations on human nature. They show us the ethics of everyday life and everyday interactions without heavy-handed ethical posturing or the kind of melodrama that virtually forces the reader to adopt a particular ethical stance. Austen does not issue edicts about the immorality of certain character traits or depict overblown villains. Instead, she describes possible consequences of someone's having the traits in question. That is, Austen observes (as Hume would say) the effects of those traits on their possessor's narrow circle. Given the romantic unions which serve to tie up every plot, however, marriage should be on the agenda of any literary or philosophical investigator who hopes to align Austen's insights with those of some particular philosopher.

It must be acknowledged at the outset, however, that Hume seems a most unlikely match for Austen where attitudes toward marriage are concerned. Few philosophers exhibit less of a taste for the maudlin and romantic. Indeed, Hume says that "whoever dreams of raptures and ecstasies beyond the honey-month is a fool. Even romances themselves, with all their liberty of fiction, are obliged to drop their lovers the very day of their marriage, and find it easier to support the passion for a dozen years under coldness, disdain and difficulties, than a week under possession and security."[1]

Hume nevertheless describes courtship as the "most agreeable scene in life" in the course of his criticism of social arrangements that render courtship impossible, arrangements in which women are "bought and

---

[1] David Hume, "Of Polygamy and Divorces," in *Essays: Moral, Political, and Literary*, ed. Eugene F. Miller (Indianapolis: Liberty Classics, 1987), Variant Readings, p. 628.

sold like the meanest animal."[2] Moreover, the passage about romance is immediately preceded by the claim that, in the happiest marriages, love is consolidated into friendship. Friendship is what makes good marriages possible for Hume, even when they are less than passionate, or when passion has faded. Friendship "is a calm and sedate affection, conducted by reason and cemented by habit; springing from long acquaintance . . . without jealousies and fears." Marriage "chiefly subsists by friendship."[3]

Nor will it do to forget that Austen herself is no friend to the maudlin or unrealistic. Indeed, the character in Austen's work most prone to raptures and ecstasies, the emotionally incontinent Marianne Dashwood, is reformed out of such tendencies well before marriage. She is said to be

> born to overcome an affection formed so late in life as at seventeen, and with no sentiment superior to strong esteem and lively friendship, voluntarily to give her hand to another! – and that other, a man who had suffered no less than herself under the event of a former attachment, whom, two years before, she had considered too old to be married, – and who still sought the constitutional safeguard of a flannel waistcoat! (SS 378)

Unusually for the period during which they wrote, both Hume and Austen portrayed the happiest marriages as relationships between equals. Although he laughs at women's love of power and control, just as Austen does when depicting the domineering Lady Catherine and Mrs. Ferrars, Hume acknowledges that "it is the fault of our sex if the women be so fond of rule . . . if we did not abuse our authority, they would never think it worth while to dispute it." Hume wishes that "there were no pretensions to authority on either side; but that every thing was carried on with perfect equality, as between two equal members of the same body."[4] Indeed, he contends that masculine sovereignty is "a real usurpation, and destroys the nearness of rank, not to say equality, which nature has established between the sexes. We are by nature . . . [women's] lovers, their friends, their patrons: would we willingly exchange such endearing appellations, for the barbarous title of master and tyrant?"[5]

---

[2] Hume, "Of Polygamy and Divorces," p. 184.
[3] Hume, "Of Polygamy and Divorces," p. 189.
[4] David Hume, "Of Love and Marriage," in *Essays: Moral, Political, and Literary*, ed. Eugene F. Miller (Indianapolis: Liberty Classics, 1987), pp. 559–60.
[5] David Hume, "Of Polygamy and Divorces," p. 184. Hume goes on here to utter surprisingly contemporary objections to fundamentalist Islamic practices, as, for example, the prohibition against women's being treated by male physicians: pp. 185–6. The practice of foot binding is also criticized (p. 186), though Hume's search for European counterparts to such examples leaves something to be desired. It may well have been that references to assorted limbs were thought indecent, but a discussion of corsets would have been far more to the point.

Just as authoritarianism and tyranny are deplored by Hume, so petty tyrants, both male and female, are held up for ridicule in Austen's writing. Almost every novel offers a portrait of such a figure. Mrs. Ferrars of *Sense and Sensibility* bullies and blackmails her son. Mrs. Churchill of *Emma* has both her husband and nephew in thrall. Sir Thomas Bertram of *Mansfield Park*, though not a villain, can be authoritarian enough to terrify his niece and offspring – even those who haven't done anything to irritate him. General Tilney of *Northanger Abbey* is a domestic tyrant who makes servants and family equally miserable. Neither he nor Lady Catherine de Bourgh are in "the habit of brooking disappointment" or opposition (PP 356, NA 247). It is said of Lady Catherine that "her manners were dictatorial and insolent." Her reputation for sense and intelligence is derived rather from rank and the opinions of those impressed by rank than from actual abilities. She is both brusque and uncivil, and combines these characteristics with a tendency to interfere whenever possible in the business of others (PP 84). Lady Catherine, of course, prefers to think that her "character has ever been celebrated for its sincerity and frankness" (PP 353).

Hume even mentions the kind of woman who is "very well pleased to take a fool [to husband], that she might govern with the less controul."[6] Jane Austen's *Lady Susan* offers an account of just such a woman. At first the wicked Lady Susan intends an alliance between the wealthy and dimwitted Sir James Martin and her daughter. Sensibly, the daughter takes against him: "And can your Ladyship wonder that she should?" cries an irate relative, "Frederica has an excellent Understanding, and Sir James has none" (MW 288). Not inclined to be wasteful, Lady Susan herself marries Sir James, who, Austen indicates, "may seem to have drawn an harder lot than mere folly merited" (MW 313). Those of Austen's characters who marry idiots are oftener motivated by greed or by the desire for greater independence than by an outright desire to rule. Maria Bertram of *Mansfield Park* weds Mr. Rushworth to conceal a personal romantic disappointment, to take advantage of Rushworth's ample income, and to free herself from the restrictions of her father's household. She marries Rushworth despite the fact that, as her brother reflects, if Rushworth "had not twelve thousand a year, he would be a very stupid fellow" (MP 40). The sensible Charlotte Lucas of *Pride and Prejudice* weds the repellent Mr. Collins, much to the distress of her friend Elizabeth Bennet, who maintains that "Mr. Collins is a conceited, pompous, narrow-minded, silly man" and that "the woman who marries him, cannot have a proper way of thinking." Elizabeth enjoins Jane not to defend Charlotte, a defense

6 Hume "Of Love and Marriage," p. 559.

that would entail changing "the meaning of principle and integrity" and persuading oneself "that selfishness is prudence, and insensibility of danger, security for happiness" (PP 135–6). Maria Bertram and Charlotte Lucas may not have selected silly men to marry with the express intention of controlling them, a proceeding of which we have seen that Hume disapproves, but at least one of them selected a silly husband with the express purpose of controlling his income, something which Hume might consider almost as bad.

As has already been indicated, Hume recommends that, in marriage, there be "no pretensions to authority on either side; but that every thing . . . [be] carried on with perfect equality."[7] With respect to equality and friendship in marriage, Austen's insights are similar to Hume's. Mr. Knightley speaks to Emma Woodhouse of their "having every right that equal worth can give to be happy together" (E 465). Later, as Mrs. Weston reflects on the promise of felicity in that union, she considers that "it was all right, all open, all equal" (E 468). Elizabeth Bennet asserts her equality with Darcy during her confrontation with Lady Catherine: "He is a gentleman; I am a gentleman's daughter; so far we are equal" (PP 356). She later contends that it was her very lack of servility, her unwillingness to treat him as a superior being, that first aroused Darcy's admiration: "the fact is, that you were sick of civility, of deference, of officious attention. You were disgusted with the women who were always speaking and looking and thinking for *your* approbation alone" (PP 380).

Marriages in Austen may even be equalizers – sources of improvement to one of the parties. It is said of Sir Walter Elliot of *Persuasion* that "His good looks and his rank had one fair claim on his attachment; since to them he must have owed a wife of very superior character to any thing deserved by his own." With the exception of the youthful lapse in judgment which we can ascribe to her decision to marry Sir Walter, Lady Elliot is shown to have been a worthy and intelligent person – someone on account of whose influence Sir Walter was restrained in his excesses and improved in his habits: "She had humoured, or softened, or concealed his failings, and promoted his real respectability for seventeen years" (P 4). *Emma*'s Mr. Knightley draws a similar conclusion about the benefits of the married state to Frank Churchill:

> I am very much of his opinion in thinking him likely to be happier than he deserves: but still as he is, beyond a doubt, really attached to Miss Fairfax, and will soon, it may be hoped, have the advantage of being constantly

[7] David Hume, "Of Love and Marriage," pp. 559–60.

with her, I am very ready to believe his character will improve, and acquire from hers the steadiness and delicacy of principle that it wants. (E 448)

Radical inequalities of ability and intellect and moral predisposition between prospective marriage partners are disparaged in Austen. Captain Wentworth of *Persuasion*, for instance, looks askance at the union of Captain Benwick and Louisa Musgrove: "I confess that I do think there is a disparity, too great a disparity, and in a point no less essential than mind. I regard Louisa Musgrove as a very amiable, sweet-tempered girl, and not deficient in understanding, but Benwick is something more. He is a clever man, a reading man; and I confess, that I do consider his attaching himself to her with some surprise" (P 182). Indeed, such inequalities are seen as positively harmful. Fanny Price of *Mansfield Park* fears for Edmund's character, when considering the possibility of his union with Mary Crawford: "God grant that her influence do not make him cease to be respectable!" (MP 424). Emma Woodhouse is horrorstruck by the prospect of a union between Mr. Knightley and Harriet Smith (E 413). Equality of ability as well as of intellectual powers is always to be sought, as well as equality of character.

It is notable, though this can only constitute a brief aside, that Jane Austen makes a few very interesting assumptions about unequal unions. Where the female partner is less endowed with wit and intellect than her husband, the husband is seen to deteriorate as a result of the marriage. We see this in the relationship between Mr. and Mrs. Bennet of *Pride and Prejudice* and in that of Charles and Mary Musgrove of *Persuasion*. Where the woman is superior to her husband, however, she doesn't sink to his level on account of a close association. Instead, she improves her husband, as Lady Elliot improved Sir Walter Elliot, as Jane Fairfax is expected to improve Frank Churchill, and as it is assumed Anne Elliot would have improved Charles Musgrove, had she accepted him. Clearly, then, men are passive and easily swayed, while women not only retain their good qualities in the face of a pernicious influence, but have the stamina and force of character to improve the characters of others.

"We need not be afraid of drawing the marriage-knot, which chiefly subsists by friendship, the closest possible," Hume indicates. "The amity between the persons, where it is solid and sincere, will rather gain by it."[8] Indeed, " 'tis easy to remark that a cordial affection renders all things common among friends; and that married people in particular mutually lose their property, and are unacquainted with the *mine* and *thine*, which are

[8] Hume, "Of Polygamy and Divorces," p. 189.

so necessary, and yet cause such a disturbance in human society" (T 494). This image of common goals and unity is echoed in Austen's depiction of some marriages. As Emma contemplates her marriage to Knightley, "his evils seem to lessen, her own advantages to increase, their mutual good to outweigh every drawback. Such a companion for herself in the periods of anxiety and cheerlessness before her! Such a partner in all those duties and cares to which time must be giving increase of melancholy!" (E 450).

But the best example of the kind of marriage which Hume and Austen find admirable is to be found in Austen's *Persuasion*. The married couple which Anne Elliot most likes and admires, Admiral and Mrs. Croft, are lovers and friends between whom "everything is carried on with perfect equality."[9] Mrs. Croft scolds her brother for speaking "as if women were all fine ladies, instead of rational creatures" (P 70), and always sails with her husband. "As long as we could be together," she tells Mrs. Musgrove, "nothing ever ailed me" (P 71). The Crofts bring with them "their country habit of being almost always together. He was ordered to walk to keep off the gout, and Mrs Croft seemed to go shares with him in everything, and to walk for her life to do him good." Anne is always delighted to observe the Crofts' happy companionship, and to "observe their eagerness of conversation when occasionally forming into a little knot of the navy, Mrs Croft looking as intelligent and keen as any of the officers around her" (P 168). Admiral and Mrs. Croft are friends and partners, and operate in tandem. They even treat the driving of their gig as a cooperative venture. "Anne, with some amusement at their style of driving," regards it as "no bad representation of the general guidance of their affairs" (P 92). Austen's perfect marriage has just the mutuality and equality, friendship and co-operation, that Hume describes. She is no more carried away by raptures than Hume is inclined to wholesale cynicism.

Without resorting to more examples and illustrations, it is at least worth noting that Hume's account of what makes a marriage happy – friendship, unity, no pretensions to authority on the part of either partner, no exploitation, common goals, equality of capacity – provides (as we will see in one other case) the best explanation of the successes and failures of the marriages we see depicted in Austen. Indeed, it seems that the more of these characteristics the marriages in Austen share, the happier they are. And conversely, the more of the aforesaid characteristics a partnership lacks, the more irritating and unpleasant an experience it seems to be. Austen presents us with the fictional premises for which Hume's claims

---

[9] Hume, "Of Love and Marriage," p. 560.

about marital happiness appear to supply the best and most convincing explanation.

Fidelity is a topic closely related to that of marriage and may be thought to herald discord between Hume and Austen. Hume is at least willing to consider the excusability of infidelities "on account of the greatness of the temptation," even though he maintains that the dictates of convention must win the day (T 572). Austen is less inclined to excuse. Yet their views are, ultimately, not dissimilar. In the *Treatise*, Hume describes chastity and modesty as artificial virtues arising from convention, education, and social interest (T 570). In regard to the particular question of the interest of society, Hume points out that the relationship between a mother and her children is far more readily ascertainable than that between them and the father. (We may happily reflect at some other time on the difference DNA tests would make to Hume's attitude.) An assurance of paternity being a necessary condition for contributions to children's upkeep, chastity comes to be required in order to guarantee paternity and, by extension, child support. Modesty is a kind of corollary virtue, serving to reinforce the conviction that a woman is chaste. Social interests lead to the development of social conventions which, given the operation of the principle of sympathy, lend the latter moral force. The "punishment of bad fame or reputation" is imposed by society on transgressors, a punishment that is "inflicted by the world upon surmizes" (T 571). Irritatingly, no one (at least on these grounds) requires men to be chaste or modest. For women, on the other hand, the social consequences of infidelity are dire: "a woman becomes cheap and vulgar, loses her rank, and is exposed to every insult, who is deficient in this particular. The smallest failure is here sufficient to blast her character" (EPM 6.14; pp. 238–9). Hume shows that he is quite aware of the double standard in conventions created by the particular social interests under review: "Men have undoubtedly an implicit notion, that all those ideas of modesty and decency have a regard to generation; since they impose not the same laws, *with the same force*, on the male sex, where the reason takes not place" (T 573). Men have *some* obligation to restrain their appetites, "but as this interest [of civil society in having men restrain said appetites] is weaker than in the case of the female sex, the moral obligation arising from it must be proportionately weaker" (T 573).

It is sometimes mistakenly believed by those who have never bothered to read Austen that her novels would never contain anything so improper as infidelities and adulterous affairs. In fact, *Sense and Sensibility, Pride and Prejudice, Mansfield Park, Persuasion*, and *Lady Susan* all feature such sensational topics. As indicated earlier, Austen was a realist about human relationships, and while disapproval of such conduct is evident in her narrative and in character reactions, a certain cynical awareness of the aforementioned double standard is also present, as is the attribution of that double standard to social convention. At the end of *Mansfield Park*, Austen reflects on the adulterous love affair between Maria Rushworth and Henry Crawford. Maria is, of course, ruined. Henry is not: "That punishment, the public punishment of disgrace, should in a just measure attend his share of the offence is, we know, not one of the barriers which society gives to virtue. In this world the penalty is less equal than could be wished; but without presuming to look forward to a juster appointment hereafter, we may fairly consider a man of sense, like Henry Crawford, to be providing for himself no small portion of vexation and regret" (MP 468).

A few more similarities between Hume and Austen are worth mentioning. Both Hume and Austen observe the importance of appearances where fidelity and chastity are concerned. "There are many particulars in the point of honor," Hume indicates,

> both of men and women, whose violation, when open and avow'd, the world never excuses, but which it is more apt to overlook, when the appearances are sav'd, and the transgression is secret or conceal'd. Even those, who know with equal certainty, that the transgression is committed, pardon it more easily, when the proofs seem in some measure oblique and equivocal, than when they are direct and undeniable. (T 152)

Mansfield Park's Mary Crawford is one such person. She deplores Maria Rushworth's affair with her brother mainly because it became public: "She saw it only as folly, and that folly stamped only by exposure . . . it was the detection, not the offence which she reprobated" (MP 455).

Both Austen and Hume even acknowledge a kind of double standard in which women are overlooked. Hume does this when considering male succession, pointing out that the imagination turns more naturally to the male partner (as the more considerable). "This is the reason why children commonly bear their father's name, and are esteem'd to be of nobler or baser birth, according to *his* family. And though the mother should be possest of a superior spirit and genius to the father, as often happens, the *general rule* prevails, notwithstanding the exception" (T 309). Austen, of course, makes us very aware of the consequences of male succession, since it disadvantages the heroines of both *Pride and Prejudice* and *Sense and Sensibility*. And the general rule of which Hume speaks certainly prevails with Mr. Price of *Mansfield Park* who, not having seen his daughter for several years, ignores her entirely in favor of a son whom he has seen very recently. After he has failed to notice her for some considerable time, Fanny's brother William tries to call her to her father's attention: "With an acknowledgment that he had quite forgot her, Mr. Price now received his daughter; and having given her a cordial hug, and observed that she was grown into a woman, and he supposed would be wanting a husband soon, seemed very much inclined to forget her again" (MP 380). The observation that the male is generally regarded as more significant or considerable than the female is certainly illustrated by the attitude of Mr. Price. It is heartening, however, that both Hume and Austen tell us such assumptions are often false.

Hume concludes his essay on love and marriage by taking liberties with Plato's account of the origin of love. The perfect restoration of the Androgyne, he suggests, is most likely to be achieved by consulting both Pleasure and Care (the respective affiliates of Love and Hymen) and obtaining their consent to the conjunction. When this procedure is followed, "the human race enjoy the same happiness as in their primaeval state. The seam is scarce perceived that joins the two beings; but both of them combine to form but one perfect and happy creature."[10] This description is reminiscent of the cooperative union of Admiral and Mrs. Croft, which has already been canvassed. However, as a final point of interest, it is worth considering the implication which Hume's story has for the identification of misalliances. Care is concerned with prospects of futurity, pleasure with gratification only. Both must be satisfied for a happy marriage. Neither is in itself sufficient. Austen concurs. Marrying for money is deplored as much as marrying without prospects. Fanny Price, for instance, considered "how wretched and unpardonable, how hopeless and how wicked it was, to marry without affection" (MP 324). Mary Crawford's reflections on a married friend tend to confirm Fanny in her views and suggest that mercenary motives in marriage do not have the best results: "I look upon the Frasers to be about as unhappy as most other married people. And yet it was a most desirable match for Janet at the time. . . . She could not do otherwise than accept him, for he was rich, and she had nothing." As it happened, Mr. Fraser had expected rather more of steadiness and affection from his wife than he got, and she was saddled with rather more expectations from him than she had bargained for. Neither was very pleased with the arrangement (MP 361). One ought, however, to give Lady Susan the final word on exclusively mercenary marriages: "My dear Alicia, of what a mistake were you guilty in marrying a man of his age! – just old

10 Hume, "Of Love and Marriage," p. 562.

enough to be formal, ungovernable, and to have the gout – too old to be agreeable, and too young to die" (MW 298).

On the other hand, marriages without prospects are equally to be deplored in Austen. Elopements are frowned upon, as are entirely imprudent marriages. Mrs. Price of *Mansfield Park* "married, in the common phrase, to disoblige her family, and by fixing on a lieutenant of marines, without education, fortune, or connexions, did it very thoroughly." To avoid the unpleasantness of familial objections to the match, Mrs. Price reserved the announcement of her marriage until after the wedding had actually taken place. Outraged objections and even more outraged replies resulted in a breach between the Prices and Bertrams until, after eleven years,

> Mrs. Price could no longer afford to cherish pride or resentment, or to lose one connexion that might possibly assist her. A large and still increasing family, an husband disabled for active service, but not the less equal to company and good liquor, and a very small income to supply their wants, made her eager to regain the friends she had so carelessly sacrificed; and she addressed Lady Bertram in a letter which spoke so much contrition and despondence, such a superfluity of children, and such a want of almost everything else, as could not but dispose them all to a reconciliation. (MP 4–5)

Austen clearly suggests here that marriages are to be delayed until sufficient comforts are available. Elinor Dashwood and Edward Ferrars of *Sense and Sensibility* reason thus:

> They were brought together by mutual affection, with the warmest approbation of their real friends; their intimate knowledge of each other seemed to make their happiness certain, and they only wanted something to live upon. Edward had two thousand pounds, and Elinor one, which, with Delaford living, was all that they could call their own . . . and they were neither of them quite enough in love to think that three hundred and fifty pounds a year would supply them with the comforts of life. (SS 369)

That is, both care and affection are crucial factors in a decision to marry.

The parallels which have been noted in this chapter make it evident that there is a resemblance between those of Hume's and Austen's endorsements, prohibitions, and assumptions that have to do with marriage and fidelity. Some of these similarities are simply the result of their being of the same era. They were both acute observers of the social scene and of their fellows. Naturally, if they reported what they observed, one would expect more than a passing resemblance in what they wrote. But it is also clear that there is a deeper similarity – in the value placed on equality and autonomy, on the awareness (albeit not wholly critical) of double standards, on the regulation of sentiment. These correspondences suggest that an investigation into the existence of further points of commonality will bear fruit.

11
Hume and Austen on Pride

Hume and Austen often use the words "pride" and "vanity" interchangeably. Roughly, both terms are used to signify a habitual pleasure
taken in some action, trait or object exhibited by, possessed by, or
associated with oneself. It should not surprise us to find that the terms
are used to refer both to a characteristic feeling – an emotional response
to a particular kind of stimulus – and to dispositions or tendencies of the
character associated with this feeling. Differences in usage of the two terms
sometimes emerge, though the distinction is not consistent. When the
terms appear to differ in meaning, "vanity" is a bit more likely to signify
a vice than is "pride" and is sometimes, though not invariably, characterized as a concern to elicit admiration from all and sundry. "Pride
relates more to our opinion of ourselves," says Mary Bennet of *Pride and
Prejudice*, and "vanity to what we would have others think of us" (PP 20).
However, the purpose of this chapter is to see which dispositions fit within
the compass of these terms as they are actually used in Hume and Austen,
not to draw distinctions which neither of them feels inclined to make
across the board. No speculations as to the meaning of these terms beyond
those canvassed by Hume and Austen will be offered.

It should first be noted that neither Austen nor Hume condemns pride
categorically as a vice. Both acknowledge a sense in which there can be
a proper pleasure in one's achievements, abilities, and condition – what
Hume sometimes calls self-respect. There is also, for both, a sense in which
pride may be inappropriate, as when, in feeling unjustified contempt for
a person, we are "elevated with the view of one below us" (T 390) or
when we estimate our talents or capacities unrealistically. Hume considers
both pride and humility in terms of "the vice or virtue that lies in their
excesses or just proportion," sounding positively Aristotelian as he does
so. "An excessive pride or over-weening conceit of ourselves is always

esteem'd vicious, and is universally hated; as modesty, or a just sense of our weakness, is esteem'd virtuous, and procures the good will of everyone" (T 310–11).

Still, Hume reminds us that the same "qualities and circumstances, which are the causes of pride and self-esteem, are also the causes of vanity or the desire of reputation" (T 332). That is, proper and improper pride have the same causes. Pride, it should be remembered, is an indirect passion. The object of this passion is always the self. Its cause is an idea or thought concerning a quality that is esteemed valuable and inheres in some subject associated with the self. That is, the causes of sentiments like pride involve those qualities which are thought to be instantiated in something affiliated with the object of the emotion. The cause of the passion, an idea, is also the cause of a sensation of pain or pleasure (T 285). This sensation is intimately connected to the quality (pleasure, in the case of pride) which the thought ascribes to a subject (which must be something related to or associated with the self). Consider pride in the ownership of a beautiful house. Hume indicates that

> the quality [beauty is used here as an example of an agreeable quality] which operates on the passion [pride], produces separately an impression resembling it [pleasure]; the subject [a house] to which the quality adheres [i.e., beautiful house], is related to self [i.e., *my* beautiful house], the object of the passion: No wonder the whole cause, consisting of a quality and a subject, does so unavoidably give rise to the passion. (T 289)

However, this does not mean that we can only feel pride on our own account. "Nothing causes greater vanity than any shining quality in our relations; as nothing mortifies us more than their vice or infamy" (T 338). This certainly holds true in Austen. Few are likely to be more mortified than Elizabeth Bennet at the conduct of her flighty sister Lydia or than Edmund Bertram at the illicit affair engaged in by his sister Maria. Each misbehaving sibling is taken to have disgraced her family. Grim prognostications are issued about the outer darkness into which the reputations of all family members will be cast by the behavior of Lydia and Maria. In the same way that the vices of one's relatives elicit a kind of global family embarrassment, one's vanity expands to encompass the accomplishments of one's relations. Mrs. Norris is in perpetual raptures over the perfections of the very niece whose misconduct will later embarrass her nearest and dearest: "Maria was indeed the pride and delight of them all perfectly faultless – an angel" (MP 39). Equally affectionate but much more honest, is Mrs. Norris' neighbor Mrs. Grant, who "having never been able to glory in beauty of her own . . . thoroughly enjoyed the power of being proud of her sister's," and Sir Thomas Bertram, who had "a desire of seeing all that were connected with him in situations of respectability" (MP 42, 4). Indeed, the affiliation between the self and the object of the emotion may be more tenuous still. Consider the kind of sympathetic pride an entire village might experience in tandem with a beloved inhabitant: Mr. Weston "saw his son every year in London and was proud of him; and his fond report of him as a very fine young man had made Highbury feel a sort of pride in him too" (E 17).

As will become evident, the causes of pride are various indeed, according to Hume, who remarks on the "vast variety of subjects, on which they may be plac'd. Every valuable quality of the mind, whether of the imagination, judgment, memory or disposition; wit, good-sense, learning, courage, justice, integrity; all these are the cause of pride; and their opposites of humility" (T 279). Jane Austen's novels confirm this. Emma Woodhouse and Elizabeth Bennet pride themselves on their perceptiveness, Mary Bennet on her learning, and Mr. Collins on his humility, though some are less justified than others in doing so. "Nor are these passions confin'd to the mind," Hume continues, "but extend their view to the body likewise. A man may be proud of his beauty, strength, agility, good mien, address in dancing, riding, and of his dexterity in any manual business or manufacture" (T 279). Again we find examples in Austen. Sir Walter Elliot of *Persuasion* is more than a little vain of his appearance, John Thorpe of *Northanger Abbey* brags about his riding, Emma Woodhouse is pleased to be as good a dancer as Jane Fairfax. "But this is not all," Hume indicates. "The passions looking farther, comprehend whatever objects are in the least ally'd or related to us. Our country, family, children, relations, riches, houses, gardens, horses, dogs, cloaths; any of these may become a cause either of pride or of humility" (T 278–9). Since there are literally hundreds of examples in Austen's work of cases such as these, given that vanity is one of her chief sources of amusement, an attempt will be made to focus on those examples which evidence the most striking similarities in ethical insight between Hume and Austen.

As has been indicated, Hume does not regard pride as inevitably vicious. On the whole, he maintains, vanity is not so bad. For one thing, it is sometimes the only reward for and the only spur to virtuous behavior.[1] Surely we will not begrudge someone a little cheerful moral smugness when there is not much else to prompt an act of kindness, especially when

[1]   David Hume, "Idea of a Perfect Commonwealth," in *Essays: Moral, Political, and Literary*, ed. Eugene F. Miller (Indianapolis: Liberty Classics, 1987), p. 525.

it is an act which might have remained undone without the inducement of self-satisfaction. "Vanity is . . . closely allied to virtue. . . . to love the fame of laudable actions approaches . . . near the love of laudable actions for their own sake."[2] Further, there are purely practical considerations to keep in mind: "'twoud be more advantageous to over-rate our merit than to form ideas of it, below its just standard," for fortune is hardly likely to favor the self-effacing or the diffident instead of the bold (T 597).

Many kinds of pride are perfectly proper, even desirable, if we take Austen's novels as a recommendation. First, there is a pride that constitutes a resistance to being humbled before others, that prevents one from advertising one's weaknesses, errors, and vulnerabilities. As Hume repeatedly points out, humility is painful and disagreeable, just as pride is agreeable. Clearly then, there is reason to avoid exposing one's mistakes and embarrassing susceptibilities, if only to prevent additional unpleasant sensations that could occur as the result of sympathy with the potentially negative reactions of others, as Hume might suggest. For instance, Elinor Dashwood urges upon her sister Marianne a "reasonable and laudable pride." That is, she urges Marianne to attempt to restrain her display of wretchedness at Willoughby's desertion and to exercise a modicum of self-control (SS 189). Interestingly, and very much in line with Hume's remark about pride in its just proportion, this particular sort of pride is not inevitably virtuous, since it can prove excessive.

Both Maria Bertram of *Mansfield Park* and Captain Wentworth of *Persuasion* are rejected by the respective objects of their affection, and subsequently suffer from a pride fueled by resentment, a pride that leads them to conceal or to deny their feelings about being spurned. The prolonged absence of Henry Crawford convinces Maria, rightly, that he was never serious in his advances. She therefore decides to marry a man whom she does not in the least care for to be "safe from the possibility of giving Crawford the triumph of governing her actions, and destroying her prospects." She "retire[s] in proud resolve," refusing to allow her father to extricate her from the unfortunate engagement (SS 201). "Henry Crawford had destroyed her happiness, but he should not know that he had done it; he should not destroy her credit, her appearance, her prosperity too. He should not have to think of her as pining in the retirement of Mansfield for *him*, rejecting Sotherton and London, independence and splendour for *his* sake" (SS 202). The results of Maria's pride are, as we know, disastrous.

---

[2] David Hume, "Of the Dignity or Meanness of Human Nature," in *Essays: Moral, Political, and Literary*, ed. Eugene F. Miller (Indianapolis: Liberty Classics, 1987), p. 86.

Captain Wentworth, on the other hand, manages to conquer his pride and resentment, though only after several years have passed. At first "the attempts of angry pride" lead him to court a woman with whom he could not be happy (P 242). Fearing he has attached her, he begins to "deplore the pride, the folly, the madness of resentment, which had kept him from trying to regain" his first love (P 242). "Six years of separation might have been spared" had Wentworth not been "proud, too proud to ask again" (P 247). He and Anne are happily united at last, but only because his pride has finally given way to an inclination to be happy.

Proper pride, however, usually involves more than a defense against externally imposed humility or self exposure. Hume indicates that "a genuine and hearty pride, or self-esteem, if well conceal'd and well founded, is essential to the character of a man of honour" (T 599). The antecedent of the conditional suggests that we are not permitted to lord it over those we consider inferior, and that pride is not considered appropriate when it is based on a mistaken apprehension of our merits, talents, or actions. However, "there is no quality of the mind," Hume continues, "which is more indispensibly requisite to procure the esteem and approbation of mankind," when it *is* well founded. For instance,

> there are certain deferences and mutual submissions, which custom requires of the different ranks of men towards each other; and whoever exceeds in this particular, if thro' interest, is accus'd of meanness; if thro' ignorance, of simplicity. Tis necessary, therefore, to know our rank and station in the world, whether it be fix'd by our birth, fortune, employments, talents or reputation. Tis necessary to feel the sentiment and passion of pride in conformity to it, and to regulate our actions accordingly. (T 599)

This isn't a defense of snobbery on account of class or wealth against which, as we will see eventually, Hume inveighs. It is more a question of being able to negotiate one's way within one's social milieu without arousing either enmity or contempt, of knowing how much one can expect from one's fellows and how much they can expect from oneself, and of knowing how much is too much or not enough.

In this context, we can consider Elizabeth Bennet's ultimate happy certainty of Darcy's having "no improper pride" (PP 376), or the "bright proud eye" of Captain Wentworth, which speaks of taste, discrimination, and a strong sense of what is his due (P 62). There is Emma's mild indictment of Frank Churchill, who has nothing of the pride or reserve of the wealthy snobs by whom he was raised: "Of pride, indeed, there was, perhaps, scarcely enough; his indifference to a confusion of rank, bordered too much on inelegance of mind" (E 198). And there is Emma's much more justifiable surprise at the ability of Jane Fairfax to tolerate the company of superficial and unpleasant intellectual inferiors: "She could not have believed it possible that the taste or the pride of Miss Fairfax could endure such society and friendship as the Vicarage had to offer" (E 285). To venture a further example, we may consider how seriously Emma Woodhouse takes her social responsibilities. She dreads meeting the repellent Elton, whose advances she has but recently repulsed, yet nonetheless pays a conventional call on his new wife. This is presented more or less as a requirement of rank and of the kind of pride that Hume describes. "Emma had feelings, less of curiosity than of pride or propriety, to make her resolve on not being the last to pay her respects" (E 270).

Of course, proper pride – the properest kind of pride – can simply involve not allowing oneself to be contemptible. Anne Elliot of *Persuasion* sets her own proper pride at odds with her family's sycophantic attentions to distant relatives of higher rank: "She had hoped for better things from their high ideas of their own situation in life, and was reduced to form a wish which she had never foreseen – a wish that they had more pride" (P 148). "I suppose . . . I have more pride than any of you," she tells her cousin, "but I confess it does vex me, that we should be so solicitous to have the relationship acknowledged, which we may be sure is a matter of perfect indifference to them. . . . I am certainly proud, too proud to enjoy a welcome which depends entirely upon place" (P 151).

Improper pride, on the other hand, is something of which both Hume and Austen offer acerbic critiques. As in the case of proper pride, there are several kinds of pride or vanity which might be termed improper or vicious. First, there is the kind of pride which Hume would not consider "well founded," a pride that is based on an unwarranted overestimation of one's merits. We see just such an overestimation in the conceit exhibited by Mr. Collins and Lady Catherine de Bourgh of *Pride and Prejudice*. Collins sets his merits so high, that he is incapable of understanding why a young woman would reject his proposal of marriage. Moreover, he exhibits a kind of false piety, an unrealistic conception of his duties as clergyman. He appears to believe that being a clergyman confers upon him the right to dictate proper conduct to others in areas of life having nothing whatsoever to do with religion, and certainly has an inflated notion as regards his own importance in being a member of the clergy: "I consider the clerical office as equal in point of dignity with the highest rank in the kingdom" (PP 97). Elizabeth Bennet finds this maddening and is ashamed even to be distantly related to him. Hume's writings contain more than one reflection on the hypocritical character of the clergy, and sometimes dwell in particular on their "great facility in entering into the views of . . . princes" and despots,[3] something that irresistibly reminds us of Mr. Collins' instantaneous, sycophantic adoption of any view put forward by his patron, Lady Catherine, whose condescension he is wont to extol at every opportunity. Lady Catherine is a petty tyrant whose own estimation of her merits is grossly inflated. She is even, as has already been indicated, vain of skills that she is certain she *would* have possessed, had she bothered to try and acquire them (PP 173).

The next species of pride to come under review will be the sort of pride that elevates the self at another's expense, that involves either unwarranted contempt toward someone else or unwarranted assumptions about one's own superiority. The bare fact that one's pride is accompanied by contempt is not enough to make it improper pride, of course. As Hume points out, in considering the qualities of another, we may regard them as they are in themselves, compare them to our own traits, or both. "The good qualities of others, from the first point of view, produce love; from the second, humility; and from the third, respect; which is a mixture of these two passions. Their bad qualities, after the same manner, cause either hatred, or pride, or contempt, according to the light in which we survey them" (T 389–90). So there is an admixture of pride in contempt (or humility in respect), which arises from "a tacit comparison of the person contemn'd or respected with ourselves. . . . These passions, therefore, arise from our observing the proportion; that is, from a comparison" (T 390).

So contempt, as well as pride, isn't inevitably vicious. Feelings of contempt can be quite appropriate, as when Captain Wentworth takes the true measure of Anne's relations, and she cannot but notice and sympathize with his disdain: "Anne caught his eye, saw his cheeks glow, and his mouth form itself into a momentary expression of contempt" (P 227). Mrs. Dashwood's contempt for the money-grubbing Fanny Dashwood in equally understandable: "The contempt which she had, very early in their acquaintance, felt for her daughter-in-law, was very much increased by the farther knowledge of her character, which half a year's residence in her family afforded" (SS 14).

It also appears to follow (both from Hume's observations and from Austen's depictions) that the proud and contemptuous will be held to have erred insofar as they have been mistaken about the badness of the other person's qualities or the preferability of their own, or insofar as they have illegitimately generalized from the superiority or inferiority of a

---

[3] David Hume, "Of the Parties of Great Britain," in *Essays: Moral, Political, and Literary*, ed. Eugene F. Miller (Indianapolis: Liberty Classics, 1987), p. 66.

single quality over the entire character. There are clear examples in Austen of wholly inappropriate contempt and pride. Consider Emma's inability to resist mocking poor Miss Bates for her interminable chatter. Knightley rebukes Emma for her contemptuous treatment of someone worthy of respect:

> It was badly done, indeed! You, whom she had known from an infant, whom she had seen grow up from a period when her notice was an honour, to have you now, in thoughtless spirits, and the pride of the moment, laugh at her, humble her . . . and before others, many of whom (certainly some) would be entirely guided by your treatment of her. (E 375)

One of Jane Austen's most believable depictions of personal shame and guilt (more convincing by far than Willoughby's declarations of regret in *Sense and Sensibility*, but then it is not clear how convincing those are meant to be) is her description of Emma's distress at her own conduct: "How could she have been so . . . so cruel to Miss Bates! How could she have exposed herself to such ill opinion in any one she valued!" (E 376).

Part of what makes this so believable, of course, is Emma's concern about what others think of her. Hume speaks of the influence of sympathy "on pride and humility, when these passions arise from praise and blame, from reputation and infamy" (T 320). We take pride in possessing those qualities we're praised for. We sympathize with people who admire some trait of ours until we've become co-admirers of our own trait and have come to treat their judgment about us as a kind of argument for our superiority (T 320). For just such reasons are infamous flirts like Austen's Henry Crawford driven to elicit admiration at all costs, even to their own eventual detriment. They simply cannot resist being found irresistible. But the same kind of process is involved in the case of less pleasant reactions like shame. When Emma considers herself in the same light in which she appears to someone who *disapproves* of her conduct, she suffers an additional pain, followed by shame and self-contempt. She enters into Knightley's disapprobation and into his judgment. There is the added irony of Emma's having committed the same error for which she held Miss Bates in contempt: self-indulgently saying more than she should have done and producing thereby an effect she didn't intend to create. That Emma was motivated by contempt makes this more contemptible rather than less. Her distress is very convincing.

Hume points out that excessive conceit on an individual's part causes uneasiness in everyone else, especially as that conceit presents observers with a disagreeable comparison in which they come out the losers. After

176 Hume and Austen on Pride

all, "'tis our own pride, which makes us so much displeas'd with the pride of other people; and that vanity becomes insupportable to us merely because we are vain" (T 596). When we look for a demonstration of this in Austen, there is no dearth of examples. For instance, Darcy "was discovered to be proud, to be above his company, and above being pleased; and not all his large estate in Derbyshire could then save him from having a most forbidding, disagreeable countenance, and being unworthy to be compared with his friend" (PP 10). It is Elizabeth's injured pride, ably assisted by Wickham's lies, that leads to her initial unflattering and inaccurate assessment of Darcy's character. Indeed, Elizabeth's pride is injured by the pride of Darcy, who at first considers her to be beneath his notice: "I could easily forgive *his* pride," she points out, "if he had not mortified *mine*" (PP 20). When various false allegations concerning Darcy are exposed for what they are, Elizabeth realizes that she has labored under a misapprehension. She blames her vanity and overconfidence in her own abilities for that mistaken assessment: "I, who have valued myself on my abilities! who have . . . gratified my vanity, in useless or blameable distrust. – How humiliating is this discovery. . . . vanity . . . has been my folly" (PP 208).

Unjustified contempt for others is also often tied to the kind of pride that is accompanied by insolence or arrogance. Characters exhibiting these traits emerge repeatedly in Austen. *Emma*'s Mr. Weston says of Mrs. Churchill that "her pride is arrogance and insolence" (E 310), a description that also applies to Lady Catherine de Bourgh of *Pride and Prejudice*. Frank Churchill speaks of the Eltons' "insolence of imaginary superiority" when he considers the air of unwarranted familiarity they adopt with Jane Fairfax (E 442). Catherine Morland reflects on the fact that there is no "apology that could atone for the abruptness, the rudeness, nay, the insolence of" General Tilney's behavior in summarily dismissing her from Northanger (NA 226). Mrs. Ferrars' "cold insolence" toward Elinor distresses Marianne, who knows that it is prompted by her disapproval of Edward Ferrars' interest in Elinor (SS 236). Emma Woodhouse reflects in regret on her own overestimation of her abilities and on what she terms arrogance: "With insufferable vanity had she believed herself in the secret of every body's feelings; with unpardonable arrogance proposed to arrange every body's destiny" (E 412–13).

Those, "who have an ill-grounded conceit of themselves," says Hume, "are for ever making comparisons" [between their own qualities and possessions and those of others], nor have they any other method of supporting their vanity. A man of sense and merit is pleas'd with himself, independent of all foreign considerations: But a fool must always find some person, that is more foolish, in order to keep himself in good humour with his own parts and understanding. (T 596)

Thus Sir Walter and Elizabeth Elliot feel the loss of the sycophantic Mrs. Clay, despite their shock at her liaison with Mr. Elliot. "They had their great cousins, to be sure, to resort to for comfort; but they must long feel that to flatter and follow others, without being flattered and followed in turn, is but a state of half enjoyment" (P 272).

It should be remembered that, according to both Hume and Austen, one may take pride in one's possessions as well as one's personal merits and accomplishments (real or imagined). External objects acquire a relation to ourselves, Hume indicates, and the "same object causes a greater or smaller degree of pride, not only in proportion to the encrease or decrease of its qualities, but also to the distance or nearness of the relation" (T 306). We can, in fact, be vain of any object that bears a relation to us. And if the ownership of anything that gives pleasure by its utility, its beauty or its novelty can produce pride, then the *power* or means to acquire those things – namely wealth – should give rise to pride as well (T 311). Hume reflects on pride in wealth and rank, and the kind of economic and class snobbery that go with them: "As we are proud of riches in ourselves," says Hume, "so to satisfy our vanity we desire that every one, who has any connexion with us, shou'd likewise be possest of them, and are asham'd of any one that is mean or poor among our friends and relations. For this reason we remove the poor as far from us as possible" (T 307).

Consider, against this backdrop, Sir Walter Elliot's outrage at Anne's choosing to spend the evening with her old schoolfellow Mrs. Smith instead of joining the family in their attentions to Lady Dalrymple:

> . . . and who is Miss Anne Elliot to be visiting in Westgate Buildings? – A Mrs. Smith. A widow Mrs. Smith. And who was her husband? One of the five thousand Mr. Smiths whose names are to be met with everywhere. . . . Upon my word, Miss Anne Elliot, you have the most extraordinary taste! Everything that revolts other people, low company, paltry rooms . . . disgusting associations are inviting to you. . . . A poor widow, barely able to live . . . a mere Mrs. Smith, an everyday Mrs. Smith, of all people and all names in the world, to be the chosen friend of Miss Anne Elliot, and to be preferred by her to her own family connections among the nobility of England and Ireland! (P 157–8)

Just as Sir Walter is ashamed of any affiliation with poverty, so *Northanger Abbey*'s John Thorpe feeds his vanity by ascribing a fictitious wealth to his connections. Flattered by General Tilney's request for information about

Catherine Morland and her family, and laboring under the conviction that Catherine will accept his proposals and his sister those of Catherine's brother, Thorpe's "vanity induced him to represent the family as yet more wealthy than his vanity and avarice had made him believe them. With whomsoever he was, or was likely to be connected, his own consequence always required that theirs should be great, and as his intimacy with any acquaintance grew, so regularly grew their fortune. The expectations of his friend Morland, therefore, from the first overrated, had ever since his introduction to Isabella been gradually increasing; and by merely adding twice as much for the grandeur of the moment, by doubling what he chose to think the amount of Mr Morland's preferment, trebling his private fortune, bestowing a rich aunt, and sinking half the children, he was able to represent the whole family to the general in a most respectable light" (NA 244–5). The financial advantages of Catherine Morland, whom Thorpe hopes to marry, are even more outrageously augmented. The severance of Thorpe's connection with the Morlands has exactly the reverse effect on their fortunes. Once Thorpe has been roundly rejected, his estimations of the family's wealth and respectability are sunk as far below what they in fact are as they were formerly exaggerated. He informs the General that the family is necessitous, "numerous too almost beyond example . . . aiming at a style of life which their fortune could not warrant; seeking to better themselves by wealthy connections; a forward, bragging, scheming race" (T 246).

What will constitute wealth or plenty for a given person is determined by comparison, according to Hume. "What is an immense fortune for a private gentleman is beggary for a prince. . . . When a man has either been acustom'd to a more splendid way of living, or thinks himself intitled to it by his birth and quality, every thing below is disagreeable and even shameful" (T 323). Nothing illustrates this better than the disinclination of Sir Walter Elliot and his daughter Elizabeth to restrain their expenditures, even though they have been living beyond their means for years. "The Kellynch property was good, but not equal to Sir Walter's apprehension of the state required in its possessor," and they search in vain for any prospect "of lessening their expenses without compromising their dignity, or relinquishing their comforts in a way not to be borne. . . . There was only a small part of his estate that Sir Walter could dispose of; but had every acre been alienable, it would have made no difference. He had condescended to mortgage as far as he had the power, but he would never condescend to sell. No; he would never disgrace his name so far" (P 9–10). To curtail lavish living entails a loss of dignity and pride, something that failing to pay one's debts apparently does not.

There are even closer parallels between Hume and Austen. For instance, Hume goes on to point out that

Every thing belonging to a vain man is the best that is any where to be found. His houses, equipage, furniture, cloaths, horses, hounds, excel all others in his conceit; and 'tis easy to observe, that from the least advantage in any of these, he draws a new subject of pride and vanity. His wine, if you'll believe him, has a finer flavour than any other; his cookery is more exquisite; his table more orderly; his servants more expert; the air, in which he lives, more healthful; the soil he cultivates more fertile; his fruits ripen earlier and to greater perfection. . . . (T 310–11)

Compare to this the professions of Anne Elliot's father and sister as they welcome her to their lodgings in Bath: "Their house was undoubtedly the best in Camden Place; their drawing-rooms had many decided advantages over all the others which they had either seen or heard of; and the superiority was not less in the style of fitting up, or the taste of the furniture" (P 137).

There are, of course, a great many other examples of improper pride in Austen. General Tilney of *Northanger Abbey*, Lady Catherine de Bourgh of *Pride and Prejudice*, and Mrs. Ferrars and her daughter of *Sense and Sensibility* all exhibit an inappropriate pride on account of rank and wealth and all get their comeuppance in the pages of Austen's work. The officious, interfering ways of Mrs. Norris of *Mansfield Park* and of Lady Catherine fall under the heading of Hume's latter observations on pride. It is not necessarily their wine which excels all others, but their judgment and their capacity to organize everyone else's life. Emma Woodhouse suffers from a less pernicious form of the same affliction.

One final example involves a connection that might be found between pride and indolence. Indolence itself might become an object of pride, for instance. Someone could have been a contender, his friends might claim on his behalf, were it not for his dislike of business or his lack of personal ambition. "And this a man sometimes may make even a subject of vanity; tho' with the air of confessing a fault: Because he may think, that his incapacity for business implies much more noble qualities; such as a philosophical spirit, a fine taste, a delicate wit, or a relish for pleasure and society" (T 587).

A very similar reversal occurs in *Pride and Prejudice*. Bingley is a sloppy, impatient correspondent: "he leaves out half his words and blots the rest." He assumes an attitude of humility and, very much with the air of confessing a fault, agrees that his letters seldom convey any ideas at all to his correspondents. He explains, however, that this failure is due to the fact that his ideas flow so rapidly. Darcy takes issue with this.

Nothing is more deceitful . . . than the appearance of humility. It is often only . . . an indirect boast. . . . you are really proud of your defects in writing, because you consider them as proceeding from a rapidity of thought and carelessness of execution, which if not estimable, you think at least highly interesting. The power of doing any thing with quickness is always much prized by the possessor, and often without any attention to the imperfection of the performance. (PP 48–9)

Here again, a flaw which ought to inspire humility is, by means of an air of humility, neatly converted into a subject of vanity. Hume and Austen think very much alike on vice and virtue and human nature, at least where the topic of pride is concerned. Notice also that the preceding examples neatly demonstrate Hume's stipulation that the contrary passions of pride and humility have the same object, the self, and that "according as our idea of ourself is more or less advantageous, we feel either of those opposite affections, and are elated by pride or dejected with humility" (T 277). When an apparent incapacity (to write coherently, or to bring oneself to attend to business) is presumed a symptom of "valuable qualities of the mind," humility is transformed into pride. Interestingly, the mental qualities in question are the kinds of intellectual traits that resist a concrete demonstration which would require effort of their possessor, whereas the flaws that are conveniently taken to signal their existence require just such an effort for their rectification.

The cases presented by Hume and Austen, respectively, provide us with a partial demonstration of Hume's analysis of the indirect passions and their underlying psychological mechanisms, and may thus be thought to provide clarification of their function and of the relevant concepts. First, a quality, which is given a positive or negative valence, inheres in a subject associated with the self, for the self is always the object of pride or humility. Qualities such as "a philosophical spirit" or "fine taste" or "rapidity of thought" have a positive valence. When associated with the self, they give rise to pride, just as they can give rise to love when associated with another, when that other person is the object of emotion. The test cases show us how a shift from a negative to a positive valence in the quality associated with the self (a shift away from the negatively valenced qualities of sloppiness and laziness to positively valenced intellectual qualities) necessitates a shift in the passion that is felt, a shift from humility to pride. It is not, strictly speaking, that individuals can be proud of what they perceive as flaws, but rather that they mine the flaws for evidence of estimable traits (with what commitment to accuracy, we should not inquire too closely), without the idea of which pride would not be possible.

12

Hume and Austen on Jealousy, Envy, Malice, and the Principle of Comparison

Both Hume and Austen sometimes use the words "jealousy" and "envy" interchangeably, as does the occasional dictionary. For that reason, and because work in the philosophy of emotion suggests such a course, we will assume that "jealous" may sometimes refer to a case of envy, but not vice versa. This is not always how Hume and Austen employ the two terms, but is roughly applicable to their usage. The word "envy" is generally taken to refer to pain or discontent aroused by another's good fortune. As Hume puts it, "envy is excited by the present enjoyment of another, which by comparison diminishes our idea of our own" (T 377). That is, another's happiness or good fortune makes us acutely aware of what we lack, and this awareness is painful. It may but will not always involve rivalry or arouse resentment.

But before venturing more fully into Humean territory, let us consider some recent analyses of the emotion. Such an investigation is particularly pressing, since approaches of this kind have already been used in interpretations of Austen. Jealousy, according to Robert C. Roberts, paradigmatically involves attachments.[1] As Daniel Farrell points out, the clearest cases of jealousy are cases where a person "not only wants to be favored in some way over . . . [another], but also believes that until now . . . she *has* been so favored."[2] When jealous, Farrell continues, one is held to be bothered in any of several ways by the very fact that one is (as one believes) not favored as one wants to be favored. The emotion arises in a three-party context. Consider an example from *Mansfield Park*. Fanny Price is jealous of Mary Crawford because the latter is favored by Edmund as Fanny

---

[1] Robert C. Roberts, *Emotions: An Essay in Aid of Moral Psychology* (Cambridge: Cambridge University Press, 2003), p. 257.
[2] Daniel Farrell, "Jealousy," *Philosophical Review* 89 (1980): 527–59, 530.

herself wishes to be (and until recently, was) favored. Roberts puts it this way (initials are replaced in what follows with character names): "It is very important [to Fanny] that [Edmund] have a special attachment to [her], but [Mary] is taking (has taken, may take) [Edmund's] special attachment away from [Fanny] with [Edmund's] responsible collusion or consent, with a result of" Mary's having Edmund's special attachment for herself.[3] This kind of core case occurs frequently in the emotional lives of Austen's characters, and a good deal less frequently in Hume's discussions.

Let us consider how a philosopher named Thomas Williams applies Farrell's account to Austen, tracking once more the initial example of *Mansfield Park*. Williams does not precisely offer an Aristotelian reading of Austen, but considers her as a virtue ethicist in the Aristotelian tradition, one whose astuteness and delicacy of perception are taken to give her the edge over most other virtue theorists. Williams' talk of Aristotle and virtue theory leads us to expect the scaffolding upon which he rests his case to be predominantly Aristotelian.

Williams is principally interested in Austen's portrayal of vices. He wishes, he indicates, to reflect on "some of the specifics of Austen's vision of the virtuous life" and intends to show that Austen, as a moralist, provides "quite as good a jumping-off point for reflection on the nitty-gritty of the virtuous life as Aristotle" does.[4] Jealousy and envy are the candidate vices, although neither is initially defined in terms which make it the deviation from some mean. Given the latter point, Williams' approach is not particularly Aristotelian. An Aristotelian approach might, for instance, treat *vicious* jealousy as an excessive reaction to others receiving favors to which one is also, but not exclusively, entitled. In such a case, a deficiency might involve a failure to recognize or assert one's own entitlement rather than a tendency to deny the entitlements of others. This, in any event, might be how one could begin to consider jealousy in an Aristotelian light. Williams does not do it. He takes note of such issues as more or less justified senses of entitlement (to another's attention) on the part of jealous people,[5] but this is not his focus in providing us with an account of jealousy. Instead, he makes use of the account of jealousy by Daniel Farrell, which treats it as an emotion rather than a behavioral disposition, offering an analysis of the circumstances in which it might arise and a catalog of the desires and

[3]   Roberts, *Emotions*, p. 261.
[4]   Thomas Williams, "Moral Vice, Cognitive Virtue: Austen on Jealousy and Envy," *Philosophy and Literature* 27.1 (2003): 223–30, at 223.
[5]   Williams, "Moral Vice, Cognitive Virtue," 225.

cognitions which might be involved. In fact, I entirely agree with Williams' contention that Farrell's "analysis of emotion is not only correct in the main but is also reflected in the usage of careful speakers of English."[6]

However, while approaches of this kind provide considerable insight into moral psychology, I cannot think that such an analysis provides much insight into virtue ethics, whether Aristotelian or generic. If jealousy is an emotion proper, it is difficult to see how *it* (rather than, say, the manner in which we deal with or control or succumb to it) would fit neatly into the ranks of the Aristotelian vices. Williams says that:

> Fanny Price is habitually jealous; that is, she can be counted on to feel jealousy in a broad range of situations. She is prone to interpret situations in a way that calls forth jealous feelings. (Note that her habitual jealousy can be described with equal accuracy as a cognitive and as an affective disposition: she is disposed to see situations as being of a kind that characteristically arouses jealousy, and she is disposed to feel jealousy in her reactions to the situations so interpreted.)[7]

But if jealousy is merely a disposition to feel and think in certain ways, it isn't a *behavioral* disposition at all. One would at least like to hear more of an analogy to Aristotle on anger – perhaps a discussion of how jealousy can be felt to the right degree toward the right object in appropriate situations. Williams mentions a couple of ways in which jealousy can become vicious – when it turns into envy or is based upon false beliefs about entitlement – but no part of this discussion is considered in light of dispositions or of the Aristotelian mean or of the most generic approaches to virtue ethics. Further, it is not clear that the application of Farrell's analysis to Austen's Fanny Price yields the conclusion with which Williams presents us.

I will take issue with the contention that Fanny's alienation can be linked, as Williams claims, to *habitual* jealousy or to any claim which draws a necessary connection between the outsider status which Williams emphasizes in his article and such a disposition. (Incidentally, I think that Williams' contrast between insiders and outsiders, especially in regard to Emma Woodhouse and Fanny Price, is both perceptive and promising. I just don't think it has anything to do with jealousy.) Fanny Price is, of course, jealous of Mary Crawford, in that Mary is the recipient of Edmund Bertram's attention and affection – attention that was formerly devoted to Fanny.

---

[6] Williams, "Moral Vice, Cognitive Virtue," 230 n. 2.
[7] Williams, "Moral Vice, Cognitive Virtue," 227.

184 Jealousy, Envy and Malice in Austen and Hume

Fanny's jealousy exactly fits Farrell's schema, for she wants to be favored over Mary and has, until the advent of the riding lessons, been so favored in the past.[8] It is not this, but the claim of habitual jealousy that I wish to challenge. Fanny's jealousy is described as not merely episodic but habitual, something that is put down to the insecurity of her position, her lack of confidence, and her diffidence. Recollect that when jealous, one is held by Farrell to be bothered in any of several ways by the very fact that one is not favored in the way one wants to be, and that this fits neatly as a description of Fanny's jealousy of Mary. But Mary is the *only* individual of whom Fanny is jealous, and jealousy does not seem in any other way to stem from Fanny's outsider status in the Bertram household. No one else's favor is ever lost to another, for Fanny is seldom favored. Nor does Fanny seem to wish to win the attention of the others – it is usually something she shrinks from. She is embarrassed and awkward when made much of or courted.

Fanny would like to be needed and loved and valued by the Bertrams (as she finally is, when people come to their senses at the end of the novel). However, her desire to be needed and depended on isn't connected to what Julia, Maria, and Tom Bertram have. They don't have what she wants, being feckless people whom no sensible parent would depend on for long. The affection Fanny craves isn't something she feels entitled to, since she is inevitably modest in any estimate of her own merits. Never having had a firm place in the elder Bertram's affections, Fanny cannot feel herself displaced in them, as Farrell's account seems to require. More to the point, I think, it is not the fact of Sir Thomas Bertram's loving his children that bothers Fanny. It is his not loving her. The Bertram offspring have something Fanny wants, but their being favored over her is not the issue. If Fanny were jealous of Maria and Julia, she would be bothered by their being loved *instead of her.* But that isn't the case at all. Fanny would happily settle for Sir Thomas loving everyone indiscriminately – she doesn't want to be specially favored by anyone but Edmund.

I think that Fanny feels a kind of non-pernicious envy toward insiders like Maria and Julia. She doesn't resent their happiness or their enjoyment of the elder Bertrams' affections. She'd just like them to be fond of her as well. Call this Envy Lite. It is not quite the darker Humean envy in the course of which one is pained by another's pleasure. Rather, it is wanting what another has got, but not wishing to get it by some transference from the other's possession to one's own, as might be the case with jealousy. Fanny is intelligent enough to see what she is missing as

8   Farrell, "Jealousy," 530.

an outsider, but generous enough not to wish to deprive others of something whose value she acknowledges. Hers is an envy that doesn't wish for the eradication of another's happiness, but only for the alleviation of personal pain. The desire to be favored over others arises when Mary Crawford begins to appropriate Edmund's attentions. I wouldn't call this a jealous *disposition*, exactly, when there is only a single object whose favor one craves, and only a single person who arouses the emotion.

I agree with Williams that jealousy sometimes makes Fanny acute. One of Austen's greatest gifts is her ability to expose poor moral reasoning and pathetic moral rationalization for what they are. In *Mansfield Park* we sometimes see this through Fanny's eyes, as when she observes with dismay Edmund's repeated attempts to demonstrate that Mary Crawford's feelings and intentions never correspond to her words and actions. One cannot read much of Austen without encountering some satirical depiction of self-aggrandizement or self-justification. The exposure of moral foibles and vices is her specialty. The problem is that Williams hasn't shown us any. It is never Fanny's jealousy that is censured as a vice in Austen.

To be fair, this was not Williams' central aim. That aim was to show how jealousy can act as an aid to discernment in Austen. I must admit, however, that I am not sure how much really convincing evidence there is for a general claim of this kind. For every Fanny Price and Mr. Knightley who are sensitized and made acute by jealousy, there is a Mary Musgrove who is as dimwitted as they are perceptive. And neither Fanny nor Mr. Knightley is uniformly acute. Note, for instance, the jealous Knightley's shifts in attitude toward Frank Churchill:

> He had found [Emma] . . . agitated and low. Frank Churchill was a villain. He heard her declare that she had never loved him. Frank Churchill's character was not so desperate. She was his own Emma, by hand and word, when they returned into the house; and if he could have thought of Frank Churchill then, he might have deemed him a very good sort of fellow. (E 433)

This is one of Mr. Knightley's more appealing moments, but jealousy does *not* appear to be "an aid to practical discernment," in this context at least.

Further, those cases in Austen in which it is clear that jealousy is really being depicted as a vice rather than a forgivable psychological condition militate outright against the claim that it is an aid to practical discernment. Jealousy and envy really are vices in the unattractive Mary Musgrove of *Persuasion*, who has only to hear of someone else's good fortune in

186 Jealousy, Envy and Malice in Austen and Hume

order to feel herself excluded or ill-used in not having been a party to it. Yet Mary is the least discerning character in the novel, and Austen has a great deal of fun at her expense by laughing at her inability to be honest with herself about her own motives. There is hardly a case to be made here for jealousy as an aid to discernment if that jealousy is to be characterized as a vice. Even if Austen's strength as a writer is to be found in her perspicacious depiction of virtues and vices, and I think it is, I do not believe Williams has provided an adequate explanation of how Austen has managed it.

The preceding has not exhausted relevant accounts of jealousy, however. There is another use of "jealous," as Roberts concedes, which denotes what one feels when one is losing out to a rival and one's vanity is wounded. He believes that this involves the kind of case in which a subject's central concern is specifically the concern "for personal worth rather than for reciprocation of an attachment."[9] Roberts ultimately rejects this reading of "jealous" as unsatisfying, but we will have to concede the relevance of such a notion of rivalrous envy to the current project, simply because Hume and Austen both sometimes employ the term "jealousy" in just this way. In this context, of course, it isn't just that someone else has something that one wants, but that one has been beaten in a competition, something which suggests an inferiority that cannot be rectified without the degradation of the other individual. A sense of entitlement to the desideratum and of resentment of the rival plays a frequent though not inevitable role.

Let us review briefly the ways in which Hume in particular employs the term "jealousy." Quite frequently, he simply uses it as a synonym for "watchfulness" or "suspicion" or even "distrust," as when he speaks of a monarch's jealousy of his subjects.[10] On other occasions, the intention is clearly to signify envious rivalry, as in the whole of the essay "Of the Jealousy of Trade," in which all trading states are said to consider others as their rivals.[11] (This is not to say that a certain amount of watchfulness and suspicion cannot be associated with envious rivalry as well.) Neither of these uses of the term need signify anything concerning attachments. The connection with personal worth is sometimes metaphorical at best, as when personal worth is transformed into national advantage in talking

9 Roberts, *Emotion*, p. 263.
10 See, for instance, "Of the Liberty of the Press," in Eugene F. Miller, ed., *Essays: Moral, Political, and Literary* (Indianapolis: Liberty Classics, 1987), pp. 9–13.
11 In *Essays: Moral, Political, and Literary*, ed. Eugene F. Miller (Indianapolis: Liberty Classics, 1987), pp. 327–31.

of trade rivalries. There are also, of course, some fairly standard references in Hume to jealousy in love. He indicates, for instance, that "too much jealousy extinguishes love,"[12] although he also maintains that without some share of jealousy "the agreeable affection of love has difficulty to subsist in its full force and violence."[13] The latter reminds us irresistibly of Jane Austen's Lady Susan reflecting on her lover: "Poor fellow! he is quite distracted by Jealousy, which I am not sorry for, as I know no better support of Love" (MW 269). Hume comes closest to the Roberts model in "Of Polygamy and Divorces," when he inveighs against societies that deny women rights and enforce complete masculine sovereignty. He inquires sarcastically about the advantages of adopting such policies:

> in what capacity shall we gain by this inhuman proceeding? As lovers, or as husbands? The lover, is totally annihilated; and courtship, the most agreeable scene in life, can no longer have place, where women have not the free disposal of themselves, but are bought and sold, like the meanest animal. The husband is as little a gainer, having found the admirable secret of extinguishing every part of love, except its jealousy. No rose without its thorn; but he must be a foolish wretch indeed, that throws away the rose and preserves only the thorn.[14]

Even here, it is rather obvious that Hume is speaking of jealousy as envious rivalry in the sense that Roberts rejects, for the kind of tyrant of whom Hume specifically disapproves is just the kind of person for whom attachment is a secondary matter, since the denial of choice precludes the possibility of attachment's being a necessary feature of the equation.

The most fruitful source of comparison will therefore lead us to focus on discussions of what Roberts would call envy, since both Hume and Austen use the term "jealous" for the most part to signify envious rivalry. Returning once more to Hume's central definition, envy involves experiencing pain on account of the contemplation of the pleasure of another. But another person's involvement isn't necessary to a demonstration of Hume's basic assumptions about how the principle of comparison works. It should not surprise us, Hume indicates, that the happiness and misery of others may on occasion arouse in us the opposite sentiments. We are more accustomed to this kind of reversal than we may think. For

---

[12]   David Hume, "Of Tragedy," in *Essays: Moral, Political, and Literary*, ed. Eugene F. Miller (Indianapolis: Liberty Classics, 1987), p. 225.

[13]   Hume, "Of Tragedy," p. 222.

[14]   David Hume, "Of Polygamy and Divorces," in *Essays: Moral, Political, and Literary*, ed. Eugene F. Miller (Indianapolis: Liberty Classics, 1987), p. 184.

instance, we often experience such a reversal of sentiments when we contemplate our past experiences. "Thus the prospect of past pain is agreeable, when we are satisfy'd with our present condition; as on the other hand our past pleasures give us uneasiness, when we enjoy nothing at present equal to them" (T 376). There are distinct parallels in Austen to the preceding. "When pain is over," says Anne Elliot to Captain Wentworth, "the remembrance of it often becomes a pleasure" (P 184). And Hume's assumption provides as precise a description as one could wish of Mrs. Dashwood's and Marianne's sad reflections on the family's bygone happy days at Norland. "A continuance in a place where everything reminded her of former delight," exacerbates the distress of the former at the death of her husband (SS 8). The principle of comparison is at work in more ways than one when Mrs. Dashwood and her daughters arrive at Barton cottage: "In comparison of Norland, it was poor and small indeed! – but the tears which recollection [of former wealth and security] called forth as they entered the house were soon banished" (SS 28).

Hume says that proximity is (at least usually) a necessary, though not a sufficient, condition for envy. "That envy, which arises from a superiority in others" isn't produced by the extent of the disproportion between oneself and another, but by "our proximity" (T 377). Roughly, the more it makes sense to think of the individual who possesses the superior qualities as a genuine rival, the more likely one is to envy that person:

> A common soldier bears no such envy to his general as to his sergeant or corporal; nor does an eminent writer meet with so great jealousy in common hackney scriblers, as in authors, that more nearly approach him. It may, indeed, be thought, that the greater the disproportion is, the greater must be the uneasiness from the comparison. But we may consider on the other hand, that the great disproportion cuts off the relation, and either keeps us from comparing ourselves with what is remote from us, or diminishes the effects of the comparison. (T 377–8)

Similarly, envious rivalry (sometimes referred to as jealousy) in Jane Austen's novels usually occurs between members of roughly the same class, with key differences in the central romantic cases often involving a surfeit of wealth or charm (or both) on the one side and a surfeit of character on the other. Mary Crawford is wealthy and charming, but Fanny is good. Frank Churchill is rich and entertaining, but Knightley has character. Mr. Elliot is well off and connected, but Captain Wentworth has an openness and honesty which Elliot entirely lacks. Wealth can be allied with character, of course: Brandon's property and rectitude ultimately trump

Willoughby's charm. Darcy's *proper* pride, whether or not Pemberley is weighed in the balance, triumphs over the personable Wickham's plausible lies. This is part of what makes Austen's novels so compelling. The key differences between romantic rivals almost always involve differences of the mind and the character: differences in intelligence or emotional accessibility or personal ethics. In *Sense and Sensibility*, neither Lucy nor Elinor is well off and both are despised by Edward Ferrars' autocratic parent, but Lucy is a thoroughgoing egoist while Elinor is both compassionate and fair. Nor are such rivalries restricted to romance. Isabella Thorpe and Eleanor Tilney are, in a manner of speaking, rivals for Catherine Moreland's friendship, in the acquisition of which intelligence and honesty win out over flattery.

Of course, as has been indicated, proximity of merit is not *sufficient* for envy. "A poet is not apt to envy a philosopher, or a poet of a different kind, of a different nation, or of a different age" (T 378). The mind is said to find itself the most uneasy "when superiority is conjoin'd with other relations" (T 379). In Austen, these relations can involve cultivation, refinement, and education (though they do not always do so, as has been indicated above). Thus, Anne Elliot cannot envy the Musgroves, though she "always contemplated them as some of the happiest creatures of her acquaintance." Though superior in spirits, they are not so in all respects and "Anne would not have given up her own more elegant and cultivated mind for all their enjoyments; and envied them nothing but that seemingly perfect . . . good-humoured mutual affection, of which she had know so little herself with her own sisters" (P 41). Here the difference in education and cultivation make comparison, and therefore envy, difficult.

To reiterate, Hume describes envy as being "excited by some present enjoyment of another, which by comparison diminishes our own" (T 377). Austen has a gift for describing characters whose besetting sin is envy. One of these is Mary Musgrove of *Persuasion*. In *Persuasion*, the prospect of other people's happiness makes Mary miserable, at least whenever she is not to partake of it herself. Missing dinner with her husband's parents when her child is injured does not distress her until her husband announces his intention of attending. His prospect of pleasure casts her circumstances at home in the worst possible light by comparison: "So here he is to go away and enjoy himself, and because I am the poor mother, I am not to be allowed to stir – and yet, I am sure, I am more unfit than anybody else to be about the child" (P 56). Her instant irritated response when she discovers that relatives may be visiting Bath is to make a comparison in which her own circumstances are rated the more unfortunate:

"Upon my word, I shall be pretty well off, when you are all gone away to be happy at Bath!" (P 42). Their prospective happiness is a source of grievance.

Mary Musgrove is always engaged in a kind of envious rivalry with others. She is accused of "jealousy of rank" by her sister-in-law, who points out that Mary insists (unnecessarily and inconsiderately, it is implied) on taking precedence over her mother-in-law on all possible occasions (P 46). Any task or position or activity in which she is *not* asked to participate is the preferable one to which she believes herself entitled, especially if someone else is asked instead. "The jealous and ill-judging claims of Mary" are decried when she insists on staying to nurse Louisa Musgrove, mainly because Anne (infinitely more competent) is asked to take on the task (P 115).

Hume pays particular attention to

> that species of envy, which men feel, when they perceive their inferiors approaching or overtaking them in the pursuit of glory or happiness. . . . A man, who compares himself to his inferior, receives a pleasure from the comparison: And when the inferiority decreases by the elevation of the inferior, what shou'd only have been a decrease of pleasure, becomes a real pain, by new comparison with its preceding condition. (T 377)

This is distinctly reminiscent of Mrs. Norris's real irritation at any improvement in the treatment or consideration of Fanny Price at Mansfield Park. "People are never respected," Mrs. Norris pointedly informs Fanny, "when they step out of their proper sphere" (MP 220).

Fanny's inferior status is impressed upon her from the beginning of her stay with the Bertrams, since it is the intention of her relations always "to make her remember that she is not a *Miss Bertram.*" It is believed that Fanny and the Bertram girls "cannot be equals. Their rank, fortune, rights, and expectations will always be different" (MP 11). Fanny is ensconced at Mansfield in the role of poor relation. And Mrs. Norris is determined to perpetuate that state of affairs. The purchase of a mare so as to enable Fanny to ride is bitterly opposed by Mrs. Norris: "She could not but consider it as absolutely unnecessary, and even improper, that Fanny should have a regular lady's horse of her own in the style of her cousins. She was sure that Sir Thomas had never intended it" (MP 36). Mrs. Norris objects to Fanny's being included in an excursion to Sotherton. She is "intent on lessening her niece's pleasure . . . as much as possible" when Fanny is invited to dine with the Grants, warning her that she ought not to be fancying that the invitation is meant as any particular compliment to *you*; the compliment is intended to your uncle and aunt, and me. Mrs. Grant thinks it a civility due to *us* to take a little notice of you . . . and you may be very certain, that if your cousin Julia had been at home, you would not have been asked at all. (MP 219–20)

Mrs. Norris is almost beside herself with irritation at a carriage's being called to take Fanny to that dinner. Her objections proving ineffective, she comforts herself with the thought that the carriage was sent for "upon Edmund's account" (MP 222). When Sir Thomas decides to hold a dance for Fanny and her brother, Mrs. Norris's "surprise and vexation required some minutes silence to be settled into composure" (MP 253). When Crawford asks Fanny to marry him, even though Fanny rejects him, Mrs. Norris is furious. She "would have grudged such an elevation to one whom she had always been trying to depress" (MP 332). This behavior continues throughout the novel.

It is Hume's account of envy which best explains this sequence of reactions to any improvement in Fanny's fortunes on the part of Mrs. Norris, and it is Austen's utterly believable account that makes Hume's claims all the more convincing. In fact, Austen has furnished us with a detailed depiction of events and psychological reactions for which Hume's account of envy, together with the principle of comparison, provides by far the best explanation, if not the only possible one. Consider other possible explanations for Mrs. Norris' conduct. Anger or vengefulness? Fanny is the most unprovoking person imaginable. Simple mean-spiritedness? Mrs. Norris doesn't evidence meanness toward others indiscriminately. Mania? Depression? A permanent bad mood? All of these explanations are unsatisfying, and most of them are simple-minded. They don't explain what it is about Fanny's initial inferior position or her elevation that seems to prompt reactions from Mrs. Norris. The case Austen has set before us practically invites us to make an inference to the best explanation. It sets the stage for an inductive argument the conclusion of which will affirm Hume's analysis.

Hume also observes that self-interest can lead us to take pleasure in a partner's or associate's happiness and to find her distress painful. Likewise, self-interest can prompt us to be pained by the pleasure of a rival, and to be pleased by his distress, "in short the same contrariety of sentiments as arises from comparison and malice." Hume further notes that "'tis impossible to do good to others, from whatever motive, without feeling some touches of kindness and good-will towards 'em; as the injuries we do, not only cause hatred in the person, who suffers them, but even

192 Jealousy, Envy and Malice in Austen and Hume

in ourselves" (T 384). The remark about injuries is perfectly echoed in Willoughby's "where I have most injured, I can least forgive" (SS 332), as well as explaining Austen's contention that Mrs. Norris of *Mansfield Park* "disliked Fanny [Price], because she had neglected her" (MP 332). It is also not unrelated to an acerbic remark made about Elinor's sister-in-law Fanny of *Sense and Sensibility*: "when people are determined on a mode of conduct which they know to be wrong, they feel injured by the expectation of anything better from them" (SS 248–9). Fanny's determination to slight her husband's sisters makes her resent them all the more, as does any claim she feels they may have on her, however legitimate that claim might be.

As we typically don't judge objects on the basis of their intrinsic value, "but form our notions of them from a comparison with other objects;" says Hume, "it follows that according as we observe a greater or less share of happiness or misery in others, we must make an estimate of our own, and feel a consequent pain or pleasure. The misery of another gives us a more lively idea of our happiness, and his happiness of our misery" (T 375). This doesn't always involve our being happy *that* another suffers of course. It may merely involve taking a certain satisfaction in the reflection that we do not suffer in that way, as a particularly apt example from *Sense and Sensibility* makes clear. Austen's Colonel Brandon clearly agrees that the misery of another gives us a more lively idea of our happiness. This becomes apparent when he informs Elinor Dashwood of Willoughby's conduct toward his ward Eliza, in the hope that the contemplation of Eliza's fate will make Elinor's sister Marianne more sanguine about her own. Marianne is, of course, desperately unhappy about Willoughby's having deserted her and proposed marriage to another woman. Colonel Brandon hopes to mitigate her misery by relating the tale of his seduced and abandoned ward:

[Marianne] . . . may now, and hereafter doubtless *will*, turn with gratitude towards her own condition, when she compares it with that of my poor Eliza; when she considers the wretched and hopeless situation of this poor girl, and pictures her to herself, with an affection for him . . . still as strong as her own, and with a mind tormented by self-reproach, which must attend her through life. Surely this comparison must have its use with her. She will feel her own sufferings to be nothing: they proceed from no misconduct, and can bring no disgrace. On the contrary, every friend must be made still more her friend by them . . . . had I not seriously . . . believed it might be of service, might lessen her regrets, I would not have suffered myself to trouble you. . . . (SS 210)

Hume's principle of comparison is very much in evidence in this passage, as are his ideas about how it functions in human nature. What is particularly interesting about the passage is that it *predicts* (correctly, as it eventually transpires) the effects of the psychological mechanism Hume describes. This is not merely a description of the principle of comparison and its psychological functions. It is a description of the therapeutic deployment of that principle. The tale of Eliza's misery is regarded as a panacea or restorative sufficient to mitigate Marianne's unhappiness. The text invites us to entertain causal assumptions and to form expectations on their basis. In a manner of speaking, it permits us to examine the concept of comparison as a psychological activity and to speculate on the possible effects of that activity in a way that brings Hume's assumptions to life.

We come now to malice. The difference between envy and malice, according to Hume, "lies in this, that envy is excited by some present enjoyment of another, which by comparison diminishes our idea of our own: Whereas malice is the unprovok'd desire of producing evil to another, in order to reap a pleasure from the comparison" (T 377). There is usually at least one example of apparently unmitigated malice in each of Austen's novels, very frequently preceded by a case of comparison which produces the reverse effect, a case in which the individual has been bested in competition, for instance, or one-upped in some other way. These examples fall somewhere in the gray area between malice and vengeance. "If our ill-will to another proceed from any harm or injury," Hume states, "it is not, properly speaking, malice, but revenge" (T 369). An example of revenge in Austen might involve Maria Rushworth's vindictive mother-in-law, who exposes Maria's affair.

> The servant of Mrs Rushworth, the mother, had exposure in her power, and supported by her mistress, was not to be silenced. [Maria and Mrs. Rushworth] . . . even in the short time they had been together, had disagreed; and the bitterness of the elder against her daughter-in-law might perhaps arise almost as much from the personal disrespect with which she had herself been treated as from sensibility for her son. (MP 451)

Here there have clearly been injuries, so Hume would classify this as revenge.

But there are any number of borderline cases. People often consider things harmful or injurious when they are not, choose to blame people for situations which they did nothing to create, and resent another's thoughts or beliefs rather than his or her conduct. Are the individuals who are resented in these circumstances to be regarded as the objects of vengeance or the objects of malice? After all, joy is taken in their miseries and sufferings "without any offense or injury on their part" (T 372). What if the desire to produce evil is really unprovoked by inappropriate conduct, even though the one who desires to produce it *believes* (falsely) there is provocation? I am not entirely sure of the answer, but suspect that vengefulness which rests on shaky grounds must prove at least a second cousin of malice for Hume. We will proceed on this assumption in considering other examples from Austen.

Mr. and Mrs. Elton collude in an attempt to humiliate Emma's friend Harriet and derive considerable amusement from her discomfiture prior to her fortuitous rescue by Knightley (E 327–329). But their malice is the direct result of Emma's belief, one Elton finds intolerably insulting, that Elton regarded Harriet as a worthy marital prospect. Diminished by Emma's and Harriet's assumption of his comparative worth, he tries to diminish Harriet. In *Sense and Sensibility*, Willoughby's wife-to-be Sophia, "jealous as the devil," discovers Marianne's letters to Willoughby and dictates a reply intended to wound Marianne to the heart. Clearly this begins with a case of envious rivalry. Sophia is made wretched by the contents of the letter, which reveals the extent of Willoughby's infatuation, but then "her passion – her malice – At all events it must be appeased" (SS 327–8). Willoughby is bullied into writing his wife's words in his own hand. Envy leads directly to malice. Marianne has never knowingly committed any offense against Sophia (nor is she favored by Willoughby any longer), so it seems a little inappropriate to claim that Sophia's behavior is vengeful rather than malicious.

Examples such as these tend to confirm Hume's contention that "All resembling impressions are connected together, and no sooner one arises than the rest immediately follow. Grief and disappointment give rise to anger, anger to envy, envy to malice, and malice to grief again, till the whole circle be compleated" (T 283). The transition from envy to malice that Austen illustrates is just what Hume has led us to expect.

13
Indolence and Industry in Hume and Austen

We can expect to find sloth or indolence featured in any catalog of western vices, from surveys of undesirable deportment to lists of deadly sins. David Hume and Jane Austen make the negative characterization of indolence interesting by going beyond familiar (and no doubt accurate) objections to laziness as injurious to the self and antithetical to ambitions and life projects. Hume and Austen both acknowledge this, but go further. Both regard indolence as being in some measure (albeit a small measure) necessary for happiness and in larger measures destructive of it. Both see in indolence the disuse and possible attrition of the faculties of the mind. Both are also inclined, though this is more evident in Austen's novels, to hold us responsible for the consequences of indolence and inaction, even when those consequences are the consequences of the actions of moral agents other than ourselves. Indolence is sometimes presented as the reason for someone's failure to intervene in a process with a morally significant outcome. That is, we see in Austen, and sometimes in Hume, precursors of a contemporary debate in which it is asked whether moral culpability is just as ascribable to a failure to intervene, to our merely allowing something to happen, as it is to an action which produces the relevant effect.

Hume draws a contrast between industry and indolence in the same way that he does "valour and cowardice, humanity and brutality, wisdom and folly."[1] That is, he clearly regards indolence primarily as a vice, falling in the same general category as do cowardice and brutality. Yet he also maintains that "human happiness . . . seems to consist in three ingredients:

---

[1] David Hume, "Of National Characters," in *Essays: Moral, Political, and Literary*, ed. Eugene F. Miller (Indianapolis: Liberty Classics, 1987), p. 203.

action, pleasure, and indolence."[2] No one of these can fall entirely into abeyance without disrupting a balance of elements requisite for happiness. Indolence is not so much believed to be in itself pleasant or enjoyable as it is to be a necessary condition for enjoyment. It is, "like sleep . . . requisite as an indulgence to the weakness of human nature, which cannot support an uninterrupted course of business or pleasure."[3] We hear something similar from Austen in *Emma*, when she reflects on the exploitation and on the overwork of women in poverty. For instance, Austen considers the prospective plight of Jane Fairfax in the "governess-trade," the distinction of which from the slave trade is, according to Jane, "widely different certainly as to the guilt of those who carry it on; but as to the greater misery of the victims, I do not know where it lies" (E 300–1). Industry is a friend of virtue, indeed a virtue itself, in both Hume and Austen. Exhaustion and abject servitude are not.

In continuing to make his point about the necessity of repose, Hume indicates that "that quick march of the spirits, which takes a man from himself, and chiefly gives satisfaction, does in the end exhaust the mind, and requires some intervals of repose, which, though agreeable for a moment, yet, if prolonged, beget a languor and lethargy, that destroys all enjoyment." Indolence is only agreeable when it "succeeds to labour, and recruits the spirits, exhausted by too much application and fatigue."[4] We cannot do without rest in our physical or our mental lives. It is rest that makes activity possible.

This is evident in Austen as well, especially when she reflects on the life of the mind. Take for instance, Edmund Bertram, worn out with civility, who longs for a little tranquil silence at the ball: "His mind was fagged, and her happiness sprung from being the friend with whom it could find repose" (MP 278). Cares must be tranquillized *before* we can, as both Hume and Austen put it, be taken out of ourselves: "Here's harmony!" says Fanny about a view of the starry heavens,

> here's repose! . . . . Here's what may tranquillise every care, and lift the heart to rapture! When I look out on such a night as this, I feel as if there could be neither wickedness nor sorrow in the world; and there certainly would be less of both if the sublimity of Nature were more attended to, and people were carried more out of themselves by contemplating such a scene. (MP 113)

---

[2]   David Hume, "Of Refinement in the Arts," in *Essays: Moral, Political, and Literary*, ed. Eugene F. Miller (Indianapolis: Liberty Classics, 1987), p. 269.
[3]   Hume, "Of Refinement in the Arts," p. 270.
[4]   Hume, "Of Refinement in the Arts," p. 270.

What Hume says about those spirits which "take a man from himself" is echoed again in a passage of *Persuasion*. Anne Elliot's unfortunate school friend Mrs. Smith "had moments only of languor" despite the loss of her husband and fortune and health. Anne reflects on her friend's resilience: "A submissive spirit might be patient, a strong understanding would supply resolution, but here was something more; here was that elasticity of mind . . . that power of turning readily from evil to good, and of finding employment which carried her out of herself, which was from nature alone" (P 154).

Only an active mind can take us out of ourselves in the sense intended by Hume and Austen. To be taken out of oneself is to move beyond the most parochial and limiting of concerns, to consider more of the world than that circumscribed by one's immediate experience, to think more and to think about more than one's immediate situation. Clearly, indolence and languor, when not involved in the kind of rest and recruitment of spirits that Hume and Austen each discuss, are associated by both with the kind of vacuous self-preoccupation that limits an individual's perceptiveness. To be taken out of oneself is to see past one's own particular experience. The passage from *Persuasion* is particularly moving because Austen may already have been ill and in pain, like Mrs. Smith, when she wrote it.

The worst thing about indolence, then, is its vitiation of an activity of the mind that is, not incidentally, a principal source of human happiness. As has been indicated, if prolonged, indolence begets "a . . . lethargy that destroys all enjoyment." Labor and industry are described as the chief ingredient of felicity in Hume's essay "The Stoic."[5] Indolence can itself become a fatigue, and "the mind, unexercised, finds every delight insipid."[6] In some of the less happy generalizations made in "Of National Characters," Hume repeatedly connects indolence with stupidity.[7] Indeed, Hume reflects on Dubos's assertion that nothing "is so disagreeable to the mind as the languid, listless state of indolence, into which it falls upon the removal of all passion and occupation."[8] Hume goes even further, and claims that indolence can make us credulous, and that laziness can make us accept evidence at face value: "Such indolence and incapacity is

---

[5]   David Hume, "The Stoic," in *Essays: Moral, Political, and Literary*, ed. Eugene F. Miller (Indianapolis: Liberty Classics, 1987), p. 149.
[6]   Hume, "The Stoic," p. 150.
[7]   Hume, "Of National Characters," pp. 205–7.
[8]   David Hume, "Of Tragedy," in *Essays: Moral, Political, and Literary*, ed. Eugene F. Miller (Indianapolis: Liberty Classics, 1987), p. 217.

there in the generality of mankind, that they are apt to receive a man for whatever he has a mind to put himself off for; and admit his overbearing airs as proofs of that merit which he assumes to himself."[9] It isn't entirely clear whether the generality of mankind is usually so incurious because it doesn't want to take the trouble to ascertain the truth, or because it accepts everything at face value with the kind of affable imbecility that can always be imposed on. Perhaps Hume means to imply, as he and Austen do elsewhere, that the two are not unrelated.

There are several famously indolent characters in the novels of Jane Austen who fit the kind of profile that can be formulated from Hume's reflections. Mr. Churchill of *Emma* has a "quiet, indolent, gentlemanlike pride that would harm nobody," and that leads him to defer all opinions and decisions to his wife. She decides what he will think, and he thinks as he is told (E 310). Dr. Grant of *Mansfield Park* is "an indolent, selfish bon vivant, who must have his palate consulted in everything; who will not stir a finger for the convenience of any one; and who, moreover, if the cook makes a blunder, is out of humour with his excellent wife" (MP 111). Lady Bertram is intellectually inert, and so lacking in imagination that she thinks "nothing can be dangerous or difficult, or fatiguing to any body but" herself (MP 32). Mr. Hurst of *Pride and Prejudice* "was an indolent man, who lived only to eat, drink, and play at cards, who, when he found [Elizabeth to] . . . prefer a plain dish to a ragout, had nothing to say to her" (PP 35). It is, as an aside, interesting to note Austen's marriage of indolence and gluttony. In the days before cholesterol and underexercise materialized as threats to the public health, Austen (with considerable prescience, or simply with keener powers of observation than most) nevertheless killed off Dr. Grant by means of his preferred vices. "Dr. Grant had brought on apoplexy and death, by three great institutionary dinners in one week," Austen informs us at the conclusion of *Mansfield Park* (MP 469).

The indolent characters in Austen, whether or not they succumb to additional vices, are for the most part mentally inactive and, frankly, boring. They lack imagination, possess no initiative, and achieve little of significance. They are the antithesis of what Austen defines (in the person of Anne Elliot) as good company: "My idea of good company," she tells Mr. Elliot, "is the company of clever, well–informed people, who have a great deal of conversation; that is what I call good company" (P 150). Indolence vitiates any such advantages and abilities. In fact this

---

[9]   Hume, "Of Refinement in the Arts," p. 270.

is made explicit in Austen's description of Dr. Grant, whom Mary Crawford castigates along with the rest of England's clergy for "indolence and love of ease; a want of all laudable ambition, of taste for good company, or of inclination to take the trouble of being agreeable, which make men clergymen" (MP 110).

Hume's views about good company are not so different, since both conversation and experience are requisite, though he is more concerned to counteract academic isolation than Austen has any need to be:

> Learning has been as great a Loser by being shut up in Colleges and Cells, and secluded from the World and good Company. By that Means, every Thing of what we call Belles Lettres became . . . barbarous, being cultivated by Men without any Taste of Life or Manners, and without that Liberty and Facility of Thought and Expression, which can only be acquir'd by Conversation. Even Philosophy went to Wrack by this moaping recluse Method of Study, and became as chimerical in her Conclusions as she was unintelligible in her Stile and Manner of Delivery. And indeed, what cou'd be expected from Men who never consulted Experience in any of their Reasonings, or who never search'd for that Experience, where alone it is to be found, in common Life and Conversation?[10]

Gallantry makes for the best company of all, and neither industry nor generosity comes amiss: "In good company, you need not ask, Who is the master of the feast? The man, who sits in the lowest place, and who is always industrious in helping every one, is certainly the person."[11] Good company is never passive company. Common life and conversation are prime sources of knowledge, neglected by misguided academics. Jane Austen would undoubtedly agree. Common life and conversation are the material of which her fictional worlds are composed.

Let us continue by entertaining the suggestion that considering indolence a vice carries with it some assumption that makes us responsible for omissions as well as actions. In "Of the Populousness of Ancient Nations," Hume equates action and inaction in a few familiar and uncontroversial ways. He inveighs against the exposure of unwanted children, and earlier in the essay against the exposure of old and no longer useful slaves, by designating exposure as outright killing:

---

[10]   David Hume, "Of Essay Writing," in *Essays: Moral, Political, and Literary*, ed. Eugene F. Miller (Indianapolis: Liberty Classics, 1987), pp. 534–5.
[11]   David Hume, "Of the Rise of the Arts and Sciences," in *Essays: Moral, Political, and Literary*, ed. Eugene F. Miller (Indianapolis: Liberty Classics, 1987), p. 133.

This practice was very common; and is not spoken of by any author of those times with the horror it deserves, or scarcely even with disapprobation. PLUTARCH, the humane, good–natured PLUTARCH, mentions it as a merit in ATTALUS, king of PERGAMUS, that he murdered, or, if you will, exposed all his own children, in order to leave his crown to the son of his brother, EUMENES.[12]

Leaving children in a foundling hospital isn't as bad as killing them, of course (despite the fact that Hume believes a very large number of French people to have done so), but

the great difference, for health, industry, and morals, between an educa-tion in an hospital and that in a private family, should induce us not to make the entrance into the former too easy and engaging. To kill one's own child is shocking to nature, and must therefore be somewhat unusual; but to turn over the care of him upon others, is very tempting to the nat-ural indolence of mankind.[13]

That is, inaction is still seen as an injury, or is seen to be as blameworthy as an injury.

Of course, some philosophers will argue that this is a special case, in which an undertaking to care for the child has been ignored, making the neglect of the child a species of outright contract violation (an action) rather than a case of inaction (an omission). But that isn't how Hume thinks of it:

We blame a father for neglecting his child. Why? because it shews a want of natural affection, which is the duty of every parent. Were not natural affection a duty, the care of children cou'd not be a duty; and 'twere imposs-ible we cou'd have the duty in our eye in the attention we give to our offspring. In this case, therefore, all men suppose a motive to the action distinct from a sense of duty. (T 478)

As we know, morality springs from sentiment for Hume. A failure of feeling can signal a moral failing. This is what we look to first in assess-ments of character, before we consider the question of whether a given negative consequence has been achieved by action instead of omission. Nevertheless, we can establish that Hume believes it can be morally incum-bent on us *not* to refrain from action or intervention. For instance, he

---

[12] David Hume, "Of the Populousness of Ancient Nations," in *Essays: Moral, Political, and Literary*, ed. Eugene F. Miller (Indianapolis: Liberty Classics, 1987), pp. 398–9.
[13] Hume, "Of the Populousness of Ancient Nations," p. 400.

points out that "exorbitant power proceeds not, in any government, from new laws, so much as from neglecting to remedy the abuses, which frequently rise from the old ones."[14] A failure to intervene can clearly be as bad as directly causing the events which the intervention would prevent. These issues are not of central concern for Hume, but it is interesting to note even an inclination toward a position that supposes less of an intrinsic moral distinction between acts and omissions than is commonly believed to be the case.

Fanny and John Dashwood's failure to assist Mrs. Dashwood and her daughters once John inherits Norland Park from his father is both mocked and condemned by Austen, who pillories both their omissions and their greedy rationalizations. Fanny Dashwood, via a sequence of ingeniously reasoned subtractions, reduces the amount John feels that he should settle on his stepmother and stepsisters, simultaneously reducing the qualms of his conscience. From three thousand pounds, to five hundred apiece, to an annuity (rejected for fear Mrs. Dashwood should prove too avariciously long-lived), to "a present of fifty pounds now and then," to occasional "presents of fish and game" (SS 8–12), the prospects of help for Mrs. Dashwood, Elinor, and Marianne are whittled down to nothing, as is (given those ingenious rationalizations) John Dashwood's sense of responsibility. Here is a clear case of Austen's holding someone accountable not just for having violated some obligation (John's promise to his father to care for his stepmother and sisters upon that gentleman's death was conveniently vague and open-ended) but for having neglected to act.

One of Austen's clearest critiques of indolence occurs in her delineation of the character of Lady Bertram in *Mansfield Park*, who is as guilty as Fanny and John Dashwood of significant omissions. Second only to Maria's vanity and the Crawfords' (not always unattractive) inability to think seriously on serious subjects, indolence is given considerable attention in this novel as a specifically moral failing. This is a failing possessed by more than one character, for Dr. Grant and the clergy in general are tarred by the same brush. However, Lady Bertram should certainly be considered the paradigm. It is not only the inappropriate interference of Mrs. Norris and the mistaken judgment of Sir Thomas, but Lady Bertram's failure to involve herself in the raising of her daughters that result in their egoism and self-destructive behavior. "Lady Bertram did not go into public with her daughters. She was too indolent even to accept

---

[14]   David Hume, "Idea of a Perfect Commonwealth," in *Essays: Moral, Political, and Literary*, ed. Eugene F. Miller (Indianapolis: Liberty Classics, 1987), pp. 515–16.

a mother's gratification in witnessing their success and enjoyment at the expense of any personal trouble, and the charge was made over to her sister" (MP 35). Lady Bertram's failure to feel for and to interest herself in her own children seems to involve just the kind of "want of natural affection" against which we saw that Hume inveighs.

More to the point, Lady Bertram's failure to defend Fanny Price from Mrs. Norris and from her husband, both omissions, are presented as moral flaws, albeit not as serious as are the envy and malice of Mrs. Norris. It isn't in the least that she isn't fond of Fanny, it is simply that "Lady Bertram never thought of being useful to any body" with the result that Fanny "had neither sympathy nor assistance from those who ought to have entered into her feelings and directed her taste" (MP 219). Passive – indeed, almost inert herself – Lady Bertram automatically expects Fanny to accept an offer of marriage from the wealthy Crawford: "it is every young woman's duty to accept" any offer of lifetime care (MP 333). The attitude is not unusual for the period, of course, though Lady Bertram's conviction that personal beauty is the factor that secures (and ought to secure) such arrangements is more than a little off-putting.

Austen makes her assessment of Lady Bertram's character explicit when comparing her to her less fortunate sister, Mrs. Price.

> Of her two sisters, Mrs Price very much more resembled Lady Bertram than Mrs Norris. She was a manager by necessity, without any of Mrs Norris's inclination for it. . . . Her disposition was naturally easy and indolent, like Lady Bertram's; and a situation of similar affluence and do-nothingness would have been much more suited to her capacity than the exertions and self-denials of the one which her imprudent marriage had placed her in.

Mrs. Price would probably have been just as imposing a lady of leisure as her wealthy sister, but Mrs. Norris would have been an infinitely more efficient mother of nine in straightened circumstances than Mrs. Price could hope to be (MP 390). That is, Lady Bertram's "capacity" does not extend either to exertion or to self-denial. If we look, as Hume advises, to the tendencies of her character as well as its actual effects, it is evident that it is a character that would not have been notably respectable in the absence of wealth and comfort. It is a character in which the absence of some, though certainly not all, obvious flaws is more a matter of moral luck than of virtue, and in which an incapacity for exertion signals an incapacity to intervene on behalf of another. (This is something that suggests, incidentally, that wealth and comfortable circumstances may aid in the concealment of any number of vices, the exhibition of which comfortable circumstances prevent. The entertainingly cynical suggestion about the well-off is never put directly, but implied by the splendid example.)

The passage cited above has already been canvassed at some length in the course of the discussion of Hume's general point of view. It is worth stressing in this new context, however, the kind of counterfactual reasoning that Austen brings to the investigation of indolence specifically. The honors are about even between Lady Bertram and Mrs. Price when it comes to the assessment of their respective characters. Each is indolent. Circumstances like Lady Bertram's prevent that vice from producing much immediate material harm, though they exacerbate an inclination toward near total inertia. In other words, Mrs. Price is a slattern and Lady Bertram is not, but only because Lady Bertram can afford a lot of servants. Austen has us consider what *would* transpire, were each sister differently placed and, more generally, what would transpire were anyone who could be regarded as constitutionally indolent to be placed in the social and economic situations under review. If literature can sometimes be a thought experiment, then literature which invites us to entertain counterfactuals certainly fits that description. Considering what effects a tendency to indolence would have in one set of circumstances or another (or considering what effects a "spirit of activity" and inclination to parsimony like Mrs. Norris' would have) invites us to consider a broader arena than that circumscribed by the fiction. In doing that, we are also led to pursue the Humean project of considering the tendencies of a character in isolation from its actual effects.

It is also worth noting that Austen compares the effects that each indolent parent has on her offspring. Each is guilty of neglect (and Mrs. Price is also guilty of favoritism) but the respective circumstances of the two families are crucially distinct, as Austen shows us when she reflects on the difference these circumstances have created between the Bertram children and the Price siblings:

> In [Susan's] . . . usefulness, in Fanny's excellence, in William's continued good conduct and rising fame, and in the general well-doing and success of the other members of the family, all assisting to advance each other, and doing credit to his countenance and aid, Sir Thomas saw repeated, and for ever repeated, reason to rejoice in what he had done for them all, and acknowledge the advantages of early hardship and discipline, and the consciousness of being born to struggle and endure. (MP 473)

Being wealthy can be regarded as a disadvantage insofar as it encourages, perhaps nourishes, the kind of indolence that inhibits achievement and abets self-centeredness. Richard Jenkyns writes that all of Austen's novels "depict the corrosive effect on the leisured classes, especially on women, of a lack of scope for their energies or a deficiency in useful or improving activity. It is an important element in *Emma*, but in *Mansfield Park* it is all pervasive."[15] Lady Bertram's listless inertia, the directionless hyperactivity of Mrs. Norris, Mary Crawford's need to entertain herself at the expense of others are all accounted for at least in part by such considerations. If indolence is something that may be more or less enforced by circumstances, than many of its ill effects can be likewise enforced. Clearly Austen does not believe that the tendency toward indolence is entirely a product of circumstances. But it is also clear that she believes different situations can inhibit or exacerbate that tendency, for Mrs. Price and Lady Bertram do not behave in exactly the same way despite the fact that they are described as having naturally indolent dispositions. This observation reminds us of Hume's claim that our assessment of a character should not depend only on a survey of its actual effects but should involve an investigation of its tendencies, given one set of circumstances or another.

Very much in line with Sir Thomas Bertram's insight about struggle and endurance, Hume maintains that exertion and industry are "the chief ingredient of the felicity to which" one aspires. "Every enjoyment soon becomes insipid and distasteful, when not acquired by fatigue and industry."[16] Indeed, "the great end of all human industry is the attainment of happiness."[17] He contends that "vigorous industry give[s] pleasure to the pursuit of even the most worthless prey," and indicates that application of similar exertions to the cultivation of the mind is equally or even more likely to prove an agreeable occupation.[18] This attitude is echoed more than once in Austen. We again see it, for instance, in *Mansfield Park*, in Henry Crawford's admiration of the less materially endowed William Price. Crawford longs to have been at sea and to have had William's adventures.

> His heart was warmed, his fancy fired, and he felt the highest respect for a lad who, before he was twenty, had gone through such bodily hardships and given such proofs of mind. The glory of heroism, of usefulness,

---

[15]   Richard Jenkyns, *A Fine Brush on Ivory: An Appreciation of Jane Austen* (Oxford: Oxford University Press, 2004), p. 112.
[16]   Hume, "The Stoic," p. 149.
[17]   Hume, "The Stoic," p. 148.
[18]   Hume, "The Stoic," p. 149.

of exertion, of endurance, made his own habits of selfish indulgence appear in shameful contrast; and he wished he had been a William Price, distinguishing himself and working his way to fortune and consequence with so much self-respect and happy ardour, instead of what he was! (MP 236)

The powers and faculties are enlarged by "an assiduity in honest industry"[19] and industry is ranked with integrity as a virtue in "Of the Middle Station in Life."[20] Hume states that "according to human sentiments, sense, courage, good manners, industry, prudence, genius, &c. are essential parts of personal merit."[21] In Austen as well, industry and exertion tend to improve the character rather than otherwise, as we have seen Sir Thomas reflect when considering the advantages Susan, Fanny, and William, all born to poverty, have over their wealthier cousins (MP 473). In a more subtle example, Emma Woodhouse is said "never to submit to anything requiring industry and patience," a failure which she later regrets, and which is regarded by Knightley as a flaw of character (E 37).

So while indolence is not regarded as the worst of vices either by Hume or by Austen, and while a modicum of inertia is even considered necessary for happiness, it is still apparent that their evaluations of the trait are mainly negative, though their reasons for believing this take us beyond conventional estimations of vice and virtue.

[19]   Hume, "Of Refinement in the Arts," p. 270.
[20]   David Hume, "Of the Middle Station in Life," in *Essays: Moral, Political, and Literary*, ed. Eugene F. Miller (Indianapolis: Liberty Classics, 1987), p. 546.
[21]   David Hume, "Of the Immortality of the Soul," in *Essays: Moral, Political, and Literary*, ed. Eugene F. Miller (Indianapolis: Liberty Classics, 1987), p. 594.

14

What Hume's Philosophy Contributes to Our Understanding of Austen's Fiction; what Austen's Fiction Contributes to Our Understanding of Hume's Philosophy

In the preceding chapters I have tried to trace out some of the correspondences – ethical, aesthetic, and epistemic – between the issues Hume and Austen address in their pursuit of very different projects. Part of the motive for this was to establish that, whether or not Austen read Hume's philosophy, the normative positions endorsed in her novels are in many respects characteristically Humean positions, often (though interestingly not always) arrived at in a characteristically Humean way. Because of this correspondence, I believe that understanding Hume's philosophy can contribute to our understanding of Austen's fiction. I am not just arguing that a Humean reading is preferable to a number of other possible readings (although I'd like to say that as well), but that Hume's philosophy provides a kind of groundwork that clarifies the normative content that is already there. In other words, it isn't just one way of interpreting Austen among many. It is a way of foregrounding material that other interpretations may misconstrue or fail to address. And now I will probably say some things that will make any number of philosophers angry. I also believe that Austen's fiction presents us with a source of thought experiments that offer demonstrations of and elaborations on Humean or at least Hume-compatible positions that are unavailable in Hume's philosophy, and that are accessible and attractive to a wider audience than that philosophy is likely to be. For we have on hand two gifted, intelligent writers, one superior in the exercise of intellectual attainments and analysis, one superior in respect of evoking emotion and sympathy in her readers, who share some intuitions and some insights about ethics, aesthetics, and methods of reasoning. These talents are both talents that enable the happy possessor not just to encourage reflection on the topics addressed, but to alter the convictions of the reader. They just achieve these ends in very distinct ways. Seeing Austen through a Humean lens helps us understand Austen, because it is easy not to take away enough from reading her if our attention is not directed in the right way. The perusal of ordinary incidents and inter-actions can become trivial if there is nothing to focus our attention on the way Austen lets us see human constants through those commonplace interactions. Likewise, seeing Humean concerns through Austen's fiction engages the emotions in a way that exposition cannot and makes such ideas accessible and comprehensible to a far wider audience. Writers of fiction are also often far more adept at deploying counterfactuals to the greatest possible advantage, and this gives them an edge when it comes to the exploration of questions that are also often relevant to philosophical investigations.

Most of the latter chapters of this book represent an attempt to uncover common concerns and perspectives in Hume and Austen. That isn't exactly the same thing, I'd like to stress, as producing a Humean reading of Austen. Just as a feminist reading would make certain things salient, would focus our attention more on women's roles relative to those of men and Jane Fairfax's reference to the "governess trade," a Humean reading would focus our attention on subject matter of interest to students of Humean philosophy: the roles of sentiment and sympathy in moral judgment, for instance, rather than all those references to principle at the end of *Mansfield Park*. Uncovering concerns that Hume and Austen share naturally gets us to material that would be highlighted in a Humean reading of Austen. The point is that one could essay a Humean reading of any number of authors who didn't harbor a single Humean insight – Nathaniel Hawthorne, say, or Eugene O'Neill. A Humean reading of *The Scarlet Letter*, while pretty radically unconventional, would not be as outrageous as it might appear at first glance (or at least not outrage-ous in a bad way). Dimmesdale's transgression, we are told, gave him "sympathies so intimate with the sinful brotherhood of mankind . . . that his heart vibrated in unison with theirs." A Humean reading might make something out of this fellow feeling, and certainly out of the relationship between humility and puritanical dogma. On the other hand, a Humean reading of literature invented expressly to corroborate Freudian assump-tions might provide us with a refreshing compatibilist approach to neuroses and complexes. I propose the possibility of such entertaining forays into interpretation mainly to demonstrate the aforementioned distinction, for a Humean reading does not necessarily depend on the identification of commonalities between Hume's philosophy and what is read. It merely requires an application of the first to the second, making salient those facets of the reading to which aspects of the philosophy are at all applicable. A Humean reading of Austen's work will be especially rich, and rather more rewarding than Humean readings of most other novels, just because a pervasive normative understructure (both in the plots of the novels themselves and in how it is we are encouraged to respond to them) is cast into vivid relief by such an interpretive approach.

Attempts were made early on to show how claims of correspondence between Austen and Kant did not pass muster, and how even contentions stressing an Aristotelian approach (and these would be taken to include Shaftesburian offshoots) failed to account for any number of aspects of ethical life that are repeatedly stressed in Austen. This is not to say that Kantian or Aristotelian readings of Austen are always inappropriate. In the absence of any overarching claims about correspondence, these are just ways of focusing attention on aspects of the action which might prove of concern to those particular philosophers. Seeing the aesthetic sensibilities of Fanny Price in a way that is informed by familiarity with Kant's *Critique of Judgment* is surely not a waste of time, any more than it is to consider the distinctly non-Kantian end of happiness that governs the deliberation of Austen's heroines in the course of an Aristotelian reading. That I consider a Humean reading of Austen preferable is less a reflection on intriguing interpretive byways such as these than it is a concern not to have significant portions of Austen drop out of our consideration altogether. In other words, my principal qualm about alternative readings is that they cannot take advantage of much that is there, and leave us, if we pursue them in isolation, with a necessarily skewed interpretation that does not account for a lot that is clearly significant and attention-worthy in Austen's work, especially as regards value and normativity.

Let us consider two such skewed interpretations, neither of which has as yet been canvassed: one philosophical and one less friendly to that enterprise. I will begin with the former and, since Aristotelian and Kantian readings have already been considered in the third chapter, will venture a prospective egoist interpretation instead. Any attempt to ascribe an egoist position to Austen herself, or any attempt to claim that such positions are endorsed in her work, is surely a mistake, of course. Yet it has been tried. For instance, a kind of Hobbesian reading of Austen seems to be offered by Avrom Fleishman in his *A Reading of Mansfield Park* in a passage that has been cited by other authors: "If this war of ego is carried out by each against all, society is indeed as Hobbes described it, *bellum omnia in omnes*. Yet for Jane Austen the amazing fact about this struggle is its constancy and continuity: society is permanent organized hostility, and for better or worse it is the only permanence we can attain."[1] Anne Crippen Ruderman discusses this in tandem with Harold Bloom's contention that Austen "writes about the triumph of the will" and the sustenance of individuality and individual integrity.[2] It is true that Austen's heroines are occasionally placed in positions in which social pressures are at odds with individual preference or in which a sense of obligation to family and friends clouds individual judgment. *Persuasion* is a prime example of the latter. But none of this makes it the case that Austen's novels endorse an egoist stance, be that stance Hobbesian or Nietzschean or Machiavellian. In fact, I cannot bring myself to believe that any such notion was at the heart of the claims just canvassed.

The absurdity of such suppositions becomes evident when we consider that almost every character in Austen whose behavior is condemned rather than endorsed is an egoist of one stripe or another. In fact, what amounts to a declaration of egoism as an ethical position – the conviction that moral duty *prescribes* acting first in one's own interest – is (with some humor) ascribed to just those characters who, if not cast as outright villains, are clearly depicted as "wanting" in the moral arena. The infamous Mr. Elliot of *Persuasion*, eventually exposed as calculating, insincere, and deceitful, has it said of him that " 'To do the best for himself,' passed as a duty" (P 202). The more entertaining but nonetheless selfish Mary Crawford of *Mansfield Park* says to the shocked Fanny Price that "it is everybody's duty to do as well for themselves as they can" when discussing mercenary motives in marriage (MP 289). And the soon-to-be dissolute Maria Bertram, whose actions are clearly condemned in the world of Austen's work, makes an obligation of potential advantage: "Maria Bertram was begin-ning to think matrimony a duty; and as a marriage with Mr. Rushworth would give her the enjoyment of a larger income than her father's . . . it became, by the same rule of moral obligation, her evident duty to marry Mr. Rushworth if she could" (MP 38–9).

Consider finally Austen's ironic reflections on Lucy Steele in *Sense and Sensibility*: "The whole of Lucy's behaviour in the affair, and the prosperity

[1] Avrom Fleishman, *A Reading of Mansfield Park* (Minneapolis: University of Minnesota Press, 1967), p. 80.
[2] Anne Crippen Ruderman, *The Pleasures of Virtue: Political Thought in the Novels of Jane Austen* (Lanham, MD: Rowman & Littlefield, 1995), p. 2; Harold Bloom, "Introduction" to *Modern Critical Views: Jane Austen* (New York: Chelsea House Publishers, 1986), p. 2.

which crowned it, therefore, may be held forth as a most encouraging instance of what an earnest, an unceasing attention to self-interest, however its progress may be apparently obstructed, will do in securing every advantage of fortune, with no other sacrifice than that of time and conscience" (SS 376). Clearly, the single-minded pursuit of self interest (at least at the expense of the welfare of others) is frowned upon.

When it comes to the imposition and exertion of one's own will and the triumph of that will over those of others, none fits the case so well as the eponymous anti-heroine of *Lady Susan*, an almost caricature villain who lies, seduces, and sometimes appears to connive at the death of inconvenient people: "I am tired of submitting my will to the caprices of others – of resigning my own judgment in deference to those, to whom I owe no duty, and for whom I feel no respect" (MW 308). Lady Susan says this after her plan to force her daughter to marry a wealthy idiot has been foiled and her further plan to deceive her relatives about her own motives has been exposed. She is, in fact, a forerunner of Thackeray's notorious Becky Sharp. Her delight in imposing her own will on others is humorously cast in the worst possible light: "There is exquisite pleasure," she says, "in subduing an insolent spirit, in making persons pre-determined to dislike, acknowledge one's superiority" (MW 254). Indeed, there is an outright declaration of an egoist stance expressed in Lady Susan's reasons for preferring one lover over another: "I infinitely prefer the tender and liberal spirit of Manwaring, which, impressed with the deepest conviction of my merit, is satisfied that whatever I do must be right; and look with a degree of contempt on the inquisitive and doubtful Fancies of that Heart which seems always debating on the reasonableness of its Emotions" (MW 269). The single-minded pursuit of personal interests and the further classification of such pursuits as virtues and duties are most often held up for scorn in Austen's work. They become targets for acerbic displays of her wit, in the same way that egregious impositions of the will become targets. No form of egoism can be associated with the ethical stance endorsed in Austen's novels. Neither can any reading informed by an egoist stance, given that it will have nothing in common with the ethical perspectives advocated in those novels, hope to do more than make salient for us the behavior and motives of Austen's villains.

But perhaps it is time to consider a non-philosophical alternative. To that end, it may be useful to have a look at the interpretation of Austen's novels which is most pervasive and which people will find most familiar. This is an interpretation that flourishes more often outside the academy than within it, one that so colors the popular perception of Austen's work that Gillian Anderson gives voice to it in introductions to Austen adaptations showcased on Masterpiece Theater. In Austen's fictional worlds, says Anderson "it's not only possible to find a soul mate – it's the point of it all." I wish to investigate that kind of an approach to Austen here because it shows what is lacking in a reading that neglects nearly all those elements which a Humean reading would render salient. By default, therefore, it also illustrates some real advantages to an understanding of Austen that a Humean reading provides. In fact, romantic interpretations were inveighed against in the first chapter, in which I claimed, armed with support from Virginia Woolf, that Jane Austen could not be regarded as a romantic novelist. That many people do so regard her demonstrates the pervasiveness of an unreflective interpretation, one which erases much that is worthwhile and more that is interesting from our consideration.

This erasure is evident in many recent film adaptations of Austen, in which content is sacrificed to fit a ninety-minute run time, leaving only those portions of the plot dealing with the principal romance relatively untouched. These adaptations are an excellent illustration of just the features of Austen's plots which will be rendered salient by the kind of romance-centered finding-one's-soul-mate-is-the-point-of-it-all reading about which we hear Gillian Anderson hold forth. I will not even claim that the more romance-centered adaptations are all bad films. Some are not. Austen's heroines are too intelligent to make for dull romances. It is simply that such adaptations often become entirely different stories, sometimes interesting in their own right, but no longer Austen's stories at all.

Here is what can happen when the focus is primarily on the female protagonist and her principal love interest. First, her perspective domin-ates everything in more respects than is the case in the original novel. The significance of each depicted event lies mainly in how it will affect the heroine and her prospects. Every character retained from the original is now presented only in relation to the heroine – as someone who inter-acts with her or affects her life. Frankly, this is a tactic of supermarket novels, an easy read because one need only park oneself within a single point of vantage and stay there. One empathizes only with a single char-acter and considers only her interests. This is the structure of the classic wish fulfillment scenario, one smooth sweep from the initial introduction of the heroine, to the introduction of the love interest, to the requisite misunderstanding, to its resolution, to the happy matrimony-oriented end-ing. In other words, reading Austen as a romance can make her boring. This isn't inevitably true, of course. Even under the preceding restric-tions, Austen's happy facility for depicting romantic misunderstandings and characters speaking at cross-purposes promises that we will often have on hand a superior specimen of the type. But adaptations will suffer from a crippling excess of excisions, and readings with the same focus as the adaptations will suffer from a kind of tunnel vision that only counts as relevant or interesting those events and interactions that facilitate the eventual uniting of the soul mates. It is a horrible waste of material far superior to the use to which it is, in such circumstances, put.

It is clearly true that there are readings of Austen that mimic the more romance-centered adaptations, though they cannot append all the additional material with which film adaptations tend to saddle us. They can, however, involve imaginative additions, as all readings do, for we inevitably supplement what is fictionally the case from our own store of imaginative assumptions. Let us consider what a romantic interpretation would involve. We have seen that only a narrow range of events will be regarded as crucially important. These will be the events on the basis of which most imaginative extrapolations and amendments will be made. We always begin, of course with those propositions that are true in the fictional world. But fictional worlds are never maximally comprehensive and not everything is made explicit. We will, again in all cases, make inferences on the basis of what an author has indicated to fill in such gaps. If our principal interest when reading *Northanger Abbey* is in the romantic involvement of Catherine Morland and Henry Tilney (which, in fact, is not represented in a majority of the fictional states of affairs) then most inferences and extrapolations will involve only those states of affairs pertaining to them. Minimal imaginative activity will be devoted to the other characters and their conversations, conduct, and effects on one another. The lion's share of the imaginative activity will center instead on the relatively few interactions between Catherine and Henry that are on offer, on assumptions about what may have motivated this or that quip or reflection, on extrapolations concerning what would occur were particular interactions depicted in the work to occur. This leaves us with a reading that is both biased and inappropriate. I have purposely employed *Northanger Abbey* as an example in order to show why: over half of Austen's text becomes irrelevant to any such reading, as does her principal thesis. One plot element among many is foregrounded without any attention being paid to what it is being used to demonstrate. What is featured in a romance-obsessed reader's understanding of the book is a thin, inadequate history of a relationship the very acknowledgement of which, as well as the triumph over adversity of which and the conclusion in marriage of which, are detailed as an afterthought only *in the last eight pages* of the novel. Few readings could be more unsatisfying.

Compare that kind of reading with one that is informed by an under-standing of Humean ethical and aesthetic norms, which lets us see at once the interconnectedness of Catherine's intellectual maturation and the maturation of the novel in its evolution from gothic melodrama to naturalism. An earlier chapter has already devoted a sufficient number of pages to an investigation of the way in which aesthetic norms may be conveyed and redirected by fiction, just as moral norms can be. The point to made here is only that, whether or not there is a precise correspond-ence between Hume and Austen along such lines, a Humean reading will bring out not only the late eighteenth-century approaches to the literary and picturesque so entertainingly canvassed by Henry Tilney and his sister, but will enable the reader to apply the theories canvassed in the novel *to* the novel. It will enable the reader to assess Catherine's transition from finding herself a prey to gothic fancies to finding herself in the grip of genuine difficulties, an assessment that can be negotiated in terms of the Humean distaste for excessive and melodramatic spectacle and in terms of Hume's position on our emotional investment in the literary.

Finally, seeing much of the novel though the kinds of ethical observa-tions Hume makes in Book II of the *Treatise* can be entertaining as well as rewarding. Consider, for example, John Thorpe's outrageous (and wildly funny) tendency to exaggerate the assets of any person with whom he is affiliated, so that this may reflect well on himself and his prospects, some-thing on which a major reversal in the plot hangs. Hume, as has already been indicated, tells us that "As we are proud of riches in ourselves, so to satisfy our vanity we desire that every one, who has any connexion with us, shou'd likewise be possest of them, and are asham'd of any one, that is mean or poor, among our friends and relations" (T 307). Thorpe's pride leads him to deceive General Tilney about Catherine's prospects, and this information leads the General, given his pride in connection, to seek a match between Henry and Catherine. It is injured pride which later leads him to evict Catherine from the Abbey, when he discovers he has been misinformed. A Humean reading, which would be a reading that sensitized us to the causes and objects of pride, that aligned with Hume's virtue ethics, and that led us to take special note of the effects of such traits on the possessor's narrow circle, has several advantages. It enables us to follow a trail of swelled heads and self-importance in tracing the path from initial exhibitions of pride and vanity to results that run exactly counter to the wishes fostered by the same trait. This is one of Austen's classic comic reversals: John's exhibition of vanity inspires the General to issue an invitation which foils John's plans; John's injured vanity then prompts him to exaggerate Catherine's poverty as he exaggerated her fortune; this picture of poverty injures the General's pride and pushes him to mistreat Catherine instead of following his initial plan of flattering and courting her; the ill treatment is something that Henry Tilney's proper pride leads him to rectify in direct defiance of his father's wishes. Thus, pride not only comes before a fall, but precipitates it. One can see it without Hume, but Hume adds considerably to our appreciation of some of the exhibitions of pride and humility on offer in a way that no other philosopher can.

And just as an understanding of Hume can complement and inform an understanding of Austen, so Austen's fiction can sometimes promote an understanding of and elaboration on Humean insights, on occasion even making new normative phenomena salient. First, I have tried to establish at length that Hume and Austen share at least some of the same normative perspectives, as evidenced in his philosophy and in fictional assumptions taken to be true in the world of Austen's novels. So one relatively simple-minded claim that should be made at the outset is clearly that Austen's fiction has the advantage in conveying some of these points to the general, philosophically inexperienced public in a way Hume's exposition cannot. That doesn't mean that people come away from Austen able to do philosophy or equipped with a better understanding of the structure of the indirect passions. It does mean that they will (unless doomed by a romantic interpretation at the outset) come away noticing the difference that sympathy can make in moral reasoning, the way vanity can serve to undermine the very desires that it helps to generate, the way sentiment seems bound up with moral judgment. That is, at the most basic level, Austen provides an emotionally accessible picture of certain Humean contentions, not just by illustrating them, but sometimes by arousing emotional and sympathetic responses in us that enable us to experience some of the phenomena that Hume describes. It is true, of course, that most fiction will arouse emotional and sympathetic responses of one kind or another. My contention has been that a combination of factors – the enlightenment sensibility, the ironic detachment, the normative stances adopted, make Austen's fiction more suitable than a lot of other literature to an enterprise that may yield understanding of some basic Humean insights without requiring a wholesale philosophical underpinning to sustain it.

Consider, for instance, the close parallels that have been drawn repeatedly between Hume's own illustrations, such as those offered throughout the *Treatise*, and those offered by Austen. When it comes to particular vices and virtues, for instance, the similarities between their respective sets of examples can be striking. Austen and Hume will point to exactly the same targets and causes of vanity to make their case, or note the identical tendency on the part of some to forge an alliance between beauty and utility in regard to exactly the same aesthetic objects. There is sometimes even a resemblance in prose style and tone that is perhaps an artifact of their being products of the same era, but that is nonetheless arresting. Numerous instances have been canvassed to establish the point. But consider now that Austen's descriptions will have the weight of emotional and imaginative investment behind them, will serve not simply to provide examples of the action of a psychological mechanism or facet of human nature, but examples of how one can feel, how one's life and relationships can turn out to be. More to the point, a reaction of moral approbation or disapprobation goes some steps further, in that it provides an example of how it is that the situation under scrutiny should be evaluated by placing one in the (imaginative) position of evaluator. Fiction can lead us to rehearse the very evaluative judgments of which it provides examples, or even to rehearse such judgments without providing a character with whose opinions we sympathize. The ability of fiction both to place us within the emotional perspective of decision makers and to summarily distance us to a bird's eye view of the multifarious consequences of a given course of action ensures a kind of active, participatory engagement that straightforward exposition simply cannot. In this sense reading Austen can enlarge on our understanding of certain of Hume's insights and ideas. Reading Austen permits us emotionally and imaginatively to inhabit and experience the kinds of situations, interactions, and reactions that philosophy of necessity can only describe from the outside.

Can Austen help us to see things in Hume that were previously unnoticed? Insofar as active imaginative engagement with fiction can be thought to be underwritten by our existing normative and conceptual commitments and can in addition be thought capable of refining or even changing them, it provides a clearer route to certain kinds of insights. Consider for a moment a different but more obvious example. The rational arguments of a social reformer may, especially if they eschew the delineation of particular cases, have less impact on the convictions of readers than will a piece by Dickens which illustrates dramatically the kinds of indignities and hardships that poverty is really likely to entail, but that are unlikely to occur to someone who hasn't experienced poverty. The fiction may do more to undermine the underinformed assumptions of the disinterested than the argument will.

Neither Hume nor Austen was a reformer in the sense that Dickens was. But both show considerable sensitivity and insight into questions involving how people are prone to interact with and affect one another. Consider, then, Hume's talk of how we may best assess people's character by seeing the effects of their traits on their narrow circle, often by sympathizing with those at the mercy of such traits. It is one thing simply to read the passages concerning pride in the *Treatise*, and quite another to linger over the effects that such arrogant bullies as Lady Catherine de Bourgh or Mrs. Ferrars or General Tilney or Mrs. Churchill have on those who are close to them. That is, imagining being at the mercy of a Lady Catherine or Mrs. Churchill makes us aware of a number of things that Hume's discussion of pride has not (though that discussion also makes us aware of any number of things that Austen's fiction doesn't). Both show us how pride in things for which one is not responsible – inherited wealth, for instance – brings in its wake notions of merit and desert and entitlement. But only Austen shows us that such attitudes are repellent by repelling us in the observation of them. Only Austen makes us laugh (though I acknowledge that Hume comes close in a few examples) at the ludicrous self-importance that attaches to all such perceptions of entitlement. Only Austen makes us see that contempt is the proper attitude toward improper pride, because only Austen makes us so alive to the effects of such pride at close quarters.

Where Hume shows us the reasoning behind assumptions about character assessment, Austen complements this by creating an imaginative venue that permits us to make such assessments ourselves in imagination, on the basis of just such grounds as Hume describes. What Hume writes in the *Treatise* and the second *Enquiry* is for the most part meta-ethical, though attempts have been made to tease out a normative system of sorts for Hume in earlier chapters. Insofar as it is meta-ethical, it does not strive to solicit judgments so much as it attempts to convey how they are made, and what prompts them, and how they may be biased, and what perspective might serve to eliminate biases. Fiction, and certainly Austen's fiction, *does* solicit normative judgments insofar as it is intended to elicit normative responses, in particular responses of approbation and disapprobation. These are useful in several ways as a kind of adjunct to philosophy. Austen's fictions provide not only particular, quite believable illustrations of phenomena that Hume describes, but go further and make cases in point of us and our own reactions as we are set through more or less the paces that Hume describes by actively imagining Austen's content. We enact at least some of Hume's assumptions by responding to fictional events in the way and for the reasons that Hume says we will respond to real ones. I defer to the first chapter on thought experiments for a more detailed account of what such a process involves. At this stage, it should be clear that fiction can complement philosophy by offering a level of emotional and imaginative engagement that philosophy for the most part does not. There are exceptions to this in philosophical writing, but not many, and Hume is not one of them.

As an addendum to the material on thought experiments offered in that earlier chapter it should be noted that fiction can also sometimes offer more readily recognizable "demonstrations" of conceptual or philosophical points, and that Austen's fiction is not an exception. I haven't been very explicit about the other ways in which fiction might add to conceptual knowledge in this concluding chapter, though I have attempted to include at least one example of such tactics in every chapter devoted to the establishment of commonalities between Austen and Hume. Let me offer a few general points here about the kinds of things that fiction can sometimes demonstrate, though the following may not satisfy adherents to the stricter sense of that word. Counterexamples to universal assertions clearly demonstrate the possible falsity of such assertions in an unambiguous way. In the ethical sphere, fictional scenarios are usually highly effective at this kind of demonstration. Consider an over-simple example. Austen clearly demonstrates that she doesn't regard a religious vocation as a bar to vice (although she is rather more sanguine than Hume about a person's ability to maintain some level of decency after having taken it up). *Mansfield Park*'s Dr. Grant is a glutton whom Austen cheerfully dispatches to a better world on account of overindulgence, the sycophantic Mr. Collins of *Pride and Prejudice* is plainly contemptible, and the grasping Mr. Elton of *Emma* is just as bad. She gets her readers to imagine the possibility of less than virtuous clergy, something which, if they regarded such an eventuality as impossible, they would be unable to do. Demonstrations of this kind have been singled out throughout the book, although they do not represent the best case that can be made when it comes to showing how Austen's fiction may provide reasons for accepting Humean insights.

The problem, of course, lies with the use of the word "demonstrate," when it is used principally to refer to the provision of a conclusive proof rather than simply the provision of evidence. It is worth admitting at this juncture that what we most frequently find in Austen's fiction that helps to establish Humean conclusions is an enhanced, highly effective version of the tried and true intuition pump. I believe that thought experiments that are so characterized have genuine philosophical value, and that they do so because imaginative engagement involves, at least at some level, our epistemic commitments. Thus, imaginative engagement can be implicated in a change to or refinement of or even validation of concepts and convictions. Since we cannot imagine what we cannot conceive, our ability to imagine that some act is acceptable signals something about the kind of conduct we believe is permissible, about our conception of what constitutes permissible behavior. Where the fiction leads us to consider exceptions or the hitherto unconsidered consequences of certain kinds of conduct or new territory altogether, it can also occasion new beliefs, the kinds of beliefs that arise out of existing convictions coupled with the additional element that the fiction leads us to bring into hypothetical consideration. Philosophers who argue that fiction in general and intuition pumps in particular do not *demonstrate* philosophical points have for the most part not considered what the ability to imagine that some normative assessment is applicable to some state of affairs tells us about an individual's actual evaluative and conceptual beliefs, especially beliefs about what is possible. In that arena, it is very clear from all that has come before that Austen provides us with additional reasons, reasons Hume himself does not provide, for accepting certain Humean conclusions.

Finally, it should be noted that Austen's novels will sometimes make new normative phenomena salient. She will, for instance, take a normative or meta-ethical contention that she and Hume both entertain in different ways in an entirely new direction. That is, Austen can sometimes elaborate and expand on Humean insights in a way that Hume himself does not, or show a consequence of Humean insights Hume himself did not explore. Consider, for instance, the scenario of virtue in rags so eloquently described by Hume when he makes the case for its sometimes being legitimate to ascribe a virtue to people prevented by their circumstances from exercising it. Having a character deemed beneficial to society has no necessary connection to the actual production of benefits, for "particular accidents" may "prevent its operation." Nevertheless, we still regard such an individual as virtuous: "Virtue in rags is still virtue; and the love, which it procures, attends a man into a dungeon or desert, where the virtue can no longer be exerted in action, and is lost to all the world" (T 584). As has already been indicated in an extended discussion of Hume's general point of view (and in the preceding chapter on indolence), Austen makes much the same point in *Sense and Sensibility*, as well as *Mansfield Park*.

I will focus here on the former, since the example in the latter has so recently been rehearsed. Colonel Brandon speaks of his orphaned relative Eliza, whom he loved in his youth, but who (on account of her fortune) was forced into marriage with his vicious older brother. He notes the resemblance of her character to that of Marianne Dashwood: "If I am not deceived by the uncertainty, the partiality of tender recollection, there is a very strong resemblance between them, as well in mind as person. The same warmth of heart, the same eagerness of fancy and spirits." Eliza even falls in love with Brandon, an attachment as "fervent as the attachment of your sister to Mr. Willoughby," Brandon tells Elinor (SS 205). Like Marianne's, Eliza's connection with the man she loves is ruptured. Unlike Marianne, she is coerced by her greedy guardian into a loveless marriage which she soon finds insupportable. She divorces her husband for a lover and proceeds to sink even deeper "in a life of sin." She is eventually discovered in a "spunging-house . . . confined for debt" (SS 207), dying of consumption and possessed of an illegitimate child. Brandon reflects on the comparison he has drawn between Marianne and Eliza, pointing out that "their fates, their fortunes, cannot be the same; and had the natural sweet disposition of the one been guarded by a firmer mind or a happier marriage, she might have been all that you will live to see the other be" (SS 208). In regard to this latter point, we should note that it is entirely unclear whether Marianne is held to have a firmer mind than Eliza. It is only clear that firmness is believed to be a crucially important quality which could have prevented Eliza's downfall, pre- sumably by fortifying her in the face of those attempting to bully her into the unwanted marriage. Firmness is never ascribed to Marianne by Brandon.

The similarities which Brandon notes are, most importantly, similar- ities of character. Eliza and Marianne are believed alike in their sweetness, warmth, enthusiasm, eagerness, and in the intensity of their passions and affections. Possession of such traits makes one extremely vulnerable to the vagaries of chance. Placing an emotional, excitable, affectionate, and naïve person in certain circumstances can have, we learn, disastrous results. Notice the point, found surprisingly unobjectionable by the eminently sane Elinor, that circumstances alone might delimit the difference between a proper young lady and a fallen woman! Not only do we learn that, given kindness and affection, Eliza might not have met her grim fate. We also learn that, without emotional support and in less fortunate circumstances, someone like Marianne – too excitable, too in need of affection and patience, too self-centered – might well have taken the route Eliza did.

What is especially interesting about this passage in *Sense and Sensibility* (and the other, similar passage that draws the same parallel in *Mansfield Park*) is that it deploys the counterfactual in both directions. It con- siders what would have happened if Eliza had not been forced into a loveless marriage, and considers also what would happen to Marianne if she were. As indicated in the previous discussion, this raises the entire question of moral luck, given that it may simply be impossible to exercise certain traits or dispositions in certain kinds of circumstances, and given that other circumstances will stimulate certain behaviors from most people who possess the traits in question. Marianne is valued as sweet and lively and good whereas Eliza is clearly seen as a fallen woman. One is virtuous and the other seemingly vicious, yet these characterizations are more a function of their situations than their characters, since we know their characters are more or less the same.

Austen has clearly *added* to the initial Humean claim about underexercised virtues by implying quite a lot about underexercised vices. And her approach suggests an interesting possible addition to Hume. If we can be credited with virtues whose effects no one will ever see when unfortunate or isolated circumstances prevent their exercise, can we not also be credited with vices which more fortunate circumstances provide no occasion for exhibiting? If circumstances (of affluence, say) can sometimes suppress vice and other circumstances prevent the exercise of virtue, we may be tempted to ask additional questions about whether some particular sets of circumstances will elicit vice and virtue, respectively, just as a matter of course. This brings us more quickly than might be expected into the arena of Philip Zimbardo's situationist ethics and contemporary psychology and the reasons for Abu Ghraib. That is, we might ask whether there are situations so unfortunate, from the moral perspective, that they will elicit vicious behavior from nearly any individual so unlucky as to be placed in them. If there are such situations, situations to which almost all are radically susceptible, further questions about responsibility arise to complicate matters. Zimbardo argues, for instance, that features of the situation in Abu Ghraib – the dehumanization and labeling of others, the relative anonymity contingent on acting as part of a uniformed group, power on one side and none on the other, reinforcement of the view that one is acting as part of a "just authority" – increase the likelihood of abuse, and that such situations will elicit abusive behavior from most people. That is, Zimbardo argues that certain kinds of situations elicit behavior from people of which they would never have believed themselves capable.

The preceding has offered the roughest possible sketch of one area in which Austen has expanded quite a lot on an insight which she and Hume can reasonably be taken to share, and expanded on it in a way in which Hume has not. Hume does not in this context consider comparing people with similar characters who are differently placed, nor does he consider one person in several hypothetical situations. Novelists are, of course, in the habit of considering hypothetical situations, and speculating about what states of affairs would follow, were certain other states of affairs to obtain. Nicholas Wolterstorff and David Lewis have even character-ized the manner in which we determine what is true in a given fictional world *counterfactually*, claiming that we follow out strings of subjunctive conditionals in fleshing out such a world in imagination.[3] So a reasonable claim can be made, I think, that novelists will at least sometimes have an edge in formulating philosophical problems that necessitate the employ-ment of counterfactuals. Austen in particular is interesting because she combines this skill with an interest like Hume's in the assessment of traits of character, where the conception of those traits does not necessitate the production of actual effects for an acknowledgment of their existence or possession. This allows her to trace out an occasional philosophically interesting route of investigation which Hume does not, though I would be the first to say that the kinds of speculations canvassed here have a distinctly Humean flavor, especially since they rely on the idea that the tendencies of a character can be considered in isolation from its actual effects.

And whatever one might think of Zimbardo and his situational ethics, it has to be acknowledged that the transition in ethical relevance from late eighteenth-century (*Sense and Sensibility*) and early nineteenth-century (*Mansfield Park*) comedies of manners to Abu Ghraib is nothing short of remarkable. If Austen's fiction shows us such universally applicable human constants as these, we cannot be surprised that her work has stood what Hume calls the test of time or that it can provide an admirable adjunct to philosophical exposition.

I have tried to establish that there are correlations between the norm-ative and meta-ethical positions variously endorsed in David Hume's philosophy and Jane Austen's fiction. I have argued that this in turn establishes that Austen's continuing popularity reflects something about the contemporaneity of Hume's ideas and further establishes her affinity for the worldview of the Enlightenment. Along more philosophical lines, I have also tried to show that Austen's novels can function as a species of thought experiment that complements the Humean project by offer-ing elaborations and sometimes demonstrations of Humean insights, by providing both illuminating illustrations and an opportunity for imaginative participation that is typically unavailable from philosophical

---

[3]   David Lewis introduces the idea of relative similarity between worlds in *Counterfactuals* (Cambridge, MA: Harvard University Press, 1973). For approaches to fiction, see David Lewis, "Truth in Fiction," *American Philosophical Quarterly* 15 (1978): 37–46 and Nicholas Wolterstorff, *Works and Worlds of Art* (Oxford: Clarendon Press, 1980), p. 120.

prose. I also believe that Hume's philosophy can enrich our understanding of Austen's fiction by calling our attention to more of what is there than do alternative readings and interpretations. If the minds of men can be mirrors to one another, then the minds of two people with different talents but similar insights may likewise prove to reflect and also to complement each other.

BIBLIOGRAPHY

Alter, Robert. Introduction, in Frank Kermode, *Pleasure and Change: The Aesthetics of Canon* (Oxford: Oxford University Press, 2004).

Ardal, Pall. *Passion and Value in Hume's Treatise* (Edinburgh: Edinburgh University Press, 1989).

Aristotle. *Nicomachean Ethics*, trans. Terence Irwin (Indianapolis: Hackett, 1985).

Auerbach, Emily. *Searching for Jane Austen* (Madison: University of Wisconsin Press, 2004).

Austen, Jane. *The Novels of Jane Austen*, 5 volumes, ed. R.W. Chapman, 3rd edition (Oxford: Oxford University Press, 1988).

Austen, Jane. *The Works of Jane Austen*, ed., R.W. Chapman, volume 6, *Minor Works* (Oxford: Oxford University Press, 1988).

Austen, Jane. *Jane Austen's Letters*, 3rd ed., D. Le Faye (Oxford: Oxford University Press, 1995).

Baier, Annette C. *A Progress of Sentiments: Reflections on Hume's Treatise* (Cambridge: Harvard University Press, 1991).

Bentham, Jeremy. *A Fragment on Government*, ed. by J.H. Burns and H.L.A. Hart (London: Oxford, 1977).

Bentham, Jeremy. *The Principles of Morals and Legislation* (Darien, CT: Hafner, 1970).

Blackburn, Simon. *Ruling Passions* (Oxford: Clarendon Press, 1998).

Bloom, Harold, ed. *Modern Critical Views: Jane Austen* (New York: Chelsea House Publishers, 1986).

Boruah, Bijoy H. *Fiction and Emotion: A Study in Aesthetics and Philosophy of Mind* (Oxford: Clarendon Press, 1988).

Butler, Marilyn. *Jane Austen and the War of Ideas* (Oxford: Oxford University Press, 1974).

Carroll, Noel. "Critical Study: Kendall L. Walton's *Mimesis as Make-Believe*." *Philosophical Quarterly* 45 (1995): 93–9.

Carroll, Noel. "Moderate Moralism." *British Journal of Aesthetics* 36 (1996): 223–38.

Carroll, Noel. "Art, Narrative, and Moral Understanding," in *Aesthetics and Ethics: Essays at the Intersection*, ed. Jerrold Levinson (Cambridge: Cambridge University Press, 1998), pp. 126–60.

Carroll, Noel. "The Wheel of Virtue: Art, Literature, and Moral Knowledge," *Journal of Aesthetics and Art Criticism* 60: 1 (2002): 3–26.

Casey, John. *Pagan Virtues: An Essay in Ethics* (Oxford: Clarendon Press, 1992).

Cohon, Rachel. "The Common Point of View in Hume's Ethics," *Philosophy and Phenomenological Research* 57.4 (1997): 827–50.

Collins, Irene. *Jane Austen and the Clergy* (Hambledon and London, 2004).

Conolly, Oliver and Bashshar Haydar. "Narrative Art and Moral Knowledge." *British Journal of Aesthetics* 41 (April 2001): 109–24.

Copleston, Frederick, S.J. "Kant (5): Morality and Religion," in *Modern Philosophy: From the French Enlightenment to Kant*, volume 4 of *A History of Philosophy* (New York: Doubleday, 1994).

Dadlez, Eva M. *What's Hecuba to Him? Fictional Events and Actual Emotions* (University Park, PA: Penn State Press, 1997).

Dadlez, Eva M. "The Vicious Habits of Entirely Fictive People: Hume on the Moral Evaluation of Art," *Philosophy and Literature* 26 (2002): 38–51.

Dadlez, Eva M. "Pleased and Afflicted: Hume on the Paradox of Tragic Pleasure," *Hume Studies* 30: 2 (November 2004): 213–36.

Dadlez, Eva M. "Knowing Better: The Epistemic Underpinnings of Moral Criticism of Fiction," *Southwest Philosophy Review* 21.1 (2005): 35–44.

Dadlez, Eva M. Review of D.A. Miller, *Jane Austen, or the Secret of Style* (Princeton University Press). *Journal of Aesthetics and Art Criticism* 64: 3 (2006): 387–9.

Dadlez, Eva M. "Only Kidding: The Connection between Amusement and Our Attitudes." *Southwest Philosophy Review* 22.2 (2006): 1–16.

Deresiewicz, William. *Jane Austen and the Romantic Poets* (New York: Columbia University Press, 2005).

Devereaux, Mary. "Beauty and Evil: The Case of Leni Riefenstahl's *Triumph of the Will*," in *Aesthetics and Ethics*, ed. Levinson, pp. 227–56.

Devereaux, Mary. "Moral Judgments and Works of Art: The Case of Narrative Literature," *Journal of Aesthetics and Art Criticism* 62 (2004): 3–11.

Farrell, Daniel. "Jealousy," *Philosophical Review* 89 (1980): 527–559.

Fleishman, Avrom. *A Reading of Mansfield Park* (Minneapolis: University of Minnesota Press, 1967).

Gallop, David. "Jane Austen and the Aristotelian Ethic," *Philosophy and Literature* 23.1 (1999): 96–109.

Galperin, William. *The Historical Austen* (Philadelphia: University of Pennsylvania Press, 2003).

Gaut, Berys. "The Ethical Criticism of Art," in *Aesthetics and Ethics: Essays at the Intersection*, ed. Jerrold Levinson (Cambridge: Cambridge University Press, 1998): 182–205.

Gendler, Tamar Szabo. "The Puzzle of Imaginative Resistance," *Journal of Philosophy* XCVII (February 2000): 55–81.

Halliwell, Stephen. *Aristotle's Poetics* (Chicago: Chicago University Press, 1998).

Harold, James. "Flexing the Imagination," *Journal of Aesthetics and Art Criticism* 61 (2003): 247–57.

Harold, James. "Infected by Evil," *Philosophical Explorations* 8 (2005): 173–87.

Harold, James. "Narrative Engagement with *Atonement* and *The Blind Assassin*," *Philosophy and Literature* 29 (2005): 130–45.

Harold, James. "On Judging the Moral Value of Narrative Artworks," *Journal of Aesthetics and Art Criticism* 64 (2006): 259–70.

Heydt-Stevenson, Jill. *Jane Austen: Comedies of the Flesh* (Palgrave Macmillan, 2005).

Hume, David. *An Enquiry Concerning the Principle of Morals*, in *Enquiries Concerning Human Understanding and Concerning the Principles of Morals*, ed. L.A. Selby-Bigge, P.H. Nidditch (Oxford: Clarendon, 1995).

Hume, David. *Essays: Moral, Political, and Literary*, ed. Eugene F. Miller (Indianapolis: Liberty Classics, 1987).

Hume, David. *The Letters of David Hume*, ed. J.Y.T. Grieg (Oxford: Clarendon Press, 1932).

Hume, David. "Of the Delicacy of Taste and Passion," in *Essays: Moral, Political, and Literary*, ed. Eugene F. Miller (Indianapolis: Liberty Classics, 1987), pp. 3–8.

Hume, David. "Of the Dignity or Meanness of Human Nature," in *Essays: Moral, Political, and Literary*, ed. Eugene F. Miller (Indianapolis: Liberty Classics, 1987), pp. 80–6.

Hume, David. "Of Essay Writing," in *Essays: Moral, Political, and Literary*, ed. Eugene F. Miller (Indianapolis: Liberty Classics, 1987), pp. 533–7.

Hume, David. "Idea of a Perfect Commonwealth," in *Essays: Moral, Political, and Literary*, ed. Eugene F. Miller (Indianapolis: Liberty Classics, 1987), pp. 512–29.

Hume, David. "Of the Immortality of the Soul," in *Essays: Moral, Political, and Literary*, ed. Eugene F. Miller (Indianapolis: Liberty Classics, 1987), pp. 590–8.

Hume, David. "Of Love and Marriage," in *Essays: Moral, Political, and Literary*, ed. Eugene F. Miller (Indianapolis: Liberty Classics, 1987), pp. 557–62.

Hume, David. "Of the Middle Station in Life," in *Essays: Moral, Political, and Literary*, ed. Eugene F. Miller (Indianapolis: Liberty Classics, 1987), pp. 545–51.

Hume, David. "Of National Characters," in *Essays: Moral, Political, and Literary*, ed. Eugene F. Miller (Indianapolis: Liberty Classics, 1987), pp. 197–215.

Hume, David. "Of the Parties of Great Britain," in *Essays: Moral, Political, and Literary*, ed. Eugene F. Miller (Indianapolis: Liberty Classics, 1987), pp. 64–72.

Hume, David. "Of Polygamy and Divorces," in *Essays: Moral, Political, and Literary*, ed. Eugene F. Miller (Indianapolis: Liberty Classics, 1987), pp. 181–90.

Hume, David. "Of the Populousness of Ancient Nations," in *Essays: Moral, Political, and Literary*, ed. Eugene F. Miller (Indianapolis: Liberty Classics, 1987), pp. 377–464.

Hume, David. "Of Refinement in the Arts," in *Essays: Moral, Political, and Literary*, ed. Eugene F. Miller (Indianapolis: Liberty Classics, 1987), pp. 268–80.

Hume, David. "Of the Rise and Progress of the Arts and Sciences," in *Essays: Moral, Political, and Literary*, ed. Eugene F. Miller (Indianapolis: Liberty Classics, 1987), pp. 111–37.

Hume, David. "Of the Standard of Taste," in *Essays: Moral, Political, and Literary*, ed. Eugene F. Miller (Indianapolis: Liberty Classics, 1987), pp. 226–49.

Hume, David. "The Stoic," in *Essays: Moral, Political, and Literary*, ed. Eugene F. Miller (Indianapolis: Liberty Classics, 1987), pp. 146–54.

Hume, David. "Of Tragedy," in *Essays: Moral, Political, and Literary*, ed., Eugene F. Miller (Indianapolis: Liberty Classics, 1987), pp. 216–25.

Hume, David. *Treatise of Human Nature*, ed. L.A. Selby-Bigge (Oxford: Clarendon Press, 1978).

Jenkyns, Richard. *A Fine Brush on Ivory: An Appreciation of Jane Austen* (Oxford: Oxford University Press, 2004).

John, Eileen. "Subtlety and Moral Vision in Fiction," *Philosophy and Literature* 19 (1995): 308–19.

John, Eileen. "Reading Fiction and Conceptual Knowledge: Philosophical Thought in Literary Context," *Journal of Aesthetics and Art Criticism* 56 (1998): 331–48.

John, Eileen. "Art and Knowledge," in *The Routledge Companion to Aesthetics*, ed. Berys Gaut (New York: Routledge, 2001), pp. 329–40.

John, Eileen. "Literary Fiction and the Philosophical Value of Detail," in *Imagination, Philosophy, and the Arts*, ed. Matthew Kieran and Dominic McIver Lopes (London: Routledge, 2003), pp. 152–4.

Jones, Darryl. *Jane Austen: Critical Issues* (Palgrave Macmillan, 2004).

Jones, Peter. "Another Look at Hume's Views of Aesthetic and Moral Judgments," *Philosophical Quarterly* 20 (1970): 53–59.

Jones, Peter. "Hume's Aesthetics Reassessed," *Philosophical Quarterly* 26 (1976): 48–60.

Kant, Immanuel. *Critique of Judgment*, trans. J.H. Bernard (New York: Hafner Press, 1951).

Kant, Immanuel. *Foundations of the Metaphysics of Morals*, ed. Robert Paul Wolff (Indianapolis: Bobbs-Merrill, 1969).

Kaufmann, David. "Law and Propriety, Sense and Sensibility: Austen on the Cusp of Modernity," *ELH* 59 (1992): 385–408.

Kieran, Matthew. "In Defence of the Ethical Evaluation of Narrative Art," *British Journal of Aesthetics* 41 (January 2001): 26–38.

Knox-Shaw, Peter. *Jane Austen and the Enlightenment* (Cambridge: Cambridge University Press, 2004).

Korsgaard, Christine M. "The General Point of View: Love and Moral Approval in Hume's Ethics," *Hume Studies* 25 (1999): 3–41.

Korsgaard, Christine M. *The Sources of Normativity* (Cambridge: Cambridge University Press, 1998).

Kristeller, Paul Oskar. "The Modern System of the Arts: A Study in the History of Aesthetics (II)," *Journal of the History of Ideas* 13 (1952): 17–46.

Lewis, David. "Truth in Fiction," *American Philosophical Quarterly* 15 (1978): 37–46.

MacIntyre, Alisdair. *After Virtue: A Study in Moral Theory* (Indiana: University of Notre Dame, 1981).

Mercer, Philip. *Sympathy and Ethics: A Study of the Relationship between Sympathy and Morality with Special Reference to Hume's Treatise* (Oxford: Clarendon Press, 1972).

Miller, D.A. *Jane Austen or the Secret of Style* (Princeton: Princeton University Press, 2003).

Mitton, G.E. *Jane Austen and Her Times* (Whitefish, MT: Kessinger, 2004).

Monk, Samuel H. *The Sublime: A Study of Critical Theories in XVIII-Century England* (Ann Arbor: University of Michigan Press, 1960).

Moran, Richard. "The Expression of Feeling in Imagination," *Philosophical Review* 103 (1994): 104–6.

Morreall, John. *The Philosophy of Laughter and Humor* (Albany: SUNY Press, 1987).

Morrow, Glenn R. "The Significance of the Doctrine of Sympathy in Hume and Adam Smith," *Philosophical Review* 32: 1 (1923): 60–78.

Morton, Adam. *On Evil* (New York: Routledge, 2004).

Mullin, Amy. "Evaluating Art: Significant Imagining v. Moral Soundness." *Journal of Aesthetics and Art Criticism* 60: 2 (2002): 137–49.

Nardin, Jane. *Those Elegant Decorums: The Concept of Propriety in Jane Austen's Novels* (Albany: SUNY Press, 1973).

Nussbaum, Martha C. "Finely Aware and Richly Responsible: Moral Attention and the Moral Task of Literature," *The Journal of Philosophy* 82: 10 (1985): 516–29.

Nussbaum, Martha C. *Love's Knowledge: Essays on Philosophy and Literature* (New York: Oxford University Press, 1990).

Nussbaum, Martha C. "Emotions as Judgments of Value and Importance," in *What Is an Emotion? Classic and Contemporary Readings*, 2nd ed., ed. Robert C. Solomon (New York: Oxford University Press, 2003), pp. 271–83. Originally published in *Relativism, Suffering, and Beyond: Essays in Memory of Bimal K. Matilal*, ed. P. Bilimoria and J.N. Mohanty (New Delhi: Oxford University Press, 1997).

Nussbaum, Martha C. "Exactly and Responsibly: A Defense of Ethical Criticism," *Philosophy and Literature* 22.2 (1998): 343–65.

Popkin, Richard H. "Hume's Racism," in *The High Road to Pyrrhonism*, ed. Richard Watson and James Force (San Diego: Austin Hill Press, 1980).

Radcliffe, Elizabeth S. "Hume on Motivating Sentiments, the General Point of View, and the Inculcation of 'Morality'," *Hume Studies* 20: 1 (1994): 37–58.

Radcliffe, Elizabeth S. *On Hume* (Belmont, CA: Wadsworth, 2000).

Raynor, David. "Hume's Abstract of Adam Smith's *Theory of Moral Sentiments*," *Journal of the History of Philosophy* 22 (1984): 51–80.

Roberts, Robert C. *Emotions: An Essay in Aid of Moral Psychology* (Cambridge: Cambridge University Press, 2003).

Rosenblatt, Louise M. *The Reader, the Text, the Poem: The Transactional Theory of the Literary Work* (Carbondale: Southern Illinois University Press, 1978).

Ruderman, Anne Crippen. *The Pleasures of Virtue: Political Thought in the Novels of Jane Austen* (Lanham, MD: Rowman & Littlefield, 1995).

Ryle, Gilbert. "Jane Austen and the Moralists," in *Critical Essays on Jane Austen*, ed. B.C. Southam (London: Routledge, 1987), p. 122.

Sayre-McCord, Geoffrey. "On Why Hume's 'General Point of View' Isn't Ideal – and Shouldn't Be," *Social Philosophy and Policy* 11.1 (1994): 202–28.

Sayre-McCord, Geoffrey. "Hume and the Bauhaus Theory of Ethics," *Midwest Studies in Philosophy* 20 (1995): 280–98.

Shields, Carol. *Jane Austen* (New York: Viking, 2001).

Shirley, Edward S. "Hume's Ethics: Acts, Rules, Dispositions, and Utility," *Southwest Philosophy Review* (1991): 129–39.

Smith, Adam. *The Theory of Moral Sentiments*, ed. D.D. Raphael and A.L. Macfie (Indianapolis: Liberty Fund, 1984).

Sorensen, Roy A. *Thought Experiments* (New York: Oxford University Press, 1992).

Spiegel, P. Keith. "Early Conceptions of Humor: Varieties and Issues," in *The Psychology of Humor: Theoretical Perspectives and Empirical Issues*, ed. J.H. Goldstein and P.E. McGhee (New York: Academic Press, 1972).

Tandon, Bharat. *Jane Austen and the Morality of Conversation* (London: Anthem, 2003).

Tanner, Tony. *Jane Austen* (Cambridge: Harvard University Press, 1986).

Tyler, Natalie. *The Friendly Jane Austen: A Well-Mannered Introduction to a Lady of Sense and Sensibility* (New York: Viking, 1999).

Van Inwagen, Peter. "Creatures of Fiction," *American Philosophical Quarterly* 14 (1977): 299–308.

Walton, Kendall. "Morals in Fiction and Fictional Morality (I)," *Proceedings of the Aristotelian Society*, suppl. 68 (1994): 27–50.

Whately, R. "Modern Novels," *Quarterly Review* 47 (1821): 352–63.

Williams, Thomas. "Moral Vice, Cognitive Virtue: Austen on Jealousy and Envy," *Philosophy and Literature* 27.1 (2003): 223–30.

Wolterstorff, Nicholas. *Works and Worlds of Art* (Oxford: Clarendon Press, 1980).

Woolf, Virginia. *The Common Reader*, First Series (1925). Project Gutenberg of Australia ebook. http://gutenberg.net.au/ebooks03/0300031.txt

Zagzebski, Linda Trinkaus. *Virtues of the Mind: An Inquiry into the Nature of Virtue and the Ethical Foundations of Knowledge* (Cambridge: Cambridge University Press, 1998).

INDEX

Abu Ghraib   220, 221
adultery   69–70, 163–4
aesthetics   114–34
Alter, Robert   92
Anderson, Gillian   211
Aristotle   30, 32, 47–8, 49, 50, 51,
    53–4, 55–7, 58, 62, 91, 101,
    153, 182, 183
Auerbach, Emily   85, 110, 111, 130

beauty   27, 114, 134
belief
    justified/unjustified   135–56
    thought experiments and   3–7, 12
Bentham, Jeremy   102–3
bias   103–4, 120–1, 139
Blackburn, Simon   8n, 73n, 91
Bloom, Harold   51, 209
Boruah, Bijoy   4
Burke, Simon   22, 24, 25
Butler, Marilyn   140

Caines, Michael   80
Calhoun, Cheshire   53n
Carroll, Noel   3, 8, 9
Casey, John   140–1
categorical imperative, Fanny Price
    and   38–9, 43, 44
clergy   199, 201, 217
    Hume on   173–4

Cohon, Rachel   90
comparison, Hume's principle of   66,
    181–94
Connolly, Oliver   9
contempt   174–5, 176
Copleston, Frederick   40–1
counterfactuals   143, 203, 207, 219,
    221

Davies, Andrew   21
Dear, Nick   22, 24, 25
delicacy (of taste)   125–6
Dennett, Daniel   6
Devereaux, Mary   9
Dickens, Charles   7, 31, 215
duty   39–41, 44–6, 49, 107, 135,
    200, 209

Edgeworth, Maria   80
Emma (E)   33, 46, 52, 53, 54–5,
    144, 145–7, 148, 149, 151,
    152, 217
    aesthetics   114, 123–4, 126
    indolence and industry   196, 198,
    204, 205
    jealousy, envy and malice   183,
    185, 194
    marriage   159, 160, 161, 162
    pleasure, sentiment and virtue   60,
    61, 62, 63, 64, 65, 66, 68, 72

Emma (E) (*cont'd*)
  pride 170, 173, 175, 176, 179
  sympathy 81, 83, 84, 86–7
  usefulness/utility 105, 107,
    108–9
emotions
  rational assessment of 53–4
  sympathy and 76, 85–6
  as value judgements 2–3
  see also passions, Hume's indirect
empathy 7, 79, 80, 81, 85
Enlightenment, Austen and 14, 80,
  214, 221
envy 147–8
  envious rivalry 186, 187–8, 190,
    194
  Hume's meaning 181, 189, 191
epistemic norms 45, 101, 135–56
epistemology 135–56
equality, in marriage 158, 161–2
ethnic stereotypes 136–8

Farrell, Daniel 181, 182–4
Fattore, Gina 13
fidelity, in marriage 163–4
  Hume and Austen compared 69,
    166
Fielding, Henry 34, 114
film/tv adaptations 13–14, 22, 25,
  211–12
First Impressions 137–8
Fleishman, Avrom 208
friendship 17–18, 158
  in marriage 160–3

Gallop, David 47, 48, 51–6, 101
Galperin, William 112–13
Gaut, Berys 9
Gendler, Tamar Szabo 10
general point of view, Hume's
  conception of 61, 88–99,
    100, 102, 125–6, 142–3,
    154
  narrow circle 56, 82, 89, 91, 93,
    94–5, 96, 99, 101, 107–8,

130–1, 136, 141, 153–4, 157,
  213, 216
gluttony 198
good company 198–9
goodness 140–1
gothic novels 33, 149
  Austen critical of 128–32

Halliwell, Stephen 56
happiness 47–8, 51–7, 58–70, 95,
  102–3, 105, 109, 112, 118, 148,
  191–3, 195–6
Harold, James 9
Hawthorne, Nathaniel 207
Haydar, Bashshar 9
Hobbes, Thomas 6, 208–9
Hough, Graham 145
Hume, David
  A Treatise of Human Nature (T)
    50, 57, 58, 59, 61, 62, 63,
    66–7, 69, 71–2, 75, 76–7,
    78–80, 82, 84, 88–90, 93–4,
    95, 97, 98, 101–7, 118, 119–20,
    131, 136, 137, 140, 144, 145,
    147–8, 151, 153, 163, 164,
    168–71, 172, 174, 175–6, 177,
    178–9, 180, 181, 188, 189,
    190, 192, 193–4, 200, 213,
    214–18
  *Enquiries Concerning Human
    Understanding and Concerning
    the Principles of Morals* (EPM)
    59, 70, 88, 89, 97, 103, 103–4,
    163
  Idea of a Perfect Commonwealth
    201
  Of Essay Writing 199
  Of Love and Marriage 158, 159,
    160, 165
  Of National Characters 136–7,
    195, 197
  Of Polygamy and Divorces
    157–8, 161, 187
  Of Refinement in the Arts 196,
    205

Of the Delicacy of Taste and
  Passion (DTP) 125
Of the Immortality of the Soul
  205
Of the Jealousy of Trade 186
Of the Liberty of the Press 186
Of the Middle Station in Life 205
Of the Parties of Great Britain
  174
Of the Populousness of Ancient
  Nations 199–200
Of the Rise of the Arts and
  Sciences 199
Of the Standard of Taste (ST) 10,
  56, 121–2, 123, 124–5, 127,
  131
Of Tragedy (OT) 20, 85, 128,
  187, 197
The Stoic 197, 204
humor, reversal of expectations 32
husbands 159–60
Hutcheson, Francis 81
hypothetical imagination 29, 91

ideal observer 90–1
imagination
  cognitive role of 3–12
  creative 121
  general rule and 78–9, 89–90
  literary devices 29
indolence 49, 179, 195–205
  agreeable in Hume 196
industry 195–205
  active mind 197
  and good company 199
  ranked with integrity 205
intellectual development, Austen's
  heroines 135–56
  Fanny Price 45
intuition pumps 6, 7, 217, 218
Inwagen, Peter van 5
irony, Austen's narrative voice 34

James, Henry 3, 12, 13, 14, 15, 18,
  30, 121

jealousy 181–90
  meaning 181
  term employed by Hume
    186–7
  vanity wounded 186
  as vice 185–6
Jenkyns, Richard 32, 204
John, Eileen 8, 9, 92
Johnson, Claudia 130
Johnson, Diane 32, 33, 34
justified/unjustified belief *see* belief

Kant, Immanuel 37–57, 208
  aesthetic ideas 115, 116–17, 118,
    120–3
  Critique of Judgment 38, 116,
    120, 121–2, 208
  ethical perspective 38–46, 115
Kantian deontology 37–8, 40
Kaufman, David 39–40, 115
Kermode, Frank 92
Kieran, Matthew 9
Knox-Shaw, Peter 80
Korsgaard, Christine 41, 89
Kristeller, Paul Oskar 114

Lewis, David 221
literary form/style 20–36, 121

MacIntyre, Alasdair 47, 48, 54, 55,
  101
male succession 164–5
malice 193–4
  envy and 148
Mansfield Park (MP) 13, 33, 38,
  39, 41, 42, 44, 45–6, 49, 53,
  93, 94–5, 98, 141, 143, 144,
  151–2, 153, 207, 208, 209, 217,
  218, 219, 221
  aesthetics 114–15, 116, 119, 124,
    126
  indolence and industry 196, 198,
    199, 201 2, 203, 204–5
  jealousy, envy and malice 181–5,
    190–2, 193

Mansfield Park (MP) (*cont'd*)
  marriage 159, 161, 163–4, 165,
    166
  pleasure, sentiment and virtue
    60, 63, 64, 65–6, 69, 70, 71,
    73
  pride 169, 170, 171, 179
  sympathy 82, 83, 84
  usefulness/utility 101, 105, 107,
    108, 109, 110
marriage 23, 44, 54–5, 98, 157–67
Masterpiece Theater 211
Miller, D.A. 26–7, 33, 34
Monk, Samuel 114
moral luck 89, 97, 99, 143, 202,
  220
morality, found in sentiment 8, 54,
  62, 63, 66–9, 88, 90–1, 140–1,
  200
Moran, Richard 29
Morrison, Paul 130
Morrow, Glen R. 79
Morton, Adam 12
Mothersill, Mary 117
Mullin, Amy 9

naturalistic fiction 130–2
Neill, Alex 77n, 100
Nicomachean Ethics 53n
Northanger Abbey (NA) 16, 33,
  41, 42, 93, 95, 148, 149–50,
  212
  aesthetics 114, 122, 123, 128–30,
    131, 134
  marriage 159
  pleasure, sentiment and virtue
    72
  pride 170, 176, 177–8, 179
  sympathy 78, 81, 82, 84–5
Nussbaum, Martha 1–7, 8, 9, 12,
  13, 15, 21, 22, 92, 121

O'Neill, Eugene 207
On the Soul 53

passions, Hume's indirect
  approbation and disapprobation 8,
    21, 56, 63–4, 67–8, 70–1, 72,
    76, 88, 90, 142, 143, 215, 216
  love and hatred 67, 71–2, 88,
    131, 174
  pride and humility 50, 71–2, 79,
    86, 145, 151, 153, 168, 170,
    175, 180, 214
Persuasion (P) 16, 17, 22–3, 25, 33,
  49, 97, 141, 144, 151, 154–5,
  209
  aesthetics 114, 118, 123, 124,
    126, 127
  indolence and industry 197, 198
  jealousy, envy and malice 185–6,
    188, 189–90
  marriage 160, 161, 162, 163
  pleasure, sentiment and virtue
    63–4, 65, 68, 73–4, 75
  pride 170, 171, 172, 173, 174,
    177, 178, 179
  sympathy 77, 82, 83
  usefulness/utility 105, 107,
    110–13
pity, compared to sympathy 76–8
Plato 165
pleasure 58–75
  sympathy and 83–4, 102–3,
    118
Popkin, Richard H. 137n
prejudice 136–8
pride 168–80
  improper 173–9
  meaning 168
  proper 172–3
Pride and Prejudice (PP) 13, 49,
  52, 94, 96, 97, 137, 138, 139,
  141, 142, 143, 144, 145, 152,
  217
  aesthetics 114, 119, 124, 126
  indolence and industry 198
  marriage 159–60, 161, 163,
    164

pleasure, sentiment and virtue 59, 61, 64, 65, 66, 68, 73
pride 168, 172, 173, 174, 176, 179, 180
sympathy 78, 81, 83
usefulness/utility 101, 106, 108

Radcliffe, Elizabeth 88, 90, 104
Raynor, David 79n
revenge 193–4
Rhetoric 53
Roberts, Robert C. 181, 182, 186, 187
Rosenblatt, Louise M. 29
Ruderman, Anne Crippen 38, 43, 47, 48, 54, 58–9, 62, 68n, 115, 116n, 209
Ryle, Gilbert 47, 48, 49–50, 101, 108, 146

Sayre-McCord, Geoffrey 89, 90, 102n
Seeley, William 128
Sense and Sensibility (SS) 14, 26, 28, 33, 39–40, 48, 52, 53, 93, 98, 141, 143, 144, 150–1, 152, 209–10, 218, 219–20, 221
    aesthetics 114, 117–18, 119, 126–7
    indolence and industry 201
    jealousy, envy and malice 188, 189, 192, 194
    marriage 158, 159, 163–4, 166
    pleasure, sentiment and virtue 60, 61, 64, 65, 70
    pride 171, 174, 175, 176, 179
    sympathy 77–8, 80, 82, 84
    usefulness/utility 107, 117–18, 119
sentiment, source of morality 62–9, 141–2, 200–1
Shaftesbury, Anthony Ashley Cooper, 3rd Earl of 48, 50, 81

shame 72, 78, 81, 86, 87, 108, 139, 148, 149–50, 175
Shirley, Edward S. 102n
Shields, Carol 149
situational ethics 220, 221
sloth *see* indolence
Smith, Adam 79, 80, 81
snobbery 172, 177
social conventions (marriage) 163–4
Solomon, Robert C. 9n, 53n
Sorensen, Roy 8, 129–30
Spiegel, P. Keith 32n
Stanford Prison Experiment 99
stupidity, indolence and 197
sympathy 56, 65, 76–87, 94, 107, 142–3, 171, 214
    Adam Smith and 79–80
    Austen and *Northanger Abbey* 128, 130, 132
    Bentham and 102–3
    and the general point of view 75, 88–9, 97, 100, 104
    Hume's principle of 62, 67, 76, 88, 102, 103, 118, 163
    influence on pride and humility 175

Thackeray, William Makepeace 210
The Scarlet Letter 207
thought experiments 2–19, 73, 92, 216–17, 221
    Northanger Abbey 128
tragedy
    Austen's comedy and 35
    paradox of 16, 20
    see also Hume, Of Tragedy
tyrants/tyranny 159

usefulness/utility 46, 58, 100–13, 120
    beauty allied with 117–19, 215
    connection with the moral 100–13
    Emma 107–9

usefulness/utility (*cont'd*)
  Hume and   59, 89, 101–7, 118
  Mansfield Park   46, 109–10, 119
  Persuasion   110–13
  and taste   123
utilitarianism   101–2, 105

vanity   139–40
  meaning   168–9
vice(s), underexercised   220
virtue in rags   52n, 89, 98, 101,
  125, 143, 218

Walton, Kendall   10
wealth   27–8, 51–2, 177–8, 202–4

Wentworth, Captain (P)   22–6, 33,
  49, 55, 64, 77, 83, 97, 110,
  111–12, 154, 155, 161, 171,
  172, 174, 188
Whately, R.   48
Whelwell, David   121n
Williams, Thomas   47, 182–3, 185,
  186
Wolterstorff, Nicholas   5, 221
Woolf, Virginia   13n, 14, 211
Wordsworth, William   117

Zagzebski, Linda   135–6
Zimbardo, Philip   220, 221
Zuckert, Rachel   121